# Cowboy Days in the Old West

# Cowboy Days in the Old West
Two Personal Accounts of Cattle Ranching in Texas

ILLUSTRATED

The Unvarnished West
J. M. Pollock

Cowboy Life
Rufe O'Keefe

*Cowboy Days in the Old West*
Two Personal Accounts of Cattle Ranching in Texas
*The Unvarnished West*
by J. M. Pollock
*Cowboy Life*
by Rufe O'Keefe

ILLUSTRATED

FIRST EDITION IN THIS FORM

First published under the titles
*The Unvarnished West*
and
*Cowboy Life*

Leonaur is an imprint of Oakpast Ltd
Copyright in this form © 2023 Oakpast Ltd

ISBN: 978-1-916535-44-2 (hardcover)
ISBN: 978-1-916535-45-9 (softcover)

**http://www.leonaur.com**

Publisher's Notes
The views expressed in this book are not necessarily those of the publisher.

# Contents

The Unvarnished West     7
Cowboy Life     169

J. M. POLLOCK.

# The Unvarnished West

# Contents

| | |
|---|---|
| The Start | 13 |
| "A Greenhorn" in Wisconsin | 15 |
| Farm Hands' Diversions | 21 |
| Off to Texas | 23 |
| Across the Prairie | 29 |
| A Lonely Tramp | 35 |
| At a Friend's Ranch | 40 |
| On a Sheep Farm | 43 |
| Starting as Stocksman | 47 |
| Hog Hunting and Well Sinking | 54 |
| The Killing of the White Bull | 60 |
| Horse Trading and a Cyclone | 66 |
| A Shooting Affair | 77 |
| Windmills and a Long Ride | 81 |
| Drought and Cattle-Doctoring | 87 |
| Improving the Breed | 92 |
| Prairie Fires | 97 |
| Skunks and Other Pests | 99 |

| | |
|---|---|
| Rattlesnakes | 105 |
| A Round-Up and a Stampede | 110 |
| A Cattle Drive Under Difficulties | 117 |
| Blizzards | 124 |
| A Hunting Trip | 128 |
| Caught by a "Norther" | 135 |
| Some Stalking | 138 |
| A Suprise Visit | 144 |
| *Al Fresco* Cooking | 148 |
| A Fighting Parson | 156 |
| Road-Making | 160 |
| A City Man's Holiday | 164 |
| Farewell | 167 |

The notes from which this little book has been compiled were written in the first place only for the perusal of personal friends. By some of those kindly critics it was suggested that others outside that limited circle might be interested and amused by a record of experiences which fell to my lot while ranching in the Far West. Thus, it comes to pass that I venture into print.

Many of the incidents here set down have to do with hardships and bad weather. I hope that no reader will form an unfavourable opinion of Texas on that account. As a rule, the climate of North-West Texas is one of the finest, brightest, and most exhilarating in the world. Hence it is with a sharp sense of contrast that one recalls the cruel pitiless "nothers" that occur several times almost every winter. When life goes smoothly under a smiling sun there is little to write about. It is the floods, blizzards, and storms that "make copy."

I take this opportunity of acknowledging with thanks the courteous permission of the editor of the *Wide World Magazine* to reprint an account of a stampede which appeared originally in that publication.

J.M.P

Cutsey House, Wellington, Somerset.

Chapter 1

# The Start

As I was not born either on a farm or on a ranch I may as well begin by telling how I got there. So here goes.

It was in the early eighties that I, after having for a brief period held Her Majesty's Commission in a Militia regiment, determined to try what Dame Fortune might be holding in reserve for me in what then appeared the far distant Western Hemisphere. The most important question to be settled was, to which point I should first direct my wanderings. To decide this weighty question, the map of North America was brought out, and much consultation ensued. Of course, patriotism pointed to Canada, as to live and work under the British flag would be more like home, but then against this advantage there is the drawback that the winters are so long and cold, and the summers so short and hot.

On the other hand, the Central American Republics have no winter at all, but have instead a long rainy season. They are, moreover, blessed (or the other thing) with the most unstable forms of government under the sun. So, they also were barred. There remained now only the United States as a happy medium between North and South. But the United States cover an enormous area, and I found great difficulty in deciding which State of the Union to try first. I finally chose Wisconsin, and at once began making ready for my new start in life.

All necessary preparations were soon made, and in a short time I found myself on board the old *City of Chester*, at that time one of the best and most comfortable of the Trans-Atlantic liners.

On arriving at Queenstown, we found we had some hours to wait before the arrival of the London mails. To pass the time, several of the passengers, including myself, made up a party to go on shore and see the town. Hardly had we stepped on to the deck of the tender when there was a loud splash in the water, and the cry was raised of "Man overboard."

On running to the side of the tender we could plainly see through the clear transparent blue water the body of a man sinking deeper and ever deeper, his frightened white face staring up at us, his mouth and eyes wide open, and his arms stretching upwards vainly clutching for support at the yielding water. There were plenty among us ready and willing to jump in to his rescue, but fortunately our help was not required, as he had little more than struck the water when a boat, manned by two or three sailors, was on the spot, and as soon as he rose to the surface, he was fished out by boat-hooks in a most ignominious manner by the seat of his trousers.

The rescued man being unable to answer the questions put to him, an interpreter was called for. As no one else came forward I offered my services, so far as French and German were of any use. By this means we got his sad story, which was as follows.

He had been a Russian Professor of Science, and had at one time held a prominent position in the literary circles of St. Petersburg. For some reason unknown to himself he was arrested, thrown into prison, accused of some political crime, and finally exiled to Siberia, where for a number of years he worked in the mines.

One day an opportunity of escape offered itself, and he was not slow to avail himself of this long-sought chance of liberty. His attempt was successful, and escaping the bullets of the guard, he got clear away.

Walking by night and sleeping by day he made the long and toilsome journey across Siberia and Russia on foot. On entering Austria, he was imprisoned for some months as a vagrant. When released he made his way to Hamburg, where he was again imprisoned for being unable to give any satisfactory account of himself. After serving the term of his sentence he worked his passage to Hull, walked across England, and was put into gaol for begging. Having worked out his time he was allowed to go, as poor as he came.

He heard the *City of Chester* was about to sail for America, so he hid himself away on board of her. But his misfortunes were not yet ended, as he was discovered before we reached Queenstown, and as is usual with stowaways, he was to be handed over to the police in that port.

He said this was more than he could stand, after all the toils and privations of his long and painful endeavour to reach America, where he had hoped to establish a new home for himself and then send for his wife and children. After all he had gone through, he could not bear up against this last stroke of ill-luck, and therefore attempted to end his miseries and his life together by jumping overboard.

This was his story, whether true or false I cannot tell.

We started a subscription to pay his fare to America but were told it was too late, as he was already in custody, and the last we saw of him was as he was marching off to gaol between two stalwart Irish policemen.

Between Queenstown and New York, the only event which broke the regular routine of the ship was the death of a steerage passenger. The few of us who had heard of it went on deck to see the solemn ceremony of committing the body to the deep. The funeral was at 4.30 a.m.

We landed safely in New York after a pleasant voyage, during which we experienced the usual North Atlantic weather, which is sometimes fine and sometimes the reverse.

During the voyage we passengers had become very friendly, and I was pleased to learn that a number among them were on the same errand as myself—going to try their luck in the States in farming, cattle-ranching, mining, or mercantile business.

Two of the intending farmers had formerly been militia officers. One of them is, I believe, now doing well on a farm of his own in Lower Canada.

The other, a jolly little fellow, told us he was not going to remain *always* a farmer; he would return to England in a few years, after he had made a little money, say £10,000. He was very much annoyed when we laughed at him for his exalted expectations. He went back home to the "Old Country" in less than two months, taking with him only the clothes on his back and no portion of his hoped-for £10,000.

During the passage I formed a close friendship, which has lasted to the present day—a period of nearly 25 years—with the occupant of the state-room directly opposite my own.

On comparing notes, we found that, whereas I was going to Wisconsin, in the extreme north of the States, he was proceeding to join his brothers in Texas, in the far south. We naturally agreed to write to each other, giving our various experiences and impressions of the prospects of success in the different localities to which we were journeying.

Chapter 2

# "A Greenhorn" in Wisconsin

As sightseeing is expensive and was not the object for which we had crossed the ocean, we did not spend much time in New York. Indeed, we found one day was enough to have a look at Broadway, Central Park, and Brooklyn Bridge. The last of these greatly excited our admiration, it is such a magnificent piece of engineering.

Very tired and truly thankful we were when we took our places that evening in the cars for Chicago, which was to be the first stage of our journey. On arriving in that city our ways separated, my friend going south and I north.

I proceeded to Madison, the chief town in the State of Wisconsin, and had not been long there when I met a farmer, who agreed to teach me farming, and at the same time pay me some small wages.

I may here mention that there were at that time many farmers always anxious to get hold of likely young men, that is to say "greenhorns," and *teach* (?) them farming, paying them nominal wages, or, if possible, none at all, in return for their work. Farm labourers at that time were hard to find, and wages ranged from $20 to $30 per month, with board and lodging. Now, when a farmer got hold of a greenhorn or "farm-pupil," he made him do all the roughest and hardest of the unskilled labour there was to be done on the place and kept him at it as long as he would stand it. He would neither give him fair wages nor let him learn the higher branches of agriculture unless absolutely forced to do so, through want of trained men or other pressing need.

The farmer that I worked for was a "*Platt-Deutscher*," unable either to read or write. Still, he was a really prosperous and upright man, but was extremely close-fisted—a trait which was carried to such an extreme that it gave his character an element of meanness and small-mindedness it would not otherwise have possessed. He worked hard and expected everyone under him to do likewise; but this is the same all over America, as a man must either work hard or become a "tramp"—millionaires and a few others excepted.

Farmwork was something I had never been accustomed to, but being active and willing I was in American phraseology "able to keep up my end of the stick" with any of them, except in hand-binding the sheaves of wheat and barley, at which the girls could beat us easily, being much more quick and nimble in the use of their hands.

If the work was hard, the food was good and plentiful, though beef of any kind seldom appeared on the table, salt pork and pickled herrings taking its place. There was general rejoicing when, every now and then, the "old man" (as our farmer boss was usually called) told us to catch a sheep and kill it, as this meant fresh meat, or rather mutton, until the sheep was all eaten, an operation which took a wonderfully short space of time.

On the first of these occasions, I was full of pity for the poor sheep, but on the second and all following similar occasions I was as keen as any of them to pick the biggest and finest mutton in the flock—and to our eyes he looked much better without his skin than in it. To people living in England, where fresh meat is looked on as a necessity, not a luxury, this may sound both barbarous and gluttonous; but the craving for fresh meat can never be forgotten by anyone who has lived for long periods on salt provisions. Especially is this the case if he is doing hard manual labour all the time.

The house, unlike most American dwellings, was built of brick, which helped it to a certain extent to resist the heat of summer and cold of winter: the latter in Wisconsin is intense, often being from 20 to 40 deg. below zero. The inside of the house was clean and comfortable, especially the beds, my only grumble being that we had not long enough time to pass in them, as the rule on the farm was "Early to rise, no matter whether you are early to bed or not."

During the winter no regular fieldwork can be done, owing to the intense cold. The work which is spread over twelve months on an English farm, has in Wisconsin to be got through in six months, *viz.* from May to October. The consequence is that both man and beast have to work as long as daylight is available in order to get as much as possible completed in the limited space of time at their disposal.

With this exception farming in Wisconsin is much the same as in England. Certainly, the weather can be relied upon to a far greater extent than at home; still even there it has a nasty way of its own of catching one at the most awkward times.

I remember one trick which it played us several times during harvesting. On a Saturday evening we would all work extra hard to get a field of grain nicely "shocked up," and go home, counting on having a good quiet rest till Monday morning. But alas, for our hopes, hardly had we turned into bed, when a violent thunderstorm would come on, followed by a high wind and a deluge of rain. Next morning, we would find all our nice neat "shocks" blown about the field, or carried by the floods into one corner and heaped up among the mud. As it would certainly ruin the grain to lie in this state on the wet ground, we had to set to, and do all our Saturday's work over again, and we would have no rest for that week. How we did long then for some of the quiet Sundays at home, which we had not half appreciated when we had them.

The farmer was prosperous, and to a very great extent he owed his prosperity to the strictest economy, which indeed was carried to such a point that absolutely nothing was lost, not even the water in which we washed our hands after acting as butchers or cleaning the beehives, of which there were a large number on the farm. This water was given to the pigs to drink.

Working in the apiary was the only form of relaxation in which the "old man" indulged himself. We all highly approved of this hobby of his, for through it we had as much honey as we cared to use. He had barrels full of honey, and the neighbours could always buy as much as they wanted for their own use (but not to re-sell) at about a penny a pint. Beyond this he sold none but kept on storing it up year after year.

Goodness knows how much he must have by this time, if he is still at it.

If our day's work lay at a distance from the house, which often happened to be the case, before starting out for the field we were each given a can of cold tea and a couple of slices of bread and honey to be taken as a kind of lunch, about ten o'clock. Our usual custom was to leave the lunch at the point of the field where we expected to arrive with our work about that hour.

One day, when cultivating an 80-acre field of corn (maize) either I had miscalculated the distance or I had worked too fast; however, that may be, I suddenly realised that I had arrived there, and that the near horse of my team, a fine young chestnut, was just in the act of upsetting my can of tea. This would have hurt me sorely in that hot and thirsty field. I sprang from my seat and in my haste stupidly forgot to speak to the horse, and dived under him for my lunch. He rewarded me for my foolishness by a kick which sent me sprawling five yards away, among the "old man's" nice young corn, leaving a track as if a cyclone had struck it. I got my clothes torn, my knee cut and bruised, and my thumb badly broken. But I saved my lunch.

Next morning, I had my five cows to milk as usual. The cows had to be milked and there was no one else to do it for me. I got through the milking somehow, but I suffered torture from my injured hand in doing it, not only that day, but for several days after, until I managed to get the "old man's" consent to exchange work with the boy who cleaned and fed the horses. The bone of my thumb was never set, and still makes an awkward, ugly joint.

Fortunately, most of the work I had to do about that time was driving, and so I was able to save my hand (the left one) to a certain extent.

Of all the different kinds of work on a Wisconsin farm, cultivating corn is by far the most agreeable. It requires a quick eye and hand, foot and team, all of which must act in regular and perfect unison, or woe betide the "old man's" growing corn. A little slowness or negligence in guiding the teeth of the machine and half a row of young plants may be torn up by the roots, as if they were the weeds which your cultivation is intended to kill.

This kind of work keeps one's attention riveted on itself and most fully engages all one's faculties. It is much better than loading a hay or grain waggon, with two men pitching bundles to you as fast as they are able and with the prospect before you of upsetting the waggon, if badly loaded, in some of the ditches or on one of the hillsides (little less steep than the roof of a house) over which one has to pass on the way to the stack-yard.

Another little event, that is considerably more amusing to the on-lookers than to the actor occurs when a snake is unwittingly thrown up to you hidden among the hay or grain. You get plenty of good advice from those on the ground: "Run your fork through him," "Pitch him down," "Stamp on him," etc., etc. The snake has most probably in the meantime hidden himself somewhere in the load of hay, and you have the comfortable feeling that any time from then on, until your arrival in the yard, he may resent your sitting on the top of the load while he is underneath, and a snake's resentment is anything but pleasant.

Once a big black and green fellow ran up the leg of my trousers, but he seemed to dislike such close acquaintanceship as much as I did, so he got down again with so little delay that I was not quick enough to do him any bodily harm. There seemed to be no fellow feeling between us. Horrid wriggling squirming brute! This was my first, but by no means my last encounter with snakes during my stay in the United States.

I remember once, as several of us were walking along a narrow forest path, the fierce black heads of two ugly-looking snakes raised themselves out of the grass to hiss at us. One of my 'companions cut off both heads with a single stroke of the sickle he was carrying—a most satisfactory blow, of which he was justly proud.

The stock on this farm were, as a rule, most orderly and well-behaved animals, and well for them that it was so, as they belonged to a man who could brook no interference with his authority, as the following incidents will illustrate.

With the herd of cows there was a fine young bull, who was supposed to be of a very gentle disposition, but from sundry rapid dives he made at one or two of us, causing us to scale the fence in a manner more hasty than elegant, our suspicions were aroused. The old man jeered at us when it was reported to him, and said he would show us how quiet the beast really was. He certainly did so, but the proof was not convincing, as he had to cross the yard for all he was worth at his very best racing speed, the bull coming in a very close second, in fact, only a short head (and horns) behind when the fence was reached. From the safe side of the palings, we received orders to drive his majesty into the barn and tie him securely there. This we did after some pretty lively work in the "heel and toe" branch of athletics, and when the "old man" had finished with the brute, the latter had no more desire to fight, the demon had gone out of him.

There was a small field close to the house, always reserved for the exclusive use of a valuable brood mare, in whose welfare every one took a lively interest, and when the time came for her to bring her foal into the world there was general excitement on the farm to see how it would turn out. The "old man" was the first to discover that the great event had occurred, but instead of bringing joy to him it only made his angry passions rise—the foal was born dead. All he said was: "Well! she'll never bring me another dead one." He went into the house, got an axe, and with one blow killed the mare.

Fortunately, not all the little events that happened in connection with the stock had such tragic endings as the above. Among the workmen on the place there was a big six-foot German, "Kaspar" by name, whose duty it was to carry a couple of buckets of milk to feed the calves, which were kept in a small paddock opposite the barn. One morning, while he was crossing the yard a large ram, that had taken a strong dislike to him, seemed to decide that as both Kaspar's hands were occupied carrying the milk-pails, now was the time to pay off old scores.

Down went his head, there was a rush, a bang, and a fountain of skim-milk flew up into the air, and one of the buckets was flattened against Kaspar's legs. But as he still stood upright the ram attempted to complete his work of destruction by a second and final charge. This time Kaspar also entered into the fun of the fight, and dashed the entire contents of the second bucket into Rammy's face, which caused him to turn tail and beat an ignoble retreat; and he appeared to us to be extremely anxious to hide himself and his milk-sodden wool among the more peaceful members of his flock.

## Chapter 3

# Farm Hands' Diversions

Of outside amusements and recreations, we had not many. One Sunday, as a special favour, I was allowed to ride an old blind horse, called *Tommy*, into Madison in time to attend church service.

Another lovely Sunday morning three of us made our way down to the lake, where we were lucky enough to find an old tub of a boat in which we started out to enjoy ourselves. We soon found the enjoyment flavoured strongly of hard work.

We rowed briskly out from the shore, the beauty of which fully engrossed our attention for a time; but not for long, as we speedily realised that the crazy old craft leaked so badly that she was rapidly filling, and would, if allowed to do so, quietly sink under us. With the start that the water had already obtained and the amount that was steadily coming in, it kept two of us busy baling, while the third pulled with all his strength for dry land.

Among our acquaintances there was a lively, jolly Irishman living on a neighbouring farm, who had a most decided weakness for boasting of his own clever performances in all kinds of work. One day he was bragging of his milking exploits, and said he could milk any cow on our farm in a remarkably short space of time; I forget now how many minutes he stated. This was our opportunity to take him down a point or two, and we determined not to miss the chance. We assured him if he would come to the yard at milking-time that evening, we would show him a cow that would beat him.

When the time arrived our friend, highly excited, was in readiness with his stool and bucket, and when we pointed out the cow, he followed her about for some time, and got very angry when she would not stand still for him to milk her. Then two of us caught her and held her, and, with a sigh of relief, he sat down to show us how very fast he could milk. But all his attempts were of no avail. The truth suddenly dawned on him—he was trying to milk a dry cow that had never had a calf. He went home in anything but a sweet temper. We heard no more of his milking powers.

There were two real holidays that I must not omit to mention, *viz.*, the fourth of July and the day on which a circus came to town. The first of these two occasions is a holiday strictly observed by everyone in the United States.

The township in which our farm was situated gave a large general picnic to everyone living in the district, and needless to say everyone attended. There was an elaborate free luncheon (well patronised); songs by the schoolchildren, stalls for the sale of beer, sweets or popped-corn, and dances for those who cared to join in them, with music supplied by two or three local musicians.

But before enjoying these innocent amusements, we had to undergo the martyrdom of listening to many long, dry, uninteresting speeches, all of which were full to overflowing of America's greatness and the insignificance of all other countries in comparison, and of the wonderful freedom of America's constitution and the tyranny of all European nations, especially Great Britain. Each speaker seemed to think he could not show his patriotism better than by making some sneering remark on England. Of course, this was easily accounted for by the fact that most of the audience were of German or Irish descent.

It is a curious fact that immediately a German sets foot in America, he becomes an American; but an Englishman, Welshman or Scotchman remains to the end, in feelings and sympathy, a Britisher, no matter how long he may live abroad, and in spite of the fact that he probably takes out his papers of naturalization very soon after landing.

Of course, the Declaration of Independence was read amid solemn silence by a worthy gentleman, who delivered it with a German accent adorned by a nasal twang. The annual reading of this does much to keep up, among the less educated classes, a strong feeling of animosity to Great Britain, which is fostered by the Irish German faction in American politics.

Almost as great an event as the "Glorious Fourth" was the arrival of a circus in the county seat. We all got there somehow, in waggons, on horseback, or on foot. Everybody went to all there was to be seen from the State Capitol down to the smallest dime side-show, and everyone struggled hard to take in everything on view, through wide-open eyes and not less wide-open mouths. Through the former we took in glimpses of Barnum's freaks and the backs of our neighbours' heads, while through the latter we inhaled clouds of filthy dust and much odour of stale beer and coarse tobacco.

After having toiled through a full season, and as the winter was fast approaching, when the work on a farm is reduced to feeding the stock and cutting wood for home use or for sale in the neighbouring towns, I set my brain to consider the prospects which a farmer's life offered.

As to the working of a small farm I felt that I had learnt all that was essential, as I had gone through it in a thorough and practical manner, carefully mastering the principal points necessary for carrying on successfully a farm of say 100 or 150 acres. The minor points could be picked up later on through paying close attention to what was being done by one's neighbours. I therefore considered that I was able to take up a farm of my own should the prospects warrant me in doing so.

But on closely going into matters and also perhaps paying too much attention to the complaints of the farmers I happened to meet, who, like their English confreres, are born grumblers, I came to the conclusion that the outlook for the small farmer was not altogether a happy one. The market value of all farm products was falling rapidly, while expenses could not be lessened in proportion. The actual summer labour was severe in the extreme. This would have been but a slight drawback if the returns had been proportionately good, but they were not; and one feels that it is a sinful waste of strength and energy to work like a slave and get little or nothing in return. I, therefore, decided to stay on where I was for some time longer, and might still to the present day have been a Wisconsin farmer had not the following event occurred.

One day, while several of us were doing some hauling, I was astonished to hear one of my companions make a joke which could only refer to a matter contained in one of my home letters. I immediately forced him to explain himself, and then, to my great amazement and vexation, learnt that while I had been working in the fields others in the house had been reading my letters from the old country, which I had not put under lock and key. I at once threw down my reins and told "the old man" he had better get someone else to take my team, as I would not stay another day on the place. He was very wrath at this, and raised all manner of objections and excuses, but go I would, and go I did.

In settling up my wages I found that he charged me with two holidays *and all Sundays* at the full rate of wages, not at the rate he was paying me, which reduced the amount coming to me to a very small figure indeed.

## Chapter 4
# Off to Texas

Having during the summer received several letters from my friend in Texas, all containing good accounts of the cheerful outlook in that country, I determined to join him there.

Without loss of time, I packed my trunks, and went over to an acquaintance, a young Englishman who was just starting an 80-acre farm on his own, and told him the cause of my sudden departure. He kindly offered to take me and my baggage into Madison in time to catch the train for the south, which left about 11.30 p.m. By midnight I was fairly started on my 1,500-mile journey, while little more than 12 hours earlier I had considered myself a fixture, at least for some considerable time to come.

I could not afford to travel by express trains and pass the nights in Pulman sleepers, so had to make the journey by slow trains, and sleep in my clothes as best I could for the three nights I passed in the cars. Under these circumstances it was not exactly a pleasure trip, still there was so much new country to be seen, with a constant change of travelling companions, that it was by no means monotonous.

We passed through Chicago and St. Louis, where for the first time I was able to see real passenger trains running up and down the middle of busy streets crowded with vehicles and people on foot, none of whom took any more notice of the trains than if they had been ordinary tram-cars.

This is very general in many eastern and all western towns of the States, as it saves the railroad companies the heavy cost of buying a right of way through the building sites of the towns and ensures a central position for the city depot.

After leaving St. Louis, we had a long straight run by the side of the Mississippi River, which was an endless source of interest, with its noisy, fussy sternwheel steamboats and long lines of log-rafts, floating down its muddy current. Presently the line branched off from the river in a south-west direction, and when we awoke next morning, we were running through the lovely Indian territory, which is on the whole the most beautiful, though not the grandest country of its kind to be found in America.

At the time of which I am writing this territory was the undisputed possession of various Indian tribes, to whom the U.S. Government had granted it as a "reservation." It has since been thrown open to settlers, and is now known as the Oklahoma territory, and has at present a white population of many thousand inhabitants, who can shoot as straight and gamble and drink as hard as the pioneers of any other brand-new settlement in the Far West. But at the time I am writing of all was peace and quietness, the unenclosed railway track being the only real sign of the white man's civilization. There were no whiskey saloons, Methodist churches, or dance-halls in those days.

Beyond the railway employees and an occasional Government "Indian agent" no white people were to be seen. There were a few scattered deer and several herds of antelope that would excite the lust for slaughter in any man who had the faintest taste of a sporting nature in his composition.

At the stations where the engine had to make a stop to take in water or fuel, a few degenerate Indian "braves" would hang around the cars begging, or offering for sale small trifles of Indian work, as, for instance, toy bows and arrows, beaded *moccasins*, or little bark canoes. The squaws also, with an eye to business, would bring their little copper-coloured babies to help their mothers to pick up an odd nickel or two. The child, entirely enveloped in a blanket, was held up to view, but for a five-cent piece the head and face would be uncovered, while for 25 cents the poor little *papoose* would be stripped of every stitch of its swaddling clothes, and, perfectly naked, be lifted about and passed from hand to hand, no matter how hot or cold the weather might be. The babies seemed to greatly appreciate, either the admiration they excited or the unusual freedom from the tight bands of cloth in which they are generally bound up.

This is quite the reverse of an experience I had a number of years later in Jamaica, when, wandering about with my Kodak, I met a big sturdy negress carrying a fine fat little black baby, which I fancied would make a good picture if divested of the rags in which it was clothed. But though only a minute before its mother had been begging for a penny, not even the temptation of a shilling would induce her to strip her darling *picannini*, as she said it would be sure to catch cold; and this in spite of the thermometer being over 100 degrees in the shade and the air as full of moisture as a steam-bath. I talked for some time, but all to no purpose. I had to take the picture of the youngster with its clothes on or do without it.

On leaving the Indian territory or "The Nation" (the name by which it is known in the west) we entered Texas, which is often spoken of as the "Lone Star State," from the fact that when it was an independent republic its national flag was blue with a single gold star in the centre.

Passing through the busy, bustling towns of Dallas and Denison, beyond which lies the Pine Belt of Texas, we came to Fort Worth, where the East meets the West.

On the streets and in the hotels, one sees an equal mixture of the

"AN INDIAN BRAVE"

Eastern business man in stiff black hat, black coat and starched white collar and shirt, and the Western rancher, in his high boots, coloured woollen shirt and white *sombrero* hat, so dear to the heart of all westerners and southerners.

Of two men one meets in the street one may be a smart wiry New Yorker, all black, oily and grimy, straight from the round-house or engine works, and walking along with quick hurried steps, so that at a glance one can see he will not allow the grass to grow under his feet. The other man may very probably be a *"greaser,"* *i.e.*, a Mexican shepherd, a picturesque figure, with his swarthy complexion and bright black eyes peering out from under the shade of his broad brimmed, high-crowned hat, which is heavily ornamented with silver beads and lace.

He usually has a bright scarlet or blue blanket thrown loosely over his shoulders and a sash of some lively colour tied round his waist above the top of his tight-fitting brown breeches. Somewhere under the sash or blanket, if one looks closely enough, the hilt of a knife or the butt of a revolver may probably be discovered. Dressed in this striking and really handsome costume he saunters along the street perfectly satisfied with himself and everyone else so long as they leave him alone, but quick to resent any affront, real or imaginary.

The true cowboy is not in very strong evidence in Fort Worth. His sphere lies further west, where he can in any of the little prairie towns spend his wages and amuse himself as he likes best in the country he knows, which is also the country that knows *him*. In fact, he often refers to it, in his conversation, as "God's country," by which he means it is the land that is all in all to him. He would feel uncomfortably restrained even in Fort Worth, as there would be the ever-present knowledge that the inhabitants (unfortunately supported by the police) would not be inclined to take his playful little jokes, such as shooting at the heels of a neighbour's boots during a dance, in the light-hearted way in which those accustomed to such sport might look upon it.

There are large numbers of negroes in Fort Worth, but they are by no means an improvement to the town from any point of view. Fort Worth was the beginning of the last stage of my railway journey. From this point the line runs almost due west over the open prairie, entirely unenclosed by either walls or fences. From the passengers' seats this is a decided advantage, as a fine view of the landscape is obtained, unobstructed by any bridges, deep cuttings or high board fences; but it is a very different matter with the engineer in charge of the locomotive, as his life, at best never a very happy one, is made miserable by the constant strain of looking out for stray stock, horses, cattle or sheep, which will insist upon wandering aimlessly on to the line in front of the advancing train. Although they had hundreds of miles of open prairie on either side to roam over, no place seemed to suit the taste of some of them nearly so well as right in the middle of the railroad track.

The day I went over this stretch of railway this seemed to be the case with an old mule, who appeared to wish for some little excitement to break the monotony of his existence. He, therefore, placed himself in front of the engine, and set off down the track at an easy hand gallop.

The whistle shrieked, the bell clanged and the men shouted and cursed him for all they were worth and a great deal more too. But it was no use, the speed had to be slackened, and on this being done he at once adapted his gait to the reduced rate of speed of the train until both finally came to a standstill, whereupon the train men attacked him with showers of stones and coal. This made him move off the line, but only just far enough to be out of range of the missiles with which he was generously bombarded, and there he stood and brayed as the train pulled slowly past him.

The railway company would much prefer to fence the line throughout, as it would be cheaper for them to do so than to pay for the stock that are killed or damaged by passing trains. But this the stockmen object to do as it would shut off and render useless large tracts of country by preventing stock from having access to the creeks and water-holes, an absolute necessity in that hot dry country.

When first the railway was built it was noticed that any old horse that could hardly be given away, if only lucky enough to be run over by a train, at once jumped up in value to $100 or $150.

The result of this was that the railway company were soon forced for their own protection to set armed men to patrol the line to note the brand and value of any animal accidentally killed, and also to prevent worthless beasts being driven on to the line with a view of obtaining compensation for their loss when killed by the train *or otherwise.*

I was very glad when late in the evening we arrived at Abilene, the end of my railway journey, and was able to wash off the various samples of dust and dirt that I had collected on my clothes and person in traversing the six or seven different States of the Union through which my journey lay. There was also a certain charm in enjoying once more a real good sit-down meal, even though neither the food nor the cooking was much to boast of.

I was not yet accustomed to the free and easy ways of Western life, and was, therefore, not a little astonished when the hotel-clerk asked me as I was on my way to bed not to bolt the door of my room, as, should anyone else arrive, he would have to share it with me. However, as no one did come I had it all to myself.

Chapter 5

# Across the Prairie

On making enquiries I found that my friend's place was over 130 miles distant across the prairie. How I was to get there was the next problem to be solved, as, after paying the hotel bill, my funds were reduced to so low an ebb that I had only five dollars and a few odd cents left in my pocket. There was a stage-coach running to San Angelo, which was the first 100 miles of my way; but that cost $10, and as two into one won't go, my five dollars would not pay the fare. Someone suggested a freightwagon, so off I set, searching over the town for one going in the desired direction. I found some were already loaded up and had no room for a passenger, while others would not be ready for a couple of days, which was longer than I could afford to wait.

At last, I met a man who was busy loading his eight-horse team with about 4,000 feet of rough lumber, and expected to be ready to pull out that evening. After a little bargaining he agreed for $5 to take my baggage and myself to San Angelo, and on the way to let me share his bed and board. I never regretted the bargain, as he was a pleasant honest man, who made an agreeable companion for the five or six days we were on the road.

In the last paragraph I mentioned my baggage before myself. I do this advisedly, as I had fallen into the mistake made by most young Englishmen going abroad, *viz.*, that of getting together, before starting, a large outfit of things which they fancy they may require, instead of taking with them only such articles as they cannot do without, and thereby reducing the amount of luggage to the smallest possible bulk.

Extra baggage is always an expensive load round a man's neck, and seldom or never pays for moving it about. One good suit and all the old clothes he possesses are all that is necessary, as he can always get on the spot the goods that are most suitable to whatever country he may find himself in. Outfits which look very nice in a London shop window are often found to be quite useless, and are generally thrown away, or, if worn, brand the wearer as a "tenderfoot" or new chum, and thereby lay him open to the practical jokes that are so often played on these unhappy individuals. Saddlery and guns should never be bought in England by anyone going to America, on account of the heavy import duties, and also because more suitable if not cheaper articles can be easily got anywhere in that country.

About three o'clock in the afternoon our train of waggons left Abilene and started out on its way across the prairie. There were no fences, and not much road, only many wheel tracks left by the numberless waggons which had formerly passed in the same direction, most of them pointing to Buffalo Gap, a depression in the clear line of bright blue hills which broke the circle of the horizon in the far distance, standing out vividly against the dull yellow of the level sun-scorched prairie-land.

This was my first close acquaintance with the true American prairie, and it was very different from the prairie one pictures to oneself from reading the stories of Fenimore Cooper and other novelists of our youth.

The reality, during the summer at least, is an apparently boundless extent of brown sun-dried earth, baked by the heat almost to the hardness of brick, and traversed by millions of cracks and fissures many feet in depth, and from one to six or seven inches broad.

Where not over stocked, the ground is covered with a dense growth of *mesquite* grass, dry as hay and of about the same colour, and in very few places more than four inches high. This kind of grass is curly and not straight like ours in England, and even when apparently dry and burnt up possesses most valuable qualities as feed for rearing and fattening stock. After a shower of rain, the dry grass will again turn green, showing that though dried up it still retains its life.

In some localities the prairie is bare of all trees, while in others it is densely covered with the *mesquite* or wild locust, which seldom attains a greater height than 20 or 25 ft. There are also, in some districts, many scattered groups of stately live oaks, which have somehow escaped the Redman's practice of destroying by fire as far as possible everything which in any way obstructs his clear view of game or enemies across the plain. These groves, in their perpetual deep green foliage, form a refreshing contrast to the all-pervading light-brown shade of the general landscape.

The positions of the few rivers and creeks which have water in them during the whole twelve months of the year are clearly seen from a long distance, well-marked by the narrow fringe of tall handsome trees which grow along the banks.

These trees are principally pecans, and are peculiar to Texas. They bear great quantities of nuts, something like our walnut in appearance and flavour, and of considerable commercial value.

The prairie, besides level plains, comprises also innumerable hills, valleys, and canons, and thousands of acres of such rough, rocky, broken land that nothing but a Texas pony or some mean old cow could ever get over it at any pace greater than a mere crawl, but it makes good galloping ground for either of the abovementioned animals, more especially the latter.

The train of waggons, on one of which I had engaged my passage for the cross-country journey, were eight in number. First came our waggon, loaded with lumber and drawn by a mixed team of horses and mules, numbering eight in all. Behind the main waggon, a smaller one, called the "trail waggon," was attached. By this means the weight of any very heavy load can be divided so as to bring less strain on the axles, but the great advantage of a trail waggon is, that when any very difficult pull has to be negotiated it can be detached and the main waggon hauled on to solid ground or to the top of the ascent as the case may be. The team then returns and brings up the "trail."

The second of our waggon train was loaded with blocks of natural rock salt, consigned to a wealthy stockman for the use of his cattle.

Next came two teams hauling heavy loads of mixed groceries, Californian canned goods and Irish potatoes. The potatoes are not suited to that part of Texas, as after the first season's growth they become quite sweet in taste, and to most people are very unpalatable. The last two waggons were loaded with lumber.

Before getting under way, we had arranged several sacks of oats to be used as feed for the horses on the trip, into the form of an armchair, on the top of the leading load of lumber. Seated in this impromptu lounge I soon found that I should make the journey much more comfortably than in the stage-coach, where one is packed in for the best part of 24 hours with some ten or twelve other unhappy passengers, stifled with the heat and choked with dust, having no air to breathe and no room to move one's legs. A person in this position may well envy the comfort of the proverbial "sardines packed in a box," for the tin will at least keep the dust out.

Smith, the driver and owner of our team, rode one of the wheel-

A STAGE COACH IN THE FAR WEST.

ers, a big brown mule, which had formerly belonged to the Army Transport Corps.

There was a slight drawback in using the sacks of oats as a seat, and that was that as they held the horse-feed the further we got on our way the thinner and harder my seat became, till by the time we arrived at San Angelo I was almost sitting on bare boards. I was thereby impressed forcibly with the many inequalities of the road.

Our first stage was only a short one, as it is always considered advisable to make a halt after the first five or six miles to straighten any loads that may have shifted, and, if necessary, to re-adjust the weights between the two waggons, and also to go over the harness to see that it is not galling the horses' backs or shoulders. As there was a waterhole about five miles out, we determined to camp there for the night. The waggons were, therefore, stopped just where they were, and the horses were unhitched, hobbled and turned out to roll in the dust and pick a little grass before they got their supper of oats and corn.

I had always been accustomed to see harness taken off, cleaned and hung up properly on the harness pegs, but here I saw it roughly thrown on the ground in a heap, just as it was taken off the horses. I soon got used to this, and, indeed, to doing the same myself before long.

The next proceeding was to get our own supper, consisting of bacon fried on the camp-fire, bread, molasses and canned tomatoes all on the same tin plate, and black coffee made with water fresh drawn from the mud-hole at which the stock were drinking.

After supper we made our beds—a very simple operation indeed. A smooth patch of ground beside the waggons was picked out and odd sticks and stones cleared off. On this a couple of blankets were spread, another couple upon them to cover us, with our boots and coats for a pillow, and all was ready.

This was my first trial of sleeping in the open without either tent or roof to shut out the beauty of the lovely star-spangled sky. How delicious it was, after the great heat of the day, to feel the cool light evening breeze blowing gently over one's face. How restful seemed the intense stillness of the vast expanse of the surrounding prairie, broken only at intervals by the hoot of an owl, the howl of a coyote, or the sound of the "lead-bell," sometimes near, sometimes distant as the horses moved their positions in grazing round the camp. When teams halt for the night it is usual to fasten a bell round the neck of whichever horse takes the lead, as it prevents the bunch from scattering and also lessens the labour of finding them in the morning.

Although camping out and sleeping in the open is one of the most enjoyable features in Texas life, still there are many nights on which the charm is entirely lost, and even a very inferior roof would be a great comfort. This chanced to be the case on our second or third night out.

We had reached a little settlement called "Reynolds" just at sundown, and had comfortably fixed our camp in the middle of one of the streets of the village. As the homes of several of the freighters were only five or six miles off, they rode over to spend the night with their wives and families, leaving only myself and one other with the waggons.

We had our smoke and turned into bed, but were very soon roused by a furious thunderstorm. The thunder and lightning did not matter much, but the torrents of rain soon set us hunting for what was just then impossible to find, *viz.*, a dry corner to shelter in. Everything was soaked, ourselves, our clothes, our bedding, and all. It soon passed over, and then we made a diligent search for some dry wood to light a fire at which we could warm ourselves, for it was too bitterly cold to stand about in our wet clothes till the sun got up. We found a *mesquite* log, which we split up, and with the inside, which was quite dry, soon had a fine fire. We passed a fairly comfortable night, sitting on our heels in the mud drying our clothing, piece by piece. And all this was in the street of a town.

Next morning, we found some difficulty in pulling out, as the lumber, soaked with the rain, had greatly increased in weight, and had thereby caused the wheels to sink deep in the mud. The horses, too, were cold, and did not like to feel the wet collars on their shoulders, and so for some time refused to pull. When the sun got up and we once more felt comfortably warmed through we forgot our troubles, and thoroughly enjoyed the light elastic feeling in the air. New life seemed to have been put into all things by the refreshing rain of the night before.

We fully expected to find all the creeks and waterholes well filled during the rest of our journey, but we discovered to our cost that this was not the case, as either the storm was only local or else, we had just come in for the tail end of it.

At times the rain storms in Texas stop so abruptly that it seems as if a line had been drawn across the country, one side of which is wet and the other dry. When this is the case, a person can stand with one foot in the mud and the other in the dust.

The next day we had determined to camp at a spot where after the late storm there ought to have been a good supply of water and grass. But on reaching it we found everything as dry as a bone. The rain had not touched it at all. Just before arriving at this point, we had been fortunate in witnessing a very fine example of that mysterious phenomenon, the mirage. Before us we could see distinctly a lovely blue lake, the little weaves rippling almost up to our feet on a yellow sandy shore, which was bordered by tall dark green trees. As we approached the vision retired, and then faded quickly away.

Without water the horses could not haul the loads any further, so as water must be found we each climbed on to the back of one of the team horses and scattered in pairs over the plain, here thickly covered with *mesquite* bush, to search for the necessary supply of water.

After riding several miles, not an extremely pleasant undertaking on a remarkably thin, bare-backed, and thirsty-worked horse, Smith and I reached Black Bull Creek, in the bed of which there was a small quantity of a brown muddy fluid, which the horses were fain to drink for lack of better. We filled the demijohns with this liquid, and from it, on getting back to camp, made some most enjoyable cups of coffee, the taste of which I have not yet forgotten. As freighters and, indeed, everyone else in Texas drink coffee very hot and very strong, the additional flavour from the stagnant water was hardly noticeable.

We had the misfortune to lose most of the afternoon of the same day, as shortly after starting one of the horses, overcome by the heat—or the water—dropped down in his tracks and lay there so stiff and motionless that we thought he had hauled his last load. But after a short time of unconsciousness, he began to tremble, then struggled to his feet, and no sooner was he in harness again than he attempted to pull the whole load by himself. By evening he was once more all right, and showed no further signs of sickness.

It was about 10 o'clock on the morning of the sixth day out that we pulled into the timber yards of San Angelo, and I had to bid goodbye to my freighter friends, none of whom I ever saw again.

Chapter 6

# A Lonely Tramp

As mentioned before, after paying for my journey from Abilene I had only a few cents left in my pocket, and it was therefore necessary either to get to my friend's ranch without delay or else to find some means of replenishing the empty exchequer. My friend had not yet received the letter which I had written him the same day as I started from Wisconsin, telling him that I was on the point of coming to join him in Texas, so no one had come into town to meet me. My only course then was to walk out the thirty miles to his place; but before starting to do so I made enquiries as to what I could get to do in town to gain my living should I for any reason have to return.

My search for work was most successful, as I soon found there was plenty of employment open to me, at which I should be able, in case of need, to earn an honest living.

Among the different jobs that were offered to me were the following:

1st.—Bricklayer's assistant, for which the pay was $3 a day, without board or lodging. The work to be done was carrying bricks in a hod on one's back up a ladder to the top of a three-storey building which was in course of erection.

2nd.—Hauling water from the river to mix with the mortar. Pay $2 *per diem*.

3rd.—Stacking and handling lumber in the timber yards. Pay about $2½ a day.

Having gained this information I started out into the unknown country with a light heart, a lighter pocket, and an empty stomach. The directions I had received in town for finding my way to my friend's ranch were vague in the extreme. They were as follows, "Go twenty miles up the Creek and ask again." There had been a great charm of novelty and freedom about the prairie when viewed from a comfortable seat on the top of a waggon, but the charm had all gone from it that afternoon while I was trudging along in the dust under a blazing hot sun and carrying a heavy overcoat, a great burden then, though I was thankful to have it before daylight came next morning.

I followed the directions as far as it lay in my power to do so, in that I went "up the creek 20 miles," or as near as I could judge a distance of 20 miles, but at the time it seemed to me, between heat and hunger, to be double the distance. Then came the trouble, I could not carry out the second half of my directions, the part in which I was told to ask again, as there was absolutely no one to ask. On my way up the only person I had met was a Mexican shepherd, who had been watering his flock of sheep at the river. He had not been able to understand my questions put to him in English, nor I his answers given in Spanish.

When I reached the 20-mile limit all was as lonely and as still as a calm day in mid-ocean. There was no sign of man, or habitation of man, so it seemed to me that the best I could do was to turn back towards town, where I could get some work to do till my friend heard of my arrival in his neighbourhood.

By now the evening was closing in rapidly, the short southern twilight fading very quickly into night, so that by the time I had walked some five or six miles on my return journey the light had all gone. I knew that the moon would not rise for a couple of hours or more, so I thought it better to camp where I then was than to struggle along any further in the dark, more especially as I was very weary with my long tramp and felt a little weak from want of food. I had had nothing to eat since my breakfast, somewhere about 4 o'clock in the morning. By accident I stumbled on an excellent place to pitch my lonely camp, where a number of "cat's claw" thorn bushes grew in a semi-circle, leaving a clear open space in the centre.

I gathered a sufficient supply of dry wood to keep up through the night the little fire which I at once lighted, then hanging my overcoat on the bushes so as to keep off the wind, I made my preparations complete. Before lying down I went to the side of a large water-hole nearby, and had a good long drink of the half-warm muddy water, then returning to the fire had a good smoke and settled myself down to get what rest and sleep I could. I fortunately had a fairly good supply of tobacco in my pocket, and a free use of this to a great extent consoled me for having to go supperless to bed.

It was not long before I dozed off. I must have been asleep for three or four hours when I was awakened by the feeling of someone gazing intently at me. On opening my eyes, I perceived, by the dull light of the almost burnt-out fire, the motionless head of an Indian regarding me intently from above the bushes, opposite to where I was lying.

I was not at that time aware of the treachery and ferocity which is characteristic of the Texas Indian, Apache and Commanche alike, or I should probably have been very nervous at the sight of my midnight visitor. As it was I had merely a feeling of curiosity as to what he could possibly want, and therefore, beyond clearing my revolver, I made no movement whatever, but lay perfectly still watching him as he watched me.

As it turned out this was the very best thing I could have done. We maintained this position for some time, till he decided it would be best for both of us to leave each other alone, and slowly and silently moved away through the brush and was speedily lost in the surrounding gloom. I then got up, made up my fire, had another smoke, and lay down again. As my Indian visitor showed no signs of returning, I made myself as comfortable as I could under the circumstances, and it was not long before I was again in the land of dreams.

I suppose I had been asleep for a couple of hours or so when I was aroused by some animals, which I mistook for dogs, sniffing at my hands and face. On my suddenly jumping up they bolted off through the bush for a distance of fifty or one hundred yards, and seating themselves on their haunches, set up a dismal, chattering howl, showing by the hideous noise they made that they were not dogs, but coyotes. This is the Spanish name for the small yellow prairie wolf, a cowardly but audacious brute widely scattered over all the Western States of America. My fire had burned very low, or they would not have come so near me. This was my first introduction to the coyote, with which I was destined to become much better acquainted in the following years of my life in America.

After piling on a large supply of fuel to make a cheerful blaze, I again went to sleep; but soon a light rain began to fall, which caused such a hissing and spluttering as it fell on the burning logs of my fire that I was soon fully awakened for the third time. After the shower passed over, I thought I had had enough sleep for that night, so sat up and smoked and nursed the fire till I considered it was time to take to the road again. Before beginning my walk, I went to the water-hole and had a most refreshing drink, as the water had cooled off during the night. It struck me then that this particular water-hole, which was as large as a small lake, must be very pretty by daylight, as it seemed to be dotted all over with small round islands, which I pictured to myself as covered with flowers and luxuriant green grass.

Before I left the edge of this charming pond the sun jumped up above the horizon and showed me the ghastly reality of the scene. The "Lake" was nothing more than a stretch of shallow muddy water, covered with a slimy green scum, much thicker in substance than ordinary ship's pea-soup. But the islands were the worst, as they were not islands at all, but only the bloated bodies of numerous dead cattle, which, on coming to drink at this veritable death-trap, had stuck fast in the mud, and in that way had perished miserably. I had had two good drinks of this "green Bovril," but I did not want a third, nor did I care to stay long to admire the scene. So, I set off at once for my second day's tramp.

I had gone only a few miles further down the creek when I met an Englishman, who at once put me on the right road and gave me landmarks that I could not well miss. It was only some 14 or 15 miles further, but these 14 or 15 miles seemed to spin themselves out interminably. I had to cross the river at a shallow ford and then strike out for a hill which stood up boldly from the surrounding prairie. As I trudged along trying to reach this hill, it appeared always to recede further and further from me until at last I began to think it must be some form of mirage and would soon fade away and be lost altogether.

As the day advanced the heat grew more intense, and my discomfort was greater now that my way no longer followed the river. I had thirst as well as hunger to contend with. The *mesquite* tree at best gives but little shade, still I was often very thankful to sit down under one of them and rest for ten or fifteen minutes. I would then mark out another tree a quarter-of-a-mile or so ahead, walk to it and rest again; then make for another one, and so on.

There were some five or six deep narrow creeks to be crossed, as they ran at right angles to the path. After the rains these channels are filled bank high with a furious rushing torrent of foaming muddy water, but now, unfortunately for me, they were all perfectly dry. Great was my disappointment, after hastening my pace almost to a run as each one came in sight, only to find on reaching it that there was no water there wherewith to assuage my burning thirst.

There was one exception, however. It was a particularly deep water-worn channel, and at the foot of a little rocky bluff a small amount of water had been retained after the rest of the stream had dried up.

I was not the first to find it, worse luck, as it had been discovered a day or two earlier by a poor old cow, which, probably as thirsty as myself, had not drunk cautiously from the edge as she ought to have done, but in her haste had plunged right into the middle of the pool (at most only some 6ft. or 8ft. wide), and sinking in the mud was unable to get out again. Her entire body was buried in the mud with the exception of her head, shoulders, and a small portion of her back. The mud, stirred up by her frantic struggles, was so thick that I could not even moisten my lips with it, and the heat was so great that it at once dried into hard cakes on my hands after I had wetted them with it in hopes of getting some relief in that way. I took hold of the poor beast's horns, and then of her tail, and tugged and pulled with what strength I had left to try to save her from the miserable death to which she was doomed.

Of course, my efforts were absolutely useless, and I learnt later on that it would have been quite a difficult job for a couple of horses and two or three men to have got her out alive. Many times, in after years in riding past the spot I looked with deep interest at the white bleached bones of this poor brute and thought of this my first experience of Texas "cow-punching."

## Chapter 7
# At a Friend's Ranch

A couple of miles further on, when I seemed to be really drawing near the ever-receding mountain, I saw a man mounted on a large grey horse approaching me at a steady gallop, and it was with great pleasure that I recognised in the rider my friend, who had only just received my letter (brought from town by a passing cowboy) and had at once saddled up his horse and started out to look for me.

On meeting him my troubles were, for the present, at an end. He mounted me on his horse, and we soon arrived at the ranch house, where at a comfortable English tea-table, I had the pleasure of recounting to his parents and brothers the various little adventures of my journey.

As the family had only a few months before arrived from England and had not long taken up their land, everything was as yet in a very unsettled condition. The house itself was so far little more than a framework, as only two rooms had been to any extent completed, one for my friend and his wife and another for his father and mother.

There was plenty of work for everyone to do, and each one did his share willingly and cheerfully, so that we were all as happy as the day was long. And by the way, the day seldom seemed long enough for all that had to be got through while it was still light. The building of the house had to be finished, and that kept some of us steadily employed for a month or more.

Then a small pasture of about 100 acres had to be fenced in, to serve as a run for the saddle horses. Into this they were turned loose when not needed, and were free to graze till the next time their services were required. Stables at that time were, except in towns, an unknown luxury.

One of the most lively and interesting pieces of work was the breaking in for the saddle of a few members of a band of almost wild horses and mares which had recently been bought. As none of these animals had ever felt the authority of man, except when the branding iron had burnt and scarred their glossy hides, they naturally did not take kindly to the training which was in future to deprive them of their liberty. But it had to be done, whether they liked it or not, so a cowboy, John Harris by name, well-known as a skilful horseman, was specially engaged for this work. And glorious fun and excitement it gave to the helpers and onlookers to see how easily and gracefully he sat on the backs of the rearing, snorting, buck-jumping fiends he had to ride.

Naturally enough in the one great struggle of their lives, against the rule and authority of man, they appeared to be possessed of the ingenuity, spite, and fury of the evil one himself. But their greatest efforts were of no avail, as not one of the brutes succeeded in unseating him, except in those cases where they themselves also fell to the ground. In such cases, disengaging himself as best he could, he would quietly stand up and was in the saddle again almost as soon as the horse had regained his feet. A horse that has been ridden three times is considered "broken."

Of course, there were also several gentle horses for the less skilful riders, and on one of these, a quiet little old white pony, I started off early one morning to search for the herd of Angora goats, which a few days before had taken it into their heads to go off for a ramble and had not yet returned. As there were few fences to interfere with their liberty the goats had a wide range to roam over. I sought them all day

A MEXICAN HORSE BREAKER.

without success.

Towards evening, being tired, I was riding home, sitting somewhat carelessly on the saddle, when a coyote suddenly dashed out from a bush. With one bound the startled pony leaped from under me, and left me spread out on the broad of my back, rifle and all, in the middle of the white dusty road. So quickly had it happened that some seconds elapsed before I realised that I had had my first fall in Texas. I do not know whether the pony or I was the more astonished of the two.

About this time of the year, *viz.*, October and November, large numbers of various kinds of wild duck used to alight in the pools in the creek, which ran close in front of the house. These ducks, being on their way to the Gulf of Mexico from their summer nesting and feeding grounds in the Far North, were in splendid condition for the table, and naturally we levied a heavy toll on their numbers. But soon our shooting became so successful that by general request we were instructed not to bring in more than one or two a day, as more could not be used without waste. We therefore laid aside our shot guns, and took to our rifles, aiming only at the heads or necks of the birds, while they were at rest on the water.

Sometimes one might fire a shot into the very middle of a bunch of ducks sitting so close together that not a square inch of water could be seen between them, and yet not touch a feather. At another time one bullet might take off the heads of five or six. We found the best plan was to pick out a single bird and aim at it alone. Stalking ducks that are fairly well on the alert is almost as difficult and quite as exciting as stalking deer or antelope, as few beasts or birds keep a better look out for danger than the American wild duck.

In speaking of shooting in general, we often remarked that some days it seemed as if no shot could be too difficult for one to take with almost certain success, while at other times it appeared as if it were impossible to hit even the proverbial haystack.

### Chapter 8

# On a Sheep Farm

Just about the time when the greatest press of work was drawing to an end, and things were becoming somewhat slack, it chanced that a man who owned about 5,000 or 6,000 sheep, and ran them on a neighbouring range, lost one of his shepherds. As he found much difficulty in filling the vacancy, I volunteered for the place till he could come across a properly trained sheep-herder.

The pay was at the rate of $20 a month and board. The "board" included the joint partnership with one of his regular shepherds in a small tent and as much bread, coffee, beans, and bacon as we liked to cook for ourselves.

How well I remember the first batch of bread I baked, and also the look on my companion's face when he saw it. It is really wonderful what one can digest with the help of the lovely fresh air in that part of the globe. I must say my first bread was very economical, it lasted a long time and the memory of it has not died within me yet.

The work I had to do was to take out before sunrise a herd of 80 or 90 merino rams or "bucks," herd them all day while they grazed, bring them back at night, and put them safely in the corral at sundown.

This seems at first sight a long day's work, but in reality, it is not at all arduous. When the weather is fine, as it usually is for say 350 days out of the 365, the sheep graze only till about 9 or 10 a.m. and then lie down in the shade and rest till somewhere about 4 in the afternoon, when they rouse themselves from their mid-day *siesta* and quietly graze their way back to camp. Thus, the herder is pretty well free to do as he likes all through the middle of the day when the heat is at the greatest. It is a curious fact that does not show well for the intellectual powers of the sheep that when resting during the heat they will with one or two exceptions, on lying down to rest, "huddle" as close together as possible. As a general rule, the hotter the day the closer together they bunch themselves, so much so that if not watched carefully there is a danger of some of the smaller or weaker animals being smothered or killed by exhaustion, from the heat and pressure of the heavier sheep.

On the days when the weather is not so hot as to deprive the beasts of their natural energy, the bucks wile away the noonday hours in pleasant little trials of strength. This they do in a most systematic manner. There is sure to be one among the herd who feels himself particularly strong and well, and as soon as he realises the fact that he is so, he becomes overpoweringly anxious to impress it upon his more peaceable neighbours. He instantly gives a challenge to the rest of the flock by butting, in no gentle manner, those standing nearest him. There is seldom any delay in accepting his invitation to battle. The two champions then retire some 12 or 15 paces from each other, halt, lower their heads, and as if at a preconcerted signal rush together with all the force they can put into their charge, striking each other evenly on the forehead with a sharp, resounding blow.

If neither of them is beaten in the first onset, they make repeated charges till one or other gives in. When the first pair have finished their encounter, another pair enter the lists and go through the same performance. Occasionally one of the combatants is rendered unconscious for a time, and now and then, though rarely, one of the fighters is killed by the blow of his opponent. While any two of the bucks are engaged, the rest stand quietly looking on, but never interfere with the principal performers. They thus appear to have a code of honour among themselves.

When things go well with the Texas sheep-herder the days run along smoothly and evenly enough. It is not the worst possible form of occupation that a man could take to, if only he can endure the dreadful monotony and extreme loneliness of his isolated position; for he is far from towns or any form of human society, with nothing beyond his sheep for company, not even a dog. It is quite usual for a month or six weeks to pass without his seeing another human being of any description.

Occasionally the monotony of his quiet life is broken by incidents which are not by any means of his own choosing. For instance, some evening after "corralling" his sheep and cooking and eating his frugal supper, he betakes himself to his lowly bed, perchance to find his blankets already occupied by a sleeping rattlesnake or tarantula, no pleasant companion in a small, dimly lighted tent. Or he may return some evening hot and tired after a long day's tramp under the burning sun to find some intrusive old cow has broken down his slender brushwood fence, upset his keg of water, chewed holes in his blankets, and generally wrought havoc to her heart's content.

Then again he may have been spared either of these tests of his fortitude, and rolling himself comfortably in his warm bedding be quietly dreaming of the good time he is going to have when next he draws his cheque and goes to town for his annual "spree" (or "whiz," as he himself would name it); when suddenly he is awakened by a terrible hubbub among his flock. Rushing out, gun in hand, he is just in time to see his usually quiet and orderly herd burst through the thorny brush fence of their corral and scatter in all directions. He well knows the cause. It is the regular trick of the hungry panther, or "mountain lion," to jump into the middle of the flock, frightening the sheep so that they break out and scatter to all points of the compass. He then

Denuding the Range.

slinks quietly away to kill as many of the stragglers as he thinks fit. Many a mile the poor shepherd has to tramp before he collects the terrified members of his flock.

But the most miserable time in the shepherd's life is when a cold, wet "nother" or "blizzard" blows up suddenly, and the lovely clear blue sky is turned into a dead, dull, leaden-coloured mass, and a bitterly cold drizzling rain begins to fall. On these occasions the sheep will not graze but keep ever wandering on and on, in vain search for shelter, which is rarely to be found on the open prairie.

The poor herder, wet through and perishing with cold, is forced to keep going, not only to hold his flock together, but also to keep up the circulation in his miserable, freezing, and usually thinly-clad body. Very thankful he is when at last the day comes to an end, and he is able to crawl into the shelter of his tent, and roll himself once more in his warm blankets.

Taken as a whole it would be difficult to find any class of men who are more faithful in the execution of their duty than the Texan sheep-herders, be they white men or Mexicans.

The herder knows every one of the 1,500 or 2,000 sheep under his charge, simply by the expression of its face, and he will never hesitate one moment to sacrifice his own comfort or well-being if by so doing he can benefit his flock.

## Chapter 9
## Starting as Stocksman

While staying with friends I met a young Irishman, who, with a compatriot of his own, had a short time before started a cattle ranch of some 15,000 acres, lying about ten or twelve miles further West. On my meeting him again, shortly after finishing my sheep-herding experiences, he gave me a very pressing invitation to pay him a visit at their new home. This I agreed to do, and he promised to pick me up on his way back from town when next he went in, a couple of weeks later.

On the appointed day he arrived with his two-horse waggon, into which I, my blankets, saddle, rifle, and a few more of my belongings were soon comfortably stowed.

He had with him also a stone-mason, whom he was bringing out to build a fireplace and chimney on to his newly erected house.

There had been heavy rain the night before, and in consequence the river was running very full. He had been delayed a long time before the water had fallen sufficiently to make the ford passable, so that it was almost dark before we started for his ranch. In consequence of his having settled on the place such a short time before, there was no well-defined road or track beaten out by passing waggons, which the horse could have followed in the dark straight to the ranch-house. It happened, therefore, that having got off the direct line, we wandered for long weary hours through the brush jolting over rocks and against trees, until it seemed as if we were destined to strike every obstacle which was to be found in those ten or twelve miles of deserted prairie.

One could almost have sworn that the waggon crossed at least twenty creeks, we seemed to come on one every half mile or so. This was in the blackness of a very dark, cold night. In the daylight one could ride over the same road and have difficulty in finding more than three creeks. It was pitch dark, and to add to our discomfort a wet "nother" had blown up soon after starting. All things come to an end sometime; even that journey did, although while on the way we were ready to doubt that it ever would. It was with an immense feeling of relief that somewhere about the middle of the night we stumbled up against the ranch-house, almost before we fully realised that we had arrived.

We were not slow in rousing the partner and several friends he had staying with him, who, after lighting the lamp, set before us what cold provisions they had. Then, spreading a couple of blankets on the floor, we were soon sound asleep, and perfectly oblivious to the half-frozen condition we had been in such a short time before. Thus, did I make my first acquaintance with what turned out to be my home for several years to come.

Next morning the "nother," being only a "young one," that is, one which comes very early in the season, had completely blown over. By the time the sun arose all Nature was once more smiling and gay, and we had soon forgotten our troubles of the night before, as one always does in that glorious, clear, and exhilarating atmosphere.

As the mason's wages were high, $5 a day, there was no time to be lost in helping him along with his work. Before daylight a little fire was built in the yard, and on it, breakfast was cooked, and was quickly disposed of, there being a plentiful supply of nature's best sauce, namely, a very keen appetite. Then while Joe, the mason, was mixing his mortar, the rest of us went off with the waggon, crowbars, picks, etc., to get out and haul down rocks and stones suitable for building purposes. These stones we cut and dug out from the side of a hill, distant about a mile from the house. Joe proved himself a quick and excellent workman, and once he got the work well in hand, he soon carried the chimney up to the required height, and in a couple of days after the first start had been made, we had the pleasure of a bright log fire in our grand 3ft. square fire place.

We found it a great deal easier, and also more satisfactory as to results, to cook on the fine broad hearthstone, than to work with a little wood fire in the open, where it was subject to every wind that blew. I soon had an opportunity to feel the benefit of this, as very shortly after the building of the fire-place there chanced to be a small "round up," or gathering of cattle, on the place, and everyone except myself attended it.

I was unable to go, as at that time I did not possess a horse, so I was left at home to prepare dinner for all the boys of the outfit, some ten or twelve in number. I managed somehow to get everything ready in time; there were potatoes to boil, bread to bake, bacon to fry, and coffee to roast and grind; and novice as I was in the art of cooking, the undertaking seemed to me a big one, as the quantities required were pretty large for such a number of hungry men. The results of my efforts cannot have been "too bad," at least if one may judge from the very small amount of fragments left over after everyone had finished.

Not caring for being "left out in the cold," as the boys say, for want of something to ride, I very soon after this bought for $40 a very nice little black horse of about 14½ hands. He was handsome, quick, and clever, but full of tricks and as knowing as a monkey. The following is an example of his powers of observation. One day when I was riding him over a flat piece of ground he got a cactus thorn in his foot, and began to go very lame. I extracted the thorn, brought him back very gently and turned him out for a week's run, using meanwhile another of my horses, of which by that time I owned five or six.

At the end of the week, he was quite well. On my taking him up again he came in for a couple of days' pretty hard work. This he did not like as well as running free on the range, so the third morning on starting out he pretended to be dead lame. Of course, I turned him loose and got up another horse, when he ran away without showing the slightest lameness. The same thing happened on two or three occasions, but I noticed that it was not always the same foot which he favoured. I decided then to try whether he was scheming or not, and after examining his foot carefully and finding nothing wrong, I continued my ride. He went very lame, first on one foot and then on another, but finally seeing it was useless, gave it up, although with a very bad grace, and went quite well the rest of the day. He tried the same dodge several times, till he found it had no effect, and then gave it up for good and all. That was one of his tricks, but he had many others.

Having a comfortable fire to cook by soon induced a taste for further luxuries, and this desire we gratified to some extent by building a rude table out of the boards that were over from the material used in constructing the house. We no longer took our meals sitting on our heels with our plates and cups on the ground in front of us, as we used to do, but had regular seats. I don't mean to imply that we had chairs: what we did have was a varied assortment of empty grocery and dry goods boxes set up on end.

These made excellent substitutes for chairs, but had a nasty habit of suddenly collapsing if sat down upon without due caution. There was also a certain amount of arrangement required at first, so that the shortest members of our company should have the tallest boxes and *vice versa*. This was particularly noticeable when we happened to have a guest, as he would at once be sized up for the height of seat necessary to bring him on a comfortable level with the table.

In making additions to the home comforts of the place, one of our party even went so far as to get a trestle bed, but this was voted too high toned by the rest of the company and he soon folded up his bed and was contented to roll down his blankets on the floor like the rest of us. The crockery, from the wash basin to the tea-pot, was all made of tin. The only exception was a cheap glass lamp, on the top of which a pet colt sat down, in trying to get out of the house backwards. This effectually smashed the lamp and somewhat damaged the colt. We next added a small cooking stove to our comforts and then the furniture of the house was complete.

In the free and easy style of life that one leads on a Texas ranch, it does not take long for men to become very well acquainted with each other. In fact, a few days will do as much there to enable anyone to know and understand his neighbour as months or even years will do in England. So much so was this the case that after a few days' stay on the ranch we were all first-rate friends, and within a month or six weeks of my first arrival, I had decided to accept my friends' invitation to join them in the ownership of the place. Before finally closing with their offer, I asked the advice of all those I knew to be well up in cattle business, but the only answer to my enquiries to be got from any of them was "Decide for yourself, and then if things do not turn out as well as you expect, you will only have yourself to blame."

So, after giving the problem what I then considered to be all due deliberation and going into figures as fully as I could, I took the plunge and threw in my lot with theirs. It was only a few days before Christmas that we all rode into San Angelo and had the deeds of partnership duly executed and recorded. I thus became a fully established stocksman, with an active interest in about 1,000 head of mixed cattle and over 14,000 acres of land.

The state of Texas has been divided into sections of 640 acres, that is to say, square miles, the proceeds of the sale of every alternate section being devoted by government to the support of the state schools or universities. The other sections have been assigned to various Railroad Companies as a bonus to encourage and aid them in developing and opening up the new country.

At the time of which I am writing any man over 21 years of age could "locate" one section of school land, on condition that he lived thereon for three years. The price was $2 per acre, payable in 40 years. Any section of Railroad land could be bought for $2¾ (11s. 5d.) per acre. This law, although apparently fair and simple, was the cause of many disputes frequently ending in bloodshed.

The cause of these quarrels was not hard to find. For obvious reasons, such as the desirability of easy access to water, grass, etc., and also to lessen the heavy expense of fencing, it was all important for the large stock-owners to get their land as much as possible situated in one connected block. On the other hand, it was a very great advantage for a small owner, or "settler" as he was called, to locate some section right in the middle of the large stockman's pasture, thus, without expense to himself, taking advantage of the latter's fences, water arrangements, and other improvements. It was a common practice for these small settlers to turn on the land far more stock than their own grass could feed, trusting to their living on their neighbour's pasturage.

Generally, when this was found to be the case, the stock if caught wandering off their own land were driven through the boundary fence on to the outside range. The small man would then probably have much trouble in gathering them and bringing them back, and most likely he would return boiling over with bad temper to discover that more of his stock was out in another direction. The big man would be equally annoyed to find the trespassers he had put out were again serenely eating off his best grass.

After this, at the first meeting of the two stockowners there was

A TEXAS RANCHHOUSE.—MOUNTING A BRONCHO.

invariably an explosion. High words would be quickly followed by blows and pistol shots, and probably one of the combatants would leave the spot with the stain of blood upon his hands, lucky if he had escaped the brand of Cain.

But human life was held very cheap in those days and seldom or never was the culprit brought to justice for these fatal fights, the usual plea of self-defence being all-powerful.

We were fortunate enough to get nearly all our land in one solid block, and so were spared any of these troublesome disputes. Besides our big pasture we owned a couple of sections on Little Rocky Creek, some six or seven miles off, but these we leased at a satisfactory figure, and had no trouble with them.

To keep our cattle from straying off our own range and getting lost, we decided to run a good stout fence all round our property. This was quite a big undertaking as the ranch was six miles long and three miles broad. To build the fence, four barbed wires had to be stretched all round the line, on cedar posts firmly set in the ground, 16 feet apart. To stiffen it, three cedar stays were fastened into each panel, that is the stretch between each two posts.

As the building of this fence required more labour than we could just then afford to give, we had to hire an outfit of men to do much of the work for us. One of the members of the gang was the Justice of the Peace for the district, who in winter, built fences or did any other odd work that he could get, and in summer drove the waggon and cooked for an outfit of cow-boys. His powers of reading and writing were very limited, but not so his capacity for imbibing raw whisky, commonly called "coffin varnish."

One of my earliest experiences of working stock, and one which left the most lasting mark was the following:—One day, about noon, finding that we would after dinner require to use the waggon for some work that had to be done, I started out on a very smart little grey cow-pony to find the team horses and drive them up to the yard, I discovered them, after a considerable amount of searching, quietly feeding in a little "draw" or valley, along with a bunch of rather wild saddle horses.

Being already pretty late I was bringing them home at a fast gallop. They came along splendidly till on nearing the corral they suddenly made a break through the brush to escape being run into the yard. Seeing this my horse, intent on heading them off, made a rapid dash over the creek, dodging through the underbrush and below the limbs of the larger trees, which at that spot grew very close together. I lowered my head to avoid one branch, and on raising it again was just in time to be caught in the face by another. At first, I thought I had got off with only a slight scratch, but soon found that a dead branch about as thick as a lady's finger had pinned my lower lip to the jaw, and was fixed into my chin hard and fast.

After corralling the horses, I got the stick out, bathed the wound, and proceeded to dinner, which that day, unfortunately, happened to consist only of potato soup, made from the water in which a rather highly seasoned ham had been boiled. The salt of the soup getting into the wound in my lip caused me to use both expressions and gestures which were certainly more forcible than elegant.

## Chapter 10
# Hog Hunting and Well Sinking

A neighbouring stockman, who hailed from the old country, had given us a warm invitation, which, of course, we accepted, to spend our Christmas at his well "fixed-up" ranch-house, along with several others of his friends, who had made their homes in the surrounding district.

Wherever one goes in Western Texas it is usual, if possible, to provide one's own bedding. On Christmas Eve we all rolled up our blankets, tied them on our saddles, and rode over the 15 odd miles to our friend's house on the river. It was a bright, frosty night, with a moon that made the scenery almost as clear as day, and tinged with a mild silvery light the vast extent of the silent, lonely prairie, broken only by the sharply defined outline of the nearer trees and rocks, and in the distance fading gently away into a white ethereal indistinctness. It was the beauty of sleeping nature unmarred by money-loving man or his handiwork.

The crisp springiness of the frosty night air made our ride a most enjoyable one, so that we were all in high spirits when we arrived at our destination. A good supper was awaiting us, and then followed a long cosy chat round the cheerful log fire. The night was far advanced when we broke up our party and rolling our blankets round us, slept soundly on the floor till morning light awoke us, and we got up to make preparations for the hog hunt which had been arranged for the Christmas Day's amusement.

Besides the peccary or musk-hog, which is native to the country, there ranged over the prairie, feeding on acorns and locust beans, large numbers of semiwild hogs. Man seldom or never attended to these in the smallest degree, beyond putting the ranch earmark on any of the little fellows that were unwary enough to allow themselves to be caught. They were a very mixed lot, being the descendants of the Berkshires, Poland Chinas, and Razorbacks, or Mexican pigs which had from time to time escaped from their owners and taken to a wild life in the open country. Being very fierce they could well hold their own against coyotes or other wild animals, or even against man himself if not well armed. They had a great turn of speed, and were quick and agile in doubling and dodging, so much so that it took a good man on a good horse to catch one of them, even with the cowboy's almost unfailing instrument of capture, *viz.*, the *riata*.

Once or twice during the year a hog hunt used to take place, when a few of the biggest and fattest pigs were shot, carried home, and salted down for future use. It was one of these hunts we had arranged for Christmas Day. After breakfast we mounted our horses and rode out on the range to look out for hogs, deer, or any other game we might come across.

We had gone several miles without seeing anything when we suddenly came on a large herd of very fine swine, which were busily engaged digging for roots in the dry bed of a creek. On our approaching them they scented danger, and dashed off helter-skelter through a belt of the thickest underbrush, where they could go much faster than a man on horseback, who had to force his way through the dense growth of catsclaw, *mesquite*, and prickly pear.

Consequently, by the time we gained the open they were a long way ahead. By dint of hard riding, we were rapidly closing on them, and were beginning to think we were going to bag our game with the greatest of ease. But while we were yet several hundred yards behind them the herd split into two parts, a few striking up towards the top of a steep hill, which was thickly strewn with sharp fragments of broken flints, ranging from the size of a man's fist downwards to the size of a walnut. Of course, they could get over ground of this description much more quickly and easily than the unshod horses we were riding. Some of the boys followed this bunch, and after much trouble succeeded in bringing down a couple of the hogs with long range shots.

The rest of the herd, with three of us close at their heels, went full speed round the flank of the hill and disappeared in a narrow gulch leading up into the mountain. The brush was so dense and the ground so rough that we could not ride further than the mouth of the canon. We dismounted, tied our horses, and followed the trail on foot, sometimes climbing over rocks and sometimes creeping on our hands and knees to avoid the tangles of thorns and undergrowth. After a scramble of half a mile or more we came out at the top of the gully, which we discovered ended in a large cave about 40ft. long and about 20ft. deep.

Directly at the back of this cave and opening into it, there was a round tunnel, about 3½ft. in diameter, running back into the mountain to a greater depth than we had any means of testing. The entrance to this tunnel, which probably at one time formed the outlet of a mighty spring, was smooth and polished, evidently from the constant passage of animals of one sort or another. We therefore judged that it was probably the home of other beasts besides our hogs, which had disappeared therein.

It would have been utter madness, if not certain death, for anyone to enter such a confined passage while the hogs were within. They most certainly would have shown fight, and a man on his hands and knees would have been entirely at their mercy, which excellent characteristic is entirely wanting in the hog. After discussing the point at some length, we came to the conclusion that if we could not go in to the hogs we ought to, if possible, induce the hogs to come out to us. In order to force them to emerge from their den we set to work to smoke them out, smoke being the only agent powerful enough to cause them to make a move. To this end we gathered large quantities of dry wood and brush, and piled it up in the outer cave, where we soon had a glorious fire in full blaze.

The tunnel where the hogs had taken refuge evidently had no exit to the open air on the other side, as was shown by the absence of any draught. Consequently, the smoke would not enter their stronghold, and our efforts to dislodge them cannot have disturbed them in any way.

But if the fire and smoke had no effect on them it certainly had a strong effect on something else, which surprised and startled us not a little. On first entering the cave it had not struck us to look at the roof, which was about 10 or 12ft. above the floor, but had we done so we should have seen that it was of a limestone formation, and as full of holes as a honeycomb is of cells.

Most of these holes had been taken possession of by the rattle-snakes of the district, being used by them as winter quarters in which to sleep away the colder portion of the year. When they felt the genial warmth of our fire, they fancied the summer had come again, and stretching themselves, they began slowly to uncoil and swing themselves gently down into the cave. At the moment we first noticed them our position in the cave seemed to bear a close resemblance to that of old Damocles and his sword, indeed it is doubtful if he did not have the more comfortable position of the two.

We quickly got outside the cave, and from a safe distance shot the reptiles as they descended. Many of these snakes were very large and old. Some of them were, we estimated, 6ft. and even 7ft. long, as thick as a man's arm, and had from 12 to 18 rattles on their tails. We were able to cut the rattles off those that fell nearest to us, but of course many fell in the fire and were lost.

My friend told me he intended to blow up the cave with dynamite, but so far as I know it has not yet been done.

The destruction of so many rattlesnakes proved a great boon to that part of the country, as many fine cattle and horses had been lost through the bite of these venomous reptiles. They had formerly been so numerous that no beast could graze in the vicinity without danger, the hog alone excepted, as it is the only animal said to be proof against the fatal effects of snake-bite.

On our way back we got a good bag of quail and rabbits, also two tiger-cats, each measuring five feet from tip of fore feet to tip of hind feet—their greatest length, as they have no tails worth speaking about.

The Christmas festivities being over, we returned home and once more set to work. Finding that the well we had dug to supply the house did not give as much water as we wanted, we went to work to sink it below the 50 feet which was its original depth. To do this we rigged up a derrick over the mouth of the well, and took it in turns to be lowered down and take our spell at digging. Stripped to the waist, with bare feet, and breeches rolled above the knee, we laboured as hard as we could, alternating the digging by filling buckets with the debris, sludge, and water which was constantly flowing in. These buckets were then hauled up and emptied by someone at the top of the well, who had to be very careful not to let the bucket strike the side and so upset some of the contents.

Even a splash of water falling from a height of some 50 or 60 feet on the bare back causes a most painful sensation, and a stone of, say the size of a pigeon's egg, striking a man on the head, would certainly prove fatal. Besides being careful the man handling the buckets had also to be pretty smart, and not lose any time, because the deeper we sank the well the more quickly the water filled in, and if the buckets were not kept going steadily it became, to say the least of it, very unpleasant for the man at the bottom of the shaft.

One of us had a narrow escape while digging one morning, for a board 4in. wide and 6ft. long by some mischance was allowed to fall down the well. By good luck it fell end on and struck the bottom between his feet. If it had hit him, he would have done no more digging in that well nor in any other.

Whenever we came to a specially hard layer of rock or natural concrete, we would break it up with a blast of dynamite. Our method of blasting was to drill a hole, charge it with Giant Powder, and fix in it one end of a good length of time fuse, the other end of which passed through a hole in a board, which was well covered with black powder. The water was then allowed to rise, carrying the board with it. We then dropped down some burning rags, which had previously been soaked in paraffin. These were sure to ignite the powder, which in exploding set fire to the fuse. We would then retire to a safe distance and await the explosion, which generally threw up volumes of water, stones, and smoke, that fell again in a muddy shower.

It was somewhat trying after working at the bottom, where it was always warm and comfortable, to come to the surface while a "nother" was blowing and run across to the house with nothing on but a thin pair of breeks and a thick coat of dirt and perspiration, and then have to wash in a tub of ice-cold water. But none of us were any the worse for it.

About the same time as we were at work on our well, some men were sinking for water at a place about 40 miles south of our ranch. They had got down about 100 feet without striking any signs of a spring, when suddenly the iron drill with which they were boring disappeared from sight *through* the bottom of the well. Thinking they had struck some crevice in the rock, they got another drill and proceeded with their work.

But they had only struck a few blows when the rock gave way and they fell through into an underground river of no great depth, but of considerable width. Nobody had the courage to explore the stream, and such experiments as throwing in chaff and straw were unsuccessful in showing its exit; so, no one knows whence it comes or whither it goes. The owner of the well fixed a small water-wheel in the stream, and this pumps a constant supply of water to the surface and is therefore almost as useful as a running stream.

Ours was a "dry pasture," that is, one in which there is no natural supply of water which can be relied upon for the whole 12 months of the year. We had, therefore, to make good this deficiency by wells, the water from which was pumped up by windmills into large tanks and troughs. One of these tanks was 20ft. long, 12ft. broad, and 9ft. deep, and made a most excellent swimming bath, and many a cool refreshing splash we had in the clear spring water.

We had six wells on our range, varying in depth from 25ft. to 140ft., and three of these gave a sufficient supply of water for from 1,000 to 2,000 head of cattle on all occasions except one, which I will tell of later on.

The water in a well is usually the one spot of moisture in a large tract of utter dryness, and it forms an irresistible attraction to all the insect and lower animal life in the surrounding district. The natural result is that if a well is neglected and is not kept in constant use, it soon becomes a veritable death-trap for these poor thirsty creatures, which jump in to get the water and are not able to climb out again. They have to remain there till they drown, their decomposing bodies soon turning the well into an evil-smelling pit of corruption. It was into a hole of this description that an acquaintance of mine, formerly a trooper in the 1st Royal Dragoons, had the misfortune to tumble.

He was out one fine morning searching for a bunch of strayed sheep, and was scanning the horizon more carefully than watching where he put his feet. By some bad luck he came on an old well that in its time had served to supply a long-deserted sheep-camp Before leaving, the herders had covered the mouth of the well with a few old boards to prevent stock falling in, but these had in time rotted or been pushed aside, and so proved no protection to an unsuspicious pedestrian. The well itself was of no great depth, probably about nine or ten feet, but it held between four or five feet of water and decayed animals.

Bob had in his time done a good deal of "roughing," and been in some pretty tight corners, but never, as he afterwards told us, had he endured such misery as he did at the bottom of that well. There he was, standing several feet below the level of the ground, with this horrible putrid water almost up to his mouth, yet thirsty in the extreme from the hot sun burning on his bare head and the dead bodies of skunks, pole-cats, possums, coons and rats, bobbing up and down about him agitated by every movement of his limbs or body.

The most serious feature of his partial immersion lay in the position of the well, which had been dug among some low hills, far from the usual track of any chance passerby, so that there was a considerable probability of his dangerous situation remaining undiscovered until it was too late. The thought that he too might soon become a member of that prairie cemetery in which he found himself cannot have added much to his comfort. However, a few hours after the accident had happened, some cowboys were, as they asserted, attracted to the well by the stream of profanity and bad language proceeding therefrom and they drew him out of his malodorous seclusion.

CHAPTER 11

# The Killing of the White Bull

The object in view, when we enclosed our pasture in a ring fence, was not only to prevent our own cattle from straying off into the wide extent of open country surrounding us, but also to keep the stock from the "free-grass" country from overrunning and eating up the feed we wished to preserve for our own beasts. The fence, being a good one, to a very great extent fulfilled the purpose aimed at in its erection. Still, in spite of all our precautions, a few head of cattle would from time to time succeed in either getting in or breaking out.

This made it necessary for some of us to attend each of the "spring" and "fall" round-ups on the range, to identify and bring back our wandering property. On the other hand, when we rounded up, our neighbours sent a representative or came themselves to take away any of their cattle that might have found their way into our land.

Between times very little notice was taken of an occasional stray cow or steer which one might come across in looking through the herd, as it was considered much better to let the owner know where his animal was to be found than to risk injury to horse and steer by turning one out alone, always a difficult and frequently a dangerous operation. So long as these non-paying guests were peaceful and orderly it answered well enough to leave them alone till the next occasion when the herd had to be rounded up for cutting out strays or branding calves.

But it happened once that we were forced to break through this rule. One fine morning one of our favourite saddle horses came up to the house with a very nasty wound in the flank, evidently inflicted by the short thick horn of a bull. The wound was a very severe one, and as 18 inches of the *viscera* was protruding from the hole, we thought the horse must die; but after a time, he recovered, although he was never very much good afterwards. Next day, to our great vexation, another horse was gored, but this time not so badly.

We did not believe that any of our own beasts would be guilty of such conduct, so we immediately instituted a strict search for strays, and were not long in finding the culprit. This was a very large, pure white bull, weighing not less than 2,400 pounds (comparing him with others I have seen weighed), and bearing a brand which none of us could recognise. Goodness only knows where this brute came from, but one thing was sure: he had evidently made up his mind to be "boss of the show," and run things according to his own sweet will. On watching his proceedings, we found he had a weakness for drinking as much water as he could swallow and would then hook, prod and drive off any other poor thirsty beast that dared approach the water for a drink.

When tired of this amusement he betook himself to the crossing over the creek, which was about broad enough for perhaps two or three cows to cross comfortably at one time. Here he would take his stand, hooking everything that came within reach of his cruel horns. He seemed to bear a special hatred to horses, and did his utmost to injure them; but this proved his undoing, as it drew our attention to his mischievous propensities.

If allowed to remain he would soon have caused us much damage for which, as his owner was unknown, there would be no chance of compensation. So, arming ourselves with the long heavy stock-whips used in the country three of us proceeded to eject the intruder. On starting out we expected that there was some real hard work and good sport ahead of us, but what was our astonishment when, on our coming up to him, he left the herd and trotted off quietly in front of us, like any gentle old milk cow. He went thus for a mile and a half, but then the devil got into him, and he refused to go another step in the right direction.

At first, he simply stood with lowered head, pawing the ground and making short rushes at us whenever we approached. We were well mounted and the quickness of our horses always saved us, if not by the "skin of our teeth," at least by the hair of their hides, from a too close acquaintance with his weapons of offence. Although he could never quite catch us, his horns several times rasped our horses' sides and flanks, and it was only by their intimate knowledge of the work in hand that they saved themselves from being ripped up.

BRANDING CALVES.

Finding that he had no success in this form of attack he headed back at full gallop towards the watering place from which we had driven him. To arrest his course, we threw ourselves in his way, energetically plying him with the stock-whips, which we had not as yet made use of. As an animal will often travel better when in company with others than when alone, two of us occupied his attention while the third brought up a bunch of cows. But to these he would have nothing to say, giving his undivided attention to chasing one or other of us at top speed, and no doubt hoping sincerely that some lucky accident would deliver us into his power.

All the time he was foaming at the mouth and "roaring like a bull." As we had still more than a mile to go, the distance was too far to drag him, and moreover at that time none of us were very expert with the *riata*.

Our next proceeding may appear to the reader to savour of cruelty. But it must be remembered that he had wantonly destroyed at least one favourite horse—and a horse in that country of long distances is a man's best friend—so in order to drive him off we felt he had to be cowed at all costs. What we did was to fire several revolver shots into the fleshy parts of his thighs and hips, knowing that the pain from these would reduce his spirit or else show us that he would have to pay the full penalty of his misdeeds.

Many a stubborn, bullying beast has been reduced to submission by this severe treatment. Had these bullet wounds been mosquito bites he could not have treated them with more contempt and indifference, simply continuing his vicious attacks and always trying to work his way back to the water troughs. At last, he stood still on a slight rise of ground, uncertain which of us to chase, as I was facing him and the other two on either side of him.

My friend on the left called out that if I would hold the bull's attention for a minute, he would shoot off the tips of his horns. When this is done successfully, it invariably subdues the most refractory animal, but it is a very difficult feat to perform. I saw the bull lower his head for the charge. I saw the pistol glint in the sun. Then came the flash and report, and immediately the powerful head sank gently forward, the knees slowly bent, and the huge brute turned softly over on his side, and with hardly a quiver of a muscle lay dead between us.

The aim had not been true, and the bullet instead of striking the horns had penetrated the brain where the skull was thinnest. By our united strength, aided by our horses, we managed to drag him into the creek, where we left him to be eaten by the coyotes and turkey-buzzards, the scavengers of the prairie. So well did they do their work, that within a few days there was nothing left of him but the bones and hide, which latter we found a short time afterwards high up in the branches of a tree, where it had been left by the next freshet that flooded the creek.

It should be borne in mind by any one reading these notes that these Texas cattle of 20 years ago bore but little resemblance to the fat, sleek animals one sees peacefully grazing in the pretty English meadows, animals which have been accustomed for countless generations to look to man as their protector and the carer for their wants and welfare. The Texas cattle on the other hand had the inborn knowledge that they had no one but themselves to depend upon for either food or protection from enemies, among whom they counted human beings, wolves, and panthers.

By descent they were Spanish, the offspring of the cattle imported into Mexico by the conquering Spaniards and become practically wild by generations of unrestrained liberty. No strain of improving blue blood coursed in their elastic veins. In figure they were long in leg and slim in body, and the head, usually carried high in air, was crowned with powerful horns, measuring often as much as 3ft. or 4ft. in length. The eye was small and fierce and for ever roving over the landscape in search of possible dangers. They were fleet of foot and could develop speed enough to put a good horse on his mettle to overtake and turn them.

To go among them on foot would have been to take one's life in one's hand, and many a man has only escaped by his agility in scrambling into the branches of some friendly tree. Of course, there were exceptions to this description of their characteristics, but these were few and far between, and the above points are fairly descriptive of them as a whole.

As soon as high-grade bulls were introduced and the herd improved by the imported strain of blood, and also to a certain extent civilized by being more cared for, they very quickly became more gentle and lost most of the wildest points of their characteristics, the great length of horn being among the first to disappear.

After one of the small Spring Round-ups on a neighbour's ranch we had gathered a little bunch of 30 or 40 head of cows into one of the large corals, and as they seemed disposed to be quiet, we left our horses, which were already pretty tired, on the outside of the gate and went into the corral on foot. We had arrived at the middle of the pen before the cattle realised that we had left our mounts outside and were more or less at their mercy.

No sooner did this fact dawn on them, than they hastened to make up for lost opportunities on former occasions and take the chance to pay off old scores. Without any hesitation or warning to us, down went their heads and up went their tails and at us they came full pelt.

We ran—ran as we had seldom run before, to the nearest point of safety, the fence, up which we scrambled. It was rather unlucky that, some four or five of us, myself among the number, in order to be well beyond the reach of the threatening horns, should have clambered up to the cross-bar connecting the two gate-posts of the corral, about 8ft. from the ground. Probably the cross-bar was good and strong when put in position, but the effects of wind, weather, and old age had greatly weakened its stability, and our combined weight was more than it could carry.

We had not even time to congratulate ourselves on having reached a safe refuge, when, with a loud snap, it broke in two, depositing us in a sprawling heap right in front of the crazy brutes. Thoroughly astonished and frightened at what must have seemed to them a most novel form of attack they turned tail and rushed off to the other side of the corral, where they stood huddled close together, snorting with fright. They fully understood the rope, the stock-whip, or the branding-iron, but they did not understand a struggling mass of arms, legs, hats, top-boots, and spurs being suddenly thrown down almost on the top of them. Next time we went into the corral we took our horses with us.

In the middle of all large, well-built corrals, a strong, heavy post is firmly fixed in the ground, which is often of the greatest service in saving the strain on a horse when holding a heavy, unruly beast. Immediately the animal is caught by the riata, the loose end of the rope can be given a couple of turns round the post, and the cow or steer held more securely than if the rope were merely made fast to the horn of the saddle. It serves another purpose, too, in providing a refuge for anyone caught on foot in the corral and charged by a fighting cow, which would be likely to catch him before he could reach the fence.

He can escape the rush of the cow by dodging to the opposite side of the post, in which case the cow usually continues her course far enough past the post to give him time to make a race to the fence before she can turn and catch him. Of course, as a rule, there is not much time to spare, and by the time one reaches the top rail of the fence, one usually hears the horns rattling against the bars somewhere about one's heels.

CHAPTER 12

# Horse Trading and a Cyclone

When first starting our ranch, our cattle were not numerous, and therefore we did not need many horses to do the required work. But our herd grew larger, both from natural increase and from our taking in some of the neighbours' cattle to pasture on our land, for which we were paid at the rate of 20 cents, or tenpence, per head per month. We accordingly found it necessary to increase the number of our cow-ponies to what was considered the least that was required by a cowboy to efficiently perform his duties. The numbers generally allowed for this were five or six "day" horses and one "night" horse. The latter is ridden exclusively during the hours of darkness, and is selected for his steadiness of disposition and general amount of common sense.

It is all-important when riding "night guard" round a herd of cattle that a horse should not be fidgety, nervous, or easily frightened, as even the smallest unusual sound during the night hours may create a panic among the cattle and cause them to stampede. During a stampede they may scatter and many of them be lost, thus undoing in a few minutes the labour of weeks of toil and exposure. I have known of a herd stampeding, frightened out of their senses by the slight noise made a horse shaking himself.

Until our numbers were fully made up, we were on the look-out for likely horses to purchase. Hearing that a man had come up from the lower countries with a bunch of horses for sale, one of my partners went over to the little rocky creek where he was camping, and was lucky enough to pick up a couple of very nice ponies at $30 or $35 apiece, which was by no means too high a price. One of these horses had formerly belonged to Kingfisher, the notorious stage-robber and *desperado*. Next day a cowboy, who was staying with us at the time, joined me, and together we rode over to the horseman's camp to see if there were any of his ponies that would suit us. We only found two that would answer our requirements, and these we bought for $22½ and $20 respectively. The latter, although the better horse of the two, was sold to me for less money, as, with the exception of one very small tuft, he had lost all the hair from his tail.

On my enquiring the cause of this, the owner explained that on his way up from San Antonio he had had much trouble in keeping his bunch of horses together. He had no one to assist him in herding them, and whenever an opportunity occurred, they strayed back towards their old homes. So, when forced at times to leave them unherded, he adopted the novel plan of tying them all in a string, the head of one horse being fastened to the tail of the animal ahead of him, leaving just sufficient rope for him to get his head down to graze.

As a rule, this answered very well, but on one occasion these two horses I bought, being fastened together in this manner, got on opposite sides of a good stout tree, and each at once proceeded to try and pull the other round to his own side. The tussle then became a trial of strength between a neck at one end of the rope and a tail at the other, and in this tug of war the tail proved the weaker, and hence the blemish to the beauty of my steed.

The above method of tying the horses together must have seriously interfered with their feeding, as they were both in a miserably poor condition; which induced me to give them the very unromantic names of "*Skin*" and "*Bones*." These names, though suitable at first, did not long remain, as after I got them, they had plenty of good feed and only a little light work. It was not very long before they fattened up and were able to take their turn of work with the other ponies, and were in no way behind them, not even in the matter of the tail, which soon grew luxuriantly. By the time I traded them off a few months later, there was every promise of a caudal appendage that any pony might be proud of.

The buying, selling, or trading, *i.e.*, exchanging of horses, holds an almost irresistible charm for the Texan, whether cowboy or stockman; and it was not long before I indulged in a little of it myself.

It happened in this way. One of an outfit of cowboys passing through our ranch took a fancy to the two ponies I have just been writing about and wanted to get them for his own use. Thereupon we started a "horse-trade" in true Texas fashion, sitting down on our heels, facing each other, each supplied with a pocket-knife and a piece of stick, which is gradually whittled away, until the bargain is struck or the trade falls through. In this case, I traded off "*Skin*" and "*Bones*" for a pair of spurs, a pair of *tapaderos*, or Mexican leggings, and a well-bred horse, which I considered worth more than my two ponies put together. His name was "*Brown Dick*."

Sometime after this, while I was with an outfit of cowboys gathering some cattle say 30 or 40 miles from our ranch, I was one morning about sunrise standing in front of a ranch-house, leaning on the yard-fence, when I heard the *tap, tap, tap* of a hobbled horse coming up behind me. As there were plenty of horses about, I paid no attention to it till I felt the warm muzzle of a horse pushed under my arm.

What was my astonishment on turning round to find poor old *Bones* nosing me all over and evidently almost as pleased to see me as a pet dog could have been.

After petting and making much of the faithful creature, I hunted up his owner and tried every means to tempt him to sell the horse back to me. But he absolutely refused to part with him. So, after some more petting I had to leave him and ride off on my own work, his owner departing in the opposite direction. I never saw him again, but to this day I have always regretted selling that horse. However, he had a good master, for which I was very thankful.

It happened on one occasion that my two partners were both absent, working on the outside range, leaving M——, a cowboy (who, by the way, was cousin to an English earl) and myself on the ranch. As our saddle horses had wandered off some distance, I told M—— he had better go and round them up, while I got dinner ready. The only horse left for him to ride was a big, lanky sorrel that none of us had ridden.

We knew nothing about him as he was a quite a late acquisition, but to all appearances he was quiet and gentle. So, M—— saddled up and rode off. But he had not been long gone, when he walked in looking very white and asserting vehemently that he could not ride that horse. I laughed at him, and telling him to finish cooking the dinner, I got on the horse and rode off to bring up the ponies. He went beautifully and was as quiet as a lamb, and I smiled to myself, think-

A BUCKING HORSE

ing of the fun we would have with M—— chaffing him about being scared by such a gentle old beast.

Thinking thus, I was riding along neglecting even the most rudimentary precautions against a "bad" horse, so that I was most horribly disgusted when after having gone some three or four miles he suddenly, on sighting the bunch of horses, stuck his head between his knees and began to buck and pitch like a full-grown cyclone. As I had been careless enough to allow him to get his head down, I knew almost from the first pitch that I was done for.

I held on as long as I could. Then I came off—when, I don't know; but *how*, I do know; and that was by a most elegant somersault straight over his head, hitting the ground with a thud as if shot from a gun, and with a very distinct impression of the brute's heels passing close over my head. Freed from all restraint, he ran like an antelope, and in the expressive language of the West, "only hitting the ground in high places." He was caught somewhere some time afterwards; I did not care when or where. I did the only thing I could under the circumstances; I got up and tramped back to dinner, wishing bad luck to the brute that had played me such a mean trick. I must say that it was not M—— who was laughed at over this affair.

This fall was a nasty, unpleasant business, but was not so bad as one that Bob had, who always seemed to come in for the worst of any ill-luck that happened to be going. He was one morning riding a young horse, which managed to get the better of him, and pitched him over its head into the middle of a large well grown plant of prickly-pear. He landed fairly in it, on his back, but in such a position that for some weeks to come the act of sitting down was to him a very painful operation, for when he crawled out of the prickly-pear his back from the knees upwards was more or less like the back of a hedgehog. The cactus spine being barbed at the point is very hard to extract, and for days after the accident all Bob's leisure hours were spent bending over a small hand-mirror armed with a pair of tweezers, and busily engaged in picking out the irritating little thorns.

It was in the month of July, when the summer heat was at its greatest, that we heard from a friendly stockman, located about 130 miles south of us, that a number of our cattle had, from time to time, been seen in his neighbourhood, and that if one of us could come for them he would gather and hold them in one of his pastures till our arrival.

As it would be a good opportunity to see much new country I gladly volunteered for the job. I was fortunate in being able to make the journey along with a man named Sam Hunter, who, having in his time had much experience as "boss" of various cow-outfits, was very well acquainted with all the country we had to pass through. As his wife was accompanying him, he made the trip in his waggon instead of on horseback. This was a great help to me, as it saved me the trouble of "packing" my bedding, provisions, coffee-pot and frying pan on one of my spare horses, as I must have done had I gone alone.

As it was I had only my three saddle horses to look after. I had taken with me my favourite *Little Roan, Brown Dick*, and another. On the second day of our trip, we were, about four o'clock in the afternoon, crossing Lipan Flats, a large level district, now completely covered with thriving farms, but at that time almost destitute of habitation of any kind. I happened to be riding a few hundred yards behind the waggon, when I noticed a very suspicious-looking black cloud, resembling nothing I had ever seen before.

It was in every respect so peculiar that it fascinated my gaze, and its gloomy threatening aspect forced me to rivet my attention upon it. The horses, too, became restless and uneasy. The surrounding sky, except in this one direction, was clear and cloudless, and the air, though unusually heavy and sultry, was calm and still. But the cloud kept coming on, as it seemed, with ever increasing speed, and as it came one could discern, at first faintly and then louder and louder a rushing, crashing sound as of some great river in flood.

As it approached, I could see distinctly the form of a swaying, swirling column, loaded with dust and debris and black as night, spread out and broad on the surface of the ground, narrowing higher up and again spreading out mushroom shape at the top. Gazing, full of wonder, at this awe-inspiring spectacle, I all at once realised that we were directly in the path of this all-destroying monster. Hunter and his wife, screened from the heat of the sun by the tent-like covering of his waggon, which shut everything out from view with the exception of the road directly ahead, were driving quietly along, totally oblivious of the devastating cyclone.

It was advancing at race-horse speed, and if it had struck them unprepared would undoubtedly have overturned and destroyed the waggon, and most probably have killed, or at least injured, both themselves and the horses. It was the work of only a few seconds for me to gallop up, shouting warning all the way. But even then, we were almost caught, for though we immediately turned off at right angles and put the horses to their utmost speed, still we had only covered a short distance when the tornado was upon us. But we had escaped the deadly centre of the whirlwind, and had only the outskirts of the storm to contend against.

First there was a slight tremor in the sultry air, then came a strong blast of icy-cold wind, followed without a pause by such a buffeting as one might expect to meet in an Atlantic gale. Without warning I was whipped off my horse and blown against a tree, where I had to stay, *nolens volens*, till the fury of the blast was over. Another stout tree served as anchorage to the two horses I was leading; one was blown round the one side of the tree and the other round the opposite side, the leading rope, to the ends of which the horses were tied, proving strong enough to resist the strain put upon it.

Although their necks must have been pretty painful from tugging at the rope, still they showed no signs of injury. The waggon had reached a hollow in the creek, the high banks of which sheltered it from the force of the wind. A heavy downpour of rain followed close on the heels of the cyclone, and lasted for a quarter of an hour, then ceased as suddenly as it had begun. The sky cleared, the sun shone out, and the air again became calm and clear, and much fresher than it had been before the storm appeared. But for seeing here and there a smashed and broken tree one might have looked back on the hurricane as some ghastly nightmare, the creation of our own imagination.

We camped that night close to the lovely Lepan Springs, which take their name from the Lepan tribe of Indians, now extinct or nearly so, but formerly a fierce and warlike people. These springs break out of the side of a ridge of low hills in a large volume of water, almost as big as the body of a horse, and the local theory is that they, like Kickapoo Springs (also named after their former owners, an Indian tribe), Dove Creek, and Spring Creek, which all take their rise from some point in this 50-mile-long ridge, are simply leakages from a large underground river, the noise of which can be distinctly heard above ground during various parts of its course.

However, that may be, the water is clear as crystal, and is deliciously cool to drink, forming a most pleasant change from the tepid muddy stuff found in the shallow waterholes, upon which travellers in this district have to a very great extent to depend. Hence the banks of Lepan Creek are a much-favoured camping ground. A party of Mexicans, who were encamped near us, very generously shared with us their supper of "*Chili con Carni*," literally pepper with meat, which I verily believe is about the hottest dish on earth. If there be anything

A COW CAMP.

hotter, I have not yet met with it in any of my travels.

In "*Chili con Carni*" the principal ingredient is the native Mexican Chili pepper, the sauce and gravy alone being formed from the meat. When properly cooked it does not burn one's mouth and tongue in the eating of it, but neither does it allow one to forget that one has swallowed something hot, indeed something very hot, which warms him with a genial glow for 24 hours or more after partaking thereof.

After leaving Lepan we went on to Kickapoo Springs and then across the long dry stretch of country to the pretty winding San Saba River, which generally meanders gently along between its thickly wooded banks, but has at times been known to rise rapidly in flood, and come down as a raging torrent, doing much damage to the towns and villages that chanced to be within reach of its devastating floods.

Another couple of days, passing through Menard and San Saba counties, brought us to our destination, where we stayed a few days in order to rest the horses before gathering the cattle and starting on our homeward journey.

While staying here we made our headquarters at a ranch not very far from a place called London, which though big in name was small in size, as it consisted of only one building—general store and Post-office combined.

Our host, Thompson, who had been gathering our cattle, was a fine, stalwart, hearty fellow, and like nearly all Texans, the embodiment of hospitality. As he had owned his ranch for many years, it was in a more advanced and homelike condition than any of our more newly-settled ranches on the North Fork of the Concho River.

Among other luxuries he had a fine garden, and we much appreciated the glorious water-melons which grew therein, especially after our accustomed home fare, the usual extent of which was bread, bacon, and beans, with occasionally a mess of potatoes and onions for a change, with rice and porridge, hot or cold, as *entrees*.

There was one pet weakness in which our friend Thompson indulged himself whenever opportunity offered, and that was "Trading," in the Texan meaning of the word. He would trade anything from a horse to a postage stamp.

The day after we arrived at his place he tackled me on the subject, and after much haggling and hectoring we succeeded in making several "trades." In one of these I recollect I traded him a plug of tobacco for a pocket-knife. In another he got a pair of buckskin gloves from me, and I in exchange got a pair of spurs from him. Then he gave me a new leather Mexican hatband for some trifle or other. Next, he wanted to trade for my saddle, bridle, or blankets, but as I needed all these, I could not part with them.

Then he worked for hours, indeed it would be more correct to say days, trying to induce me to trade for my pet, my *"Little Roan,"* but this of course was useless, as not even his whole ranch would have tempted me to part with my favourite. So, he turned his eyes on *"Brown Dick,"* whom I had not owned long enough to become deeply attached to, and the trading for him lasted out the rest of our visit to Thompson's ranch. Finally, I let him have *Brown Dick* in exchange for a fine big strong horse (which I afterwards named *Eli*) and two yearlings and $5 in cash, and both of us were satisfied.

In making the trades and exchanging bills of sale for the horses, each of us described his horse as being "gentle." I believe this was genuine in his case; it certainly was in mine, as *Brown Dick* had come to me with a good character, and while in my possession I had never seen anything to the contrary. But as it turned out the word "gentle" could not be fairly applied to either horse, at least in so far as it referred to pitching or buck-jumping. Sometime after I had arrived back on our own place, I heard by chance that Thompson had on our departure turned *Brown Dick* out to grass for a month or six weeks to fatten up, and when he took him up and rode him, he pitched like an unbroken colt. And Eli was not altogether innocent either.

While on our way back with the cattle, our camp chancing one night to be near a little town, Kernville I think it was called, I thought I would "bust" my $5 in getting a few luxuries for my fellow-campers, and with this object in view rode *Eli* into town. The hour was early, somewhere about daybreak, and I had much trouble in rousing the sleepy store-keeper from his bed. I made my purchases of tinned meats, canned fruits, and a large paper bag full of oranges, and climbed on to my horse to ride back to camp. But no sooner was I mounted and my pockets, saddle, and arms all well loaded with these various items, than *Eli* tucked his head between his forelegs and began to buck and pitch all up the main street, turning my progress into a John Gilpin-like ride.

A tin of sardines was lost in one jump and a can of peaches disturbed with the next. These were quickly followed by the oranges, and soon the street was strewn with the various articles which had been intended for our feast. The rattle and din created by the catastrophe brought many sleepy heads to the windows to see who or what it was that had disturbed their peaceful slumbers.

Much of the country through which we had to pass was covered every here and there with impenetrable thickets of oak, catsclaw, and various kinds of low underbrush. These thickets ranged in size from half an acre to four or five acres in extent, and were the favourite resort of the panther, coyote, wildcat, skunk, and rattlesnake. Through the tangle of these miniature forests the native cattle had in the course of time beaten out narrow winding paths, which were in reality nothing more nor less than tunnels, as the overhanging brush and branches interlaced and closed over them at the height of a cow's back, making it impossible for a man on horseback to pass.

This made the handling of cattle in this district a very troublesome affair as, when driven, they always tried to take refuge in these tunnels, well knowing the difficulty there would be in turning them out again. To dislodge the brutes the usual plan adopted was for one of the cowboys to run in on his hands and feet, barking like a dog. This generally answered well enough, but not always, as the cow sometimes ran the wrong way, which was very awkward and was sometimes followed by a funeral.

The chance of this happening, and the uncertainty of what one might meet in the form of snakes, *peccaries*, tarantulas, etc., in the half darkness of one of these semi-tropical thickets, always added much excitement to this form of "cow-punching." In travelling through this district, we managed to keep our little bunch of cattle very well together, but in spite of all our care one of the yearlings I had got in trade succeeded in breaking away and diving into one of these dense mots of brushwood, from which our utmost efforts to dislodge her were unavailing; we never saw her again.

On our return journey the number of our party was increased by two cowboys, who, wishing to make their way north and having horses, but no camping outfit, were glad to help us in driving the cattle in return for their board and—I was almost going to say lodging, but the lodging was of course free to all, for our beds were the prairie and our roof the open sky. For pillows we had our saddles, or our boots rolled in our jackets, and our saddle-blankets, often soaked with the day's perspiration from the horse's back, served for covering. The making of one's pillow with a pair of boots requires a certain amount of care and attention as you have to look in which direction the spurs point.

One of the boys who accompanied us had a beast of a horse to ride. It used to pitch every time the saddle was put on its back. Un–

der ordinary circumstances this would not have mattered much, but unfortunately the boy was just recovering from a bad abscess on the underside of the thigh. The abscess had been roughly lanced by a man who chanced to be in the neighbourhood, and who described himself as a doctor. The wound was still open for two inches or more; and the patient suffered excruciating pain every time the horse buck-jumped. Still, he would not change it with any of us, though we begged him to do so, and he continued to ride the brute as long as he was with us.

The heat was extreme during the nine or ten days it took us to journey back to our ranch. We were able to drive the cattle only for a short distance in the early morning; then camp during the middle of the day; and drive again in the cool of the evening, and as far into the night as the light would allow.

There was one little calf, about three weeks old, that we soon saw could not make the journey on its own legs. It became a question either of killing or carrying him. Greatly to his mother's terror and indignation we roped the little beggar and hoisted him into the waggon, setting him free on his legs to be fed by his mother when we pitched our camp.

At first both cow and calf were terribly upset by our arrangements for their comfort, but as soon as it dawned upon them that we did not wish to hurt either one or the other, they appreciated the benefit. On striking camp, the little fellow was always to be found standing close to the tail-end of the waggon, and after the first time or two there was no necessity to catch him with a rope. He was anxious not to be forgotten. As long as we had him in our possession this beast always remained gentle and friendly to us. We finally sold him (by that time a fine three-year-old steer) along with a number of others, which were going up the trail to the Indian nation to fatten for the Chicago market.

Chapter 13

# A Shooting Affair

Fifteen or twenty years ago it was the usual custom for all men on the Western frontier to go about armed, that is to say, carrying wherever they went a pistol, carbine, or rifle, in defiance of various laws and police regulations. The unsettled state of the country at that time and the antecedents of many of the population (as to which it was etiquette not to enquire) made a revolver a useful companion. Still, I always found that so long as a man treated those he met in an honourable, friendly, and open manner he was as safe, or more so, on the prairie than in the streets of London or New York. Nevertheless, shooting affairs did occur frequently—sometimes from the most trivial causes.

Disputes, which in our colder English climate would be referred to the slow and ponderous machinery of the law courts, were there settled in a speedy manner by a couple of pistol shots, followed by a funeral, with or without an inquest, according to the ease or difficulty in finding a Justice of the Peace or other officer authorised to act as Coroner. This state of affairs was no doubt due partly to the vivacity engendered by the lightness of the air, which gives a force and intensity to the mere fact of living; and partly also to the practice of habitually carrying weapons.

There is not much use in carrying a pistol if the man who carries it does not know how to use it; and as proficiency can only be gained by constant practice, the cowboys availed themselves of every opportunity of improving themselves in the art of shooting. Thus, for instance, when riding across the country they would take shots at the mischievous little prairie dogs which abound all over the Western plains of America. Or if by chance their way should lead them by the side of a river, they would keep their hand and eye in practice by trying to shoot off the heads of the mud-turtles which in the middle of the day climb on the rocks and fallen logs to bask in the warmth of the sunshine.

If three or four boys happened to be staying for a few days at some ranch house they were pretty certain to take as a mark an empty paraffin tin or an old fruit can, and have an impromptu shooting match at that. So, a very fair proportion of the men one met could be counted as first-rate shots, and many of them attained to such proficiency that it was a rare event for them ever to miss their mark. Some of the boys used the heavy Colt revolver, shooting a .450 ball, but more of them preferred the lighter Smith and Wesson's .380 six-shooter. Besides these there was a varied assortment of weapons, comprising almost every pattern of revolver made by the present-day gunsmith.

The first shooting affair that happened while I was present fortunately ended without any great damage being done. We had been helping in a cattle drive and round-up one day in May when the heat was intense, making the cattle hard to hold together. They continually kept on trying to break for shade or water, thereby delaying the work, so that it was already late in the day when we were able to turn loose those that were not wanted. The cattle that had been parted out, or—as they would be called in cattle parlance "the cut"—numbered about 400 head, a mixed bunch of cows, calves, and steers. Three of us were detailed to drive them off to a fenced-in pasture lying about ten miles back from the river and there turn them loose.

The cows had been sullen and bad-tempered all day, and no doubt thought that they too should have been allowed to go free when their companions were liberated at the end of the round-up. We knew they were thirsty, but we dared not let them get down to the river to drink as they would have taken advantage of the thick growth of trees on the river banks to escape from us and mix with the others from which they had just been separated. If this had happened, the whole of our day's work would have to be done over again. So, we determined to push them on as fast as we could in the direction they ought to go.

But with the best intentions and our greatest efforts the progress we made was slow, and for us and our horses very trying, because no sooner did we think we had got the cattle fairly started and going well, than some old cow would try to get off by lagging behind. Then while we were away bringing her up to the herd, a couple of steers in the lead of the bunch would make a determined attempt to escape. While they were being brought back others would slip away in another direction. All this meant constant hard riding, and was by no means calculated to soothe tempers already a little bit upset by a long fast.

We had had neither food nor drink since breakfast, a light repast at 4 a.m., consisting of a cup of cold black coffee, a bit of cold bacon, and a stale soda-biscuit, followed by twelve hours in the saddle, riding hard all the time under a broiling sun shining out of a clear blue cloudless sky. The horses were not over happy either, as they had reached the stage when the flanks are drawn thin and tight, and the hips and thighs lose the beauty of their roundness, and the eye looks with a wistful gaze out of a sunken socket, or else has a puffed and swollen appearance round the edge; and to keep the saddle tight the cinch or girth has been pulled many inches shorter than it was in the early morning.

In an ordinary way the cowboy looks on these slight discomforts as all in the day's work; and even though the parched and dust-choked condition of his lips and mouth has put a stop to the song or merry whistle with which he started, and he is able to do no more than give utterance to a low muttered curse, he usually contents himself by biting another piece off his plug of tobacco, or rolls another cigarette of the dry tobacco and brown corn-leaf paper, dear to the heart of the prairie rider, and then pushes on to get through his task as quickly and as thoroughly as may be.

But the disposition and temper of at least one of my companions would not allow him to take things in this philosophical manner. Although in many ways a very good fellow, "Sam" was of an overbearing and quarrelsome nature, and could ill brook opposition. On this occasion he seemed to treat the contrariness of the cattle as a deliberate insult aimed specially at himself.

So much so was this the case that by the time we had proceeded some six or seven miles on our way he had worked himself up into a boiling passion. He could get no relief from abusing the cattle; so, galloping round the end of the herd he swung up to my other companion, "Tom," charging him roundly with being the cause of the obstinacy of the beasts we were driving. Had he restrained himself to words he would only have been laughed at for the stupidity of his accusations; but instead of this he was foolish enough to aim a blow with the butt end of his heavy lead-weighted quirt at his opponent's head. Had it struck the spot intended a fractured skull would have been the result. Fortunately for both parties a quick movement of one of the ponies saved Tom's head; and the force of the stroke fell with a dull thud on the arm and shoulder.

From where I was riding, a few yards away, it seemed that almost simultaneously with the descent of the quirt Tom's pistol glanced in the sun, followed immediately by the flash and report; and a bullet whistled close past my ear, more nearly hitting me than the man it was intended for. I expected to see Sam fall to the ground. Instead of this his horse, startled by the blaze of light caused by the brilliant rays of the setting sun catching the nickel-plated revolver saved his rider's life by rearing and bolting to a safe distance, carrying his rider, perhaps against his will, out of range of further pistol shots. Sam then rode off in the gathering darkness, leaving us to finish the drive as best we could.

We heard afterwards that he next day rode into town and applied for a summons against Tom for attempted murder, but this was peremptorily refused, as it was clearly a case of self-defence. He was further advised to leave town as soon as he could or he would probably be arrested for carrying concealed weapons; for while he was in the office of the Justice of the Peace his horse, in giving himself a shake, threw out of his saddle-pocket an enormous old cavalry revolver, which lay in full view on the sidewalk.

Sam came back very crestfallen, and no reference was ever made to the affair. But these two men, be it noted, were never friendly afterwards. Their nearest approach to amity was a sort of armed neutrality.

Chapter 14

# Windmills and a Long Ride

Windmills are, as a rule, faithful and useful servants. A well-behaved mill, if properly attended to, say twice in each week, will keep on pumping away merrily night and day, raising many thousands of gallons of water every 24 hours, to supply the needs of the thirsty cattle. But occasionally the mill will get out of order, of course at some inopportune moment, either when the caretaker's presence is urgently needed elsewhere, or when a particularly large herd of cattle is requiring water.

Our best and most trusted windmill served us thus on one occasion, when there were something like a thousand head of stock depending on it for their drinking supplies. Without warning it suddenly ceased working. On searching for the cause, we found that the plunger of the pump had snapped close to the bottom of the well, and the whole of the piping and the cylinder would have to be withdrawn before the break could be repaired. We did not at that time possess the necessary apparatus for holding and unscrewing the pipe, or the blocks and tackle to pull the tubing up to the surface. The nearest place where they could be borrowed was from a well-digger, who was supposed to be boring a well some 25 miles west from us.

The break occurred in the evening of a very hot day. Next morning it was decided that I should ride over and get what we wanted, bring back the various articles, and then on my return we would fix the pump during the following night so as to renew the supply of water in the tank, which was already getting very low.

As time was precious, and I had a long lonely ride before me, I had to make an early start. Saddling my horse before daylight and eating a little cold breakfast, as I did not wish to waste time in lighting a fire, I set off, intending to reach the well-borer's camp before the heat of the day, and make the return journey in the cooler part of the evening.

It did not take very long to get over the first eight or nine miles of my way, most of which ran up the valley of the Big Mulberry Creek. After that the land was all new to me; and as the directions I had received for finding the 7D ranch house, the first object of my ride, were of the vaguest outline, when I reached the top of the divide or watershed separating the Mulberry, Kiowa, Mackenzie, and several smaller creeks, I lost a lot of time in working out in my own mind which route I ought to follow. There seemed to be a regular network of little draws and valleys, which could only be compared in arrangement to the form of a very irregular spider's web. I had to do a great deal of riding up and down these hills and valleys before at last striking the right creek.

Besides this unavoidable delay I wasted a considerable amount of time trying to capture a particularly fine badger, whose hide I wanted to add to the pile of furs which formed my bed in a corner of our ranch house. The animal escaped me, for which I am not sorry now, no matter what my feelings were at the time.

Before leaving the Divide and riding down into the creek bottom, I came on an old dead tree, on one of whose projecting limbs there was a large nest belonging to an uncommon kind of crow, which I had not seen before. It had white patches on each wing and tail, and was probably a freak of nature. As I had been at one time an ardent collector of birds' eggs, I could not pass this nest without seeing what was in it. At the risk of my neck, I climbed up and found that the nest contained five eggs, unlike any crow's eggs that I had known before. Three of the eggs I left for the parent birds and two of them I took as specimens. These, after blowing them, I wrapped in my pocket handkerchief and stowed away inside the breast of my shirt, where I carried them in safety all that day and the next.

Although this diversion occupied a considerable amount of time it could hardly be counted as altogether lost, because while I was engaged in my ornithological pursuits my pony was busy feeding on the rich curly *mesquite* grass which grew luxuriantly all over the Divide. This feed and short rest helped to keep up his spirits for the rest of the day.

It was well on in the afternoon before I reached the 7D ranch-house, near which I expected to find the man I was looking for. I was disappointed to learn that he had a few days previously moved to another camp about 16 or 17 miles further on, where he was boring for water near the head of a small creek which was little known and seldom visited.

I asked the cook at the house how I was to find the well-borer's camp, and was told to ride due west for ten miles, and then turn north west for five miles more. I would strike the creek where he was at work, and would easily find him.

As there was none too much daylight left for my further ride, I had to refuse the hospitable invitation "to get down, come in and have something to eat." Had the country over which I had to pass been level, or even fairly so. *Little Roan* and I could have got over it at a pretty respectable pace. But instead of being flat and even, it consisted entirely of sparsely wooded rolling hills, intersected by the dry beds of numberless little nameless creeks, which had to be taken just as they came, as I was afraid to leave my due westerly course to search for an easier way. If once you lose your bearings on the prairie you may hunt for days before finding them again, so much alike is one part of the country to another. It was a case of climbing up one hill, then diving into a draw, across a creek-bed, and scrambling up the opposite side; and the same thing over and over again until I was heartily sick of it, and wished that some good *genii* would roll the hills out flat.

However, by the guiding help of the sun, having held pretty correctly to the directions given at the 7D ranch I arrived, just as the sun was setting, on the top of a high ridge of bluffs overlooking the valley of the creek of which I had been in search. As I stood on the highest point of the cliff, I scanned the valley closely both up and down, but could not discern any signs of the well-borer's camp. When I started from home in the morning, I did not expect to be away more than ten or twelve hours at most, and therefore had taken no provisions with me. I now saw that as the sun had already set, and the twilight in Texas is of very short duration, if I did not find the camp, I was looking for in the next ten or fifteen minutes I should be forced to camp where I was supperless.

Just as I was preparing to descend into the valley of the creek a doe and fawn jumped up quite close to me, and after running 80 or 100 yards stood still to inspect the disturber of their rest. Here, I thought, was a good chance to provide myself with both supper and breakfast, but it was not to be, for though I aimed as carefully as I could at the fawn, I missed him, either through the dimness of the failing light or, perhaps, through my own eagerness.

A few minutes' scramble down an old cattle trail which led down one of the breaks in the line of bluffs soon brought me to the bottom of the creek valley, which was closely covered with a scattered growth of *mesquite* trees, interspersed with a dark green bunch of live oaks standing tall and stately above their more lowly companions, the locust trees.

I followed down the course of the creek bottom for a couple of miles or more, searching in and out among the trees for some sign or track that might guide me to Fox's camp; but nothing could I find, and no living creature was to be seen. Yet I knew instinctively that numbers of prairie wolves were watching eagerly every movement that I made.

I turned my pony's head and rode back to a spot a short distance beyond the point where I had entered the valley. There finding what seemed to me a convenient place, I determined to camp for the night and continue my search in the morning. Although a full moon was shining, owing to the many cross shadows among the trees it was difficult to distinguish objects any distance off from the path.

I can well remember the spot where I fixed my lonely camp, just about the middle of a small circle of ground, some half-an-acre in extent, and clear of trees with the exception of two, which stood nearly in the centre of the circle and a short distance apart. To one of these I tied my horse, giving him the full length of his rope so that he could feed on the grass within his reach. The foot of the other tree I reserved as my own resting place. Beyond the clear space everything was shut off by a dense growth of brush, except on the side nearest the bluff, where were some low rocky hillocks. Towards the westerly side of my bedroom "*au naturel*," there lay a heap of whitened bones where some old buffalo had in times gone by ended his career. I recollect how brilliantly white the skull with its black empty sockets shone in the moonlight.

After the great heat of the day, the evening felt at first delightfully cool, but as the night advanced the temperature continued to fall till it became uncomfortably chilly. As I had only my blue flannel shirt on my back, having omitted to bring with me either jacket or coat, I was thankful for the genial warmth thrown out by the little fire I lighted, which to a certain extent took away the feeling of oppressive loneliness. Crouching over the fire I smoked my goodnight cigarette, then placing my saddle at the foot of the tree as pillow, and covering myself with the extremely moist saddle-blanket, I passed into the land of dreams.

I slept peacefully till somewhere in the small hours of the morning, when I was aroused by *Little Roan* tugging at his stake rope and snorting violently. Jumping up and going over to see what was the cause of his uneasiness, I found he was frightened at something he had seen or smelt, and was shivering all over. I fancy some animal, probably a panther, had been prowling around After petting and pacifying *Little Roan*, I made up my fire and again lay down, but did not get much more sleep as the coyotes came close round among the rocks and bushes, keeping up a dismal chattering howl till break of day sent them off to their hiding places among the rocks.

With the first peep of daylight, I saddled up and continued my ride up the creek. I did not need to lose time in cooking a breakfast or performing ablutions, as I had no breakfast to cook, and even with the best will in the world one cannot wash without water.

I had not ridden more than half a mile from my camping ground, when on turning round a thick clump of trees I suddenly came on the camp I had been looking for, and was delighted to see the cheery face of Fox, the well-borer, appearing at his tent door in answer to my hail.

While chatting over a substantial breakfast of venison steaks and boiled rice, to which I did full justice, he told me that the evening before he felt certain that someone was seeking for him. So sure was he that this was the case that he was going to hang his lantern at the top of the mast pole of his drilling machine so that the light might act as a guide for anyone wandering about in the vicinity. But the boys of his outfit laughed so much at the idea that he gave up his intention and turned into bed.

A knowledge of the road made the homeward journey simpler, but not much quicker as, owing to the awkward load of pipe tongs, single and double blocks, rope, etc., which I had to carry, I was compelled to ride slowly. This would have mattered little had I been able to start immediately after breakfast, but I was not able to begin my return journey till nearly dinner-time, as Fox was using some of the tools which I most wanted to borrow, and I had to wait till he had finished with them. The afternoon was well advanced by the time I reached the Big Divide.

In crossing this plateau, I was riding along not far from the edge of one of the numerous gulches when five fine buck antelope raced past. I could not resist the temptation of having a shot at them. Hastily pulling my rifle from its scabbard I fired at the last buck in the line, apparently without effect, as all five disappeared over the edge of the draw. Pushing the rifle back into its sheath I lamented my bad luck and continued on my way. But I had not ridden more than a few yards when I saw the antelopes pop their heads up above the edge of the gulch, some distance further along, and then quickly disappear again. They did this several times, and on each occasion, I noticed that only four heads showed.

Thinking that perhaps the fifth buck was wounded and that I might still bag him, I got off my horse and creeping quietly to the edge of the Divide, looked over. There was my prize lying dead on a little ledge of ground which ran along the hillside nearly parallel with and a little lower than the crest. I could not well get my horse down to where he was lying nor could I without great difficulty lift him up to where the horse was standing. The only course open to me was to cut him up where he lay and carry him up piecemeal.

My pocket knife, totally unsuited to the work in hand, snapped short off while the work was in process, and I had to finish as best I could with the small blade alone, which was a slow and tedious task. However, I managed to get the beast all cut up and tied on to my saddle by the time the sun went down. *Little Roan*, well loaded up before, had now a double load to carry, but he was a stout, willing little fellow and jogged along to all appearances as happy as before.

When the sun had finished setting and the moon began to rise, the solemn silence which had hitherto pervaded the scene was quickly broken by the long drawn chattering howls of numbers of prowling coyotes attracted to the vicinity by the fresh smell of blood. I had no reason to complain of loneliness for any part of the remainder of my ride.

These brutes seemed to appear out of the ground as if by magic, by twos and threes, but always keeping at a safe distance of from 75 to 100 yards either in front or behind or on either side. It was of little use to shoot at them, so cunning are they. Immediately on my raising my rifle they disappeared, only to show themselves again at some other point. In the moonlight they looked like evil spirits flitting about, and the melancholy of their voices was as the wailing of lost souls.

The last few miles of my ride were soon got over. To the music of antelope steaks fizzing on the fire and the howls of the coyotes outside, I gave the "boys" an account of my ride and the cause of my late return. Then we all turned out, repaired the pump, and soon had a good stream of water flowing into the now empty tanks.

I have given in full the foregoing description of my ride, not on account of any adventure connected therewith, but simply as an example of the many little expeditions which have to be made by anyone settling on one of the frontier ranches.

CHAPTER 15

# Drought and Cattle-Doctoring

For the stockman to be short of water is worse than to be short of food. The sudden stopping of the supply of water for the stock is the one calamity which the stockman dreads more than anything else. This misfortune occurred to us once and once only; but that was quite sufficient.

We depended entirely upon windmills for raising the water needed for our cattle, and windmills will not run without wind. The conditions of the climate in our part of Texas are such that it very rarely happens that there is not, during some part of the twenty-four hours, a breeze sufficiently strong to work an ordinary 1½ horse-power windmill.

Once only during the years that I spent in Texas we had four consecutive calm days, when the wind was so light that the mills had only power to raise a mere fraction of their usual amount. This naturally happened at the same time as two of our mills were under repair, and we had to trust to one windmill alone for all our supplies.

This mill did the best it could under the circumstances, but its best was not enough. Still this, added to the water stored in the tanks and troughs, was sufficient for the first few days; and if all had gone well, we need have had no uneasiness. But on the third day of the calm, while we were all absent from the ranch, taking part in a fourth of July Barbecue at a point on the river about twelve miles off, some evil-disposed cow or steer succeeded in smashing the ball-tap arrangement for automatically filling the troughs from the tanks. The whole of the reserve stock of water ran out on the ground, and was wasted; and when we returned about 10 o'clock in the evening there were over 1,000 head of thirsty bellowing brutes stamping about in an immense muddy puddle. They had to be appeased somehow or other, and we had not a drop of water to give them.

As the wind would not blow the mill could not go. So, we had ourselves to work the pump by relays to raise as much water as we could. But oh! what never ending work it seemed! More than one thousand head of stock, and each one of them ready for half a barrel of water at the very least. It was like pouring water on the sand. As quick as it ran into the troughs it disappeared, sucked up by a few of the biggest and strongest animals, which after they had got what they wanted kept hooking and driving off the smaller and weaker ones. Most likely it was one of these mischievous brutes which had caused all the trouble.

There seem to be some cattle (as there are people) born into the world expressly to give trouble. They are never happy unless they are on the wrong side of the fence. And as to drinking, when once they have had all they want themselves, they wreck and destroy everything so that none can drink after them. They will get into the trough and stand there cooling their dirty feet and polluting the water, hoping all the time, I feel sure, that their weight will force out the bottom of the trough. This treatment often succeeds in producing leaks. Another of their little games is to hook some quiet inoffensive beast and lift her into the trough, when they playfully begin to jump on her. Finally, if she is not dead already, they leave her there to drown, if help does not come in time to save her; and it seldom does.

Sometimes, to create a diversion, they spend hours together raking with their horns as far as they can under the protecting superstructure, in hopes of being able to destroy the ball-taps or stop-cocks which automatically fill the troughs from the tanks and at the same time prevent the water from overflowing and being lost. If successful in this latter attempt their joy is complete—until they themselves once more begin to feel the effects of thirst.

After many experiments we found the only way to get the better of these mischievous rascals was to divide each trough into small compartments, each of which was only just large enough for a cow to put her nose into while drinking.

But to resume the narrative: To work the pump there were in all eight of us—our four selves, a neighbour who was pasturing some stock with us, and three of his boys. We worked in relays, two of us pumping while the others did what they could to regulate the cattle and bring them up to the troughs in batches. The well was a deep one—70 to 80 ft.—and it was heavy work lifting the water so far; but we stuck to it the first day. Then seeing that there appeared to be no prospect of any wind coming to our aid we decided that the best plan was to gather the stock and drive them to the nearest point on the river, about ten miles distant. It was trying work driving the half-crazed brutes away from the place where they had always been accustomed to get water.

When they had arrived at a point where they could see and smell the river the strongest animals broke into a run which only stopped when they plunged bodily into the water and could drink to their heart's content. So fast and in such disorder did they go, in their haste to reach the water, that most of the boys had to gallop hard to keep up with them in order to preserve some sort of order. Otherwise, the first arrivals would have been jumped upon, crushed down, and drowned by others plunging in on the top of them. A couple of us remained behind to collect any animals that seemed inclined to stray and to drive on those that lagged behind either through weakness or natural laziness of disposition.

While pushing these latter along as best we could, we chanced to come across a fine three-year-old steer, who was so famished with thirst that he had given up the struggle, and was lying on his side stretched out upon the ground to die. His deeply sunken eyes were already blue and filmy, his flanks drawn in and hollow, and his legs stretched out. His coat, no longer sleek and glossy, was standing out rough and shaggy. This is one of the worst of signs as to the condition of any animal of the cow tribe, denoting either extreme cold or some bad sickness.

Hoping there might still be some chance of saving him M——— and I jumped off our horses, and after a good deal of hard lifting, got him up on his feet and steadied him there, hoping that once on his legs again he might recover strength to reach the river. But as soon as we left him alone and moved off towards our horses, he made a wild staggering rush at our backs and fell again, almost at our feet. With more hoisting and pulling we again got our ungrateful patient into an upright position, and propped him up against a good stout tree, as we saw that his remaining strength was hardly sufficient for him to stand alone.

Hardly had we left him when he again charged us, this time almost catching my companion who only saved himself by dodging to one side. In trying to turn after him the beast's legs gave way, and down he came with a heavy fall, striking a sharp point of projecting rock, which probably stunned him. We had to leave him, and there he died, making a feast for the coyotes and turkey-buzzards.

We had not much more than finished watering the stock and were quietly moving them out from the river, when the sky became black and threatening, a strong wind began to blow, and in a few minutes one of the wildest thunderstorms I have ever experienced was raging over the country.

This was followed by torrents of rain which filled bank full every creek and waterhole for miles around, so that for days and weeks to come there was no fear of any shortage of water for man or beast. Had this rain only come one day sooner it would have saved us the loss of some thirty head of fine cattle, besides the wastage on the beef steers which were being got ready for market.

Occasionally one would come across an animal which appeared to realise that what we did for them, although not pleasant at the time, was in reality for their good, as the following incident will show.

We were engaged one scorching hot summer's day in driving home to our ranch a little bunch of 40 or 50 head of cattle which we had been gathering on the outside range. Among them there happened to be a very big four-year-old steer of a pure white colour—a most unruly beast, who took advantage of every opportunity to give us as much trouble as possible, always endeavouring to run in an opposite direction to that in which we were driving him. All went well until we reached the pasture fence. The rest of the bunch went quietly through the gate in the usual manner, thuswise:—

On arriving at a gate all the cattle make a dead stop; then ensue much snorting and sniffing to see if the gate is some terrible trap laid to ensnare them. When they decide that it is safe enough, one or two of the boldest spirits among them pass the dreaded entrance with a run and a jump over an imaginary barrier; whereupon the rest rush after them and if not too closely crowded they each make a jump as they pass between the gate-posts.

The herd went through all right, but nothing would induce the white steer to follow them. Backwards and forwards along the fence he galloped, varying his route by a break across the open country; till finding that it was useless to try to escape, as we always brought him back again, he dashed straight at the fence, without even attempting to jump it. No ordinary post and wire fence could withstand such a weight suddenly hurled against it; he went through and fell on the other side. When he stood up again his pretty white skin was stained with streams of blood, which were trickling from the wounds inflicted by the barbed wire of the fence.

Once on the inner side he quietly trotted up and joined his companions, which we drove on to the water troughs and turned loose.

A couple of mornings after this, we noticed our friend, the white steer, hanging round the corral quite alone, and every now and again walking up to the house yard and then back to the corral, all the time looking very dejected and woebegone. This was most unusual conduct for any of the stock, which generally hate the corral like poison. The cause of his uneasiness was not hard to find. The wounds caused by the barbed wire had been attacked by screws-worm, and the poor beast must have been suffering intense pain.

There is a species of fly, peculiar to some parts of the Western States of America, which attacks any open wound or break in the skin on a living animal and there lays its eggs, which by the natural heat of the body are quickly hatched out, and soon develop into grubs or maggots about ¾ of an inch long and of an inch in thickness. Each one of these forms a cell in the flesh of the victim, and quietly remains there eating out the very life of the animal it has attacked, until some vital point is reached or sheer exhaustion puts an end to the tragedy.

On discovering the cause of his restlessness, we drove him up to the corral, into which he walked as quietly as if he had been accustomed to go into it every day of his life. Once inside and the gate closed, we looked for a tough trial of strength with him; but we were mistaken. When I threw my rope on him, he took it quietly and stood still instead of rushing off struggling and bellowing as we had expected him to do. With two or three twists of the rope round his legs I soon had him down and tied fast.

He hardly uttered a groan when we cleaned out his wounds and dressed them with chloroform and chrysillic ointment. When we let him up, we did not even have to run to the fence, as he simply got up and shook himself and then quietly walked out of the corral. The same performance was gone through twice more, and then he discontinued his visits. When next we saw him two or three weeks later, he was completely cured. He had the sense to know that we alone could help him in his trouble, and came to us of his own accord so long as our help was needed.

Of course, there is no danger from screw-worm if the wounds are in such a position that the animal can reach them with his tongue, as by licking the injured part he can keep it perfectly clean.

We had, later on, another instance of animal sagacity. A Hereford bull, about six years old, had been gored under the flank by another bull. The wound was attacked by screw-worm and was in a bad condition when we found him, so that it took a long course of doctoring to get him well. Though on each occasion we had to throw him on his side, after the first time we did not require to use a rope as he seemed to understand what had to be done, and allowed us to throw him by hand, never showing any resentment towards us for any pain we may have caused him in our somewhat rough doctoring.

## Chapter 16

# Improving the Breed

During rather a cold spell of weather which came on shortly after Christmas, two of us took out our guns one afternoon and went off for a stroll, intending to shoot a few quail for our supper. We had gone about a couple of miles from the house and were busily engaged in looking for game in a clump of brush which grew among a lot of loose rocks at the foot of a little bluff when we came on a fine young cow, lying on her back, with her four feet in the air, and jammed tight in between the stems of a number of small trees. The discomfort of her position must have been intense, especially as she was lying downhill, that is, her tail was higher than her head.

She had evidently been grazing above the bluff, and in reaching over for some tempting mouthful of grass had lost her balance and fallen into the awkward position in which we found her. She was perfectly helpless, as she was unable to touch the ground with her legs, and therefore could not regain her feet. A cow cannot rise from a recumbent posture except hind quarters first, being in this respect the reverse of the horse, which when wishing to rise always puts out his fore feet first, and only uses his hind legs after he has raised his head and fore quarters by straightening out his front legs.

Although the heifer was alive when we found her, she was very weak and emaciated, and had evidently been a prisoner for a good many days, as she was literally reduced to skin and bone. With our knives we soon hacked away the saplings that held her, and rolling to one side the rocks between which she lay, we had her free once more. On dragging her out to the level ground and lifting her to her feet, we found she was too weak to stand by herself, let alone travel to food and water. To leave her where she was meant that she would die; so, we determined to take her up to the house.

With one of us supporting her she could stand; but as soon as she took a step forward her legs would double under her, and she would quietly collapse to one side or the other. What we did was this. My companion, who was bigger and stronger than I (he stood 6ft. 3in. and was proportionately well built, and a handsome fellow to boot), supported her at the shoulder while I held her up and guided her by the tail passed over my shoulder and under my arm, so as to combine support and guidance. So long as she went in the right direction it was simply a matter of keeping her from falling down, and the more ready she was to fall the faster we got along. If she seemed inclined to tumble over to the right, I hauled the tail over to the left; and if she threatened to take a header towards the left, I pulled the rudder, or rather the tail, over to the right.

We got her up to the corral, after an eventful little journey, the worst incident in which was when in spite of all we could do she insisted on subsiding quietly in the middle of a prickly pear bush—from which I am sure the three of us must have carried away in our skins nearly all the thorns. We gave her a bucket of water, which she swallowed greedily, and then a nice warm bran mash. Like all other prairie cattle, she did not understand a bran mash, and seemed to look upon it as an insult or injury. To teach her that it was not a new form of persecution we smeared handfuls of the bran over her lips and nose, which she tried to clean off by licking, and so got the taste of the bran on her tongue. This was enough, and she quickly ate up the mash. Never afterwards could she hear a bucket rattle within a mile of her without running up to see if there were a mouthful of bran in it for her.

Although we had among our herd of mixed cattle perhaps as many as 500 cows, milk was a luxury which we seldom indulged in: in fact, only when the grass was very good and when we felt certain that at least two of us would be at home together for several weeks. To milk an old-fashioned Texas cow was a serious undertaking. The native cow at best gives very little milk, only about two quarts a day; and even this small amount she absolutely refuses to give unless her calf be sucking at the same time. The calf, too, knows well enough that he has the best right to the milk, and tries his hardest to get it.

When a cow is to be milked, she is put into a corral and tied to a post if she has not learnt to stand still; then the calf is let in with her, and immediately starts his meal. The milker then plants his head firmly in the cow's right flank to prevent her from kicking him over. With the one hand he milks as fast as he can into the tin cup which he holds in the other hand, all the time keeping one foot ready to give the calf a reminding tap on the nose if he either bumps too hard or attempts to steal more than his fair share of the precious fluid.

I have known cows that had to be thrown on the ground and tied down before they could be milked. A cow belonging to one of our neighbours on getting up after being milked in this way dashed out of the corral, straight across the prairie, and was never seen again.

If our milking did not prove a remarkable success our butter-making was even less so, for during the summer the heat was so great that the butter turned into oil, and during the winter we had neither milk nor cream to make butter with. Dairying is not the strong point of Texas cattle ranching; at least this was our experience.

Soon after stocking our ranch with cattle, we began to take steps to improve the breed by getting rid of the long-horned old patriarchs and introducing higher class bulls. The first few we got were Durhams, raised by a local breeder. But finding that their calves, although a great improvement on the old native stock, did not run sufficiently to beef qualities to suit our purpose, we decided to try some Herefords. These we afterwards found to be by far the most suitable breed of cattle for a somewhat rough country, as they could pick up a living and keep fat where other well-bred stock would starve. So, we joined one of our neighbours in importing from the northern farming states a couple of car-loads of fine young Hereford bulls, all of them nearly full blood, and in some cases registered animals.

These were delivered the last day of January at the nearest railway depot, about ninety miles north of our ranch, and three of us went up to town to bring them back—two to drive the bulls and one the camping waggon.

They had been three or four days in the cars and a couple of days more standing in the livery stable when we arrived, and being young and well-fed and full of spirits were not unnaturally inclined for a frolic. When the gates of the stable yard were thrown open, they raced off pell-mell down the main street of the town, to the consternation of all the pedestrians and more timid buggy drivers. It was not till they were beyond the limits of the town that we were able to get them under control. After they had stretched their legs in this first grand race, they came back quietly enough as far as the river, but in spite of all we could do, we could neither coax them nor force them to cross the massive iron bridge, which hung high above the river bed.

Finding that we were determined that they must cross the river somehow or other, and not liking the look of the bridge, they made a sudden rush and jumped over the bluff into the water. As there was no easier way down, we had to take the jump too. There were very few spots in the river banks where this could have been done with any degree of safety. Luckily, they had chosen one of these places. There were no rocks below to break their legs, and the sand, although yielding enough to soften the fall, was yet not so unsubstantial as the quicksands often to be found along the river's course

With much splashing and floundering in the muddy yellow water we got them over to the other side and fairly started on the road to their new home. They travelled beautifully, and by evening we had reached Rendrebrook Springs, the point we had fixed upon for our first camp. But no waggon appeared, and we began to think we were going to have rather a cheerless camp. Although water was plentiful wood was scarce, and without fire, food, or bedding a February night in the open did not seem attractive. However, about 8 or 9 o'clock we were gladdened by hearing the wheels of the waggon rattling along over the hard ground, and it was not long before we had the coffee and bacon cooking over a cheerful fire.

The delay had been caused through the obstinacy of the horses, a young team of greys, spoiled in the breaking, which had baulked at starting (*i.e.*, refused to pull the waggon). It was hours before they would make a move, but when they once started, they set off at a run, which they kept up almost the whole way. They played the same trick next morning, and, indeed, each time we camped until we reached the ranch. This behaviour made the driving of the waggon a troublesome matter, as, of course, the bulls could not travel at the express rate of speed which the horses chose to adopt.

Yet we had to time our arrival at the various gates which crossed the road so as not to keep the waggon waiting, as, if once stopped, it was doubtful when we could prevail upon the horses to go on again. On the other hand, we could not pass through and leave the gate open as the driver dared not get down to close it after him, for this also would have necessitated stopping the team. Fortunately, the gates were a good many miles, apart, as the ranches we had to pass through were few and far between.

These young bulls having been raised entirely on small farms had not the roving instincts of the native cattle, and generally gave us no trouble during the night. It was enough for one of us to get up two or three times during the dark hours to see that they were all right, and head them back to camp if they seemed inclined to wander off.

One evening, about the fifth or sixth day on the road, we made our camp close to an old disused corral, into which we turned the bulls. It was not a very secure lodging for them as the gate had disappeared from its position, and opposite the opening thus formed, there was a gap large enough to drive a waggon through. To prevent the animals escaping by either of these openings we made our beds across them, one of us sleeping in the one gap and the other in the opposite one.

Under ordinary circumstances this plan would have acted very well. But unfortunately, about midnight a prowling puma or panther, which might easily have found some better occupation, crept up into the branches of a large oak tree which overhung half the corral, and there set up his melancholy wailing note, which much resembles the crying of a child in distress. The bulls had never in their lives come into such close proximity to so dangerous a member of the cat tribe, and promptly stampeded, fortunately not over us, but straight through the fence nearest the place where they happened to be standing. Of course, we were after them at once and soon had them gathered in again, but they had been badly frightened and nothing would induce them to re-enter the corral. We had to stay with them till morning as with us near them they were quiet and gentle, enjoying the sense of protection which our presence gave them.

On reaching the end of our journey we divided the bulls into two equal bunches, one for our neighbour and one for ourselves, tossing for the first choice and then picking turn about. In the end there were two as pretty little bunches as one could wish to see, all well, lively, and in fine condition. But alas! this happy state of affairs did not last long; the fates seemed to be against them.

First of all, there was a lengthy strike on the railway, which cut off the supplies of feed we had arranged to have sent down. Our poor beasts, taken straight from the comfortable, well-supplied barns of their Eastern owners, were forced to find what living they could on the scanty remains of the winter grass, as the spring feed had not yet made its appearance. Then on the top of this came a cold, wet blizzard, the last but not the least severe of the season, against which they had no protection, for we had neither shed, nor stable, to put them in. And worst of all, before they had had time to recover from the effects of exposure and starvation, they were attacked by distemper, or Texas fever, which killed them off one after another till, we only had five left out of the whole car-load. Our neighbour's loss was still worse, for he succeeded in saving only three.

Many a night we spent nursing and doctoring the poor patient invalids. Although the doctoring generally did very little good, still one could not see the beasts suffer without trying to do something to give them relief. In the morning we would take the hides off the dead ones, thus saving say $2 out of the $80 or $90 that the bull had been worth the day before. Those which managed to pull through their original trials got on very well, and became a most profitable element in our herd.

## Chapter 17
# Prairie Fires

If the Texas stockman sometimes has his happiness interfered with by the dread of a water famine, he knows also that for several months in the year he has the terrible danger of a prairie fire always before him. Against this agent of destruction, he may at any moment be called upon to fight for his very existence.

During the hot dry months of summer, the *mesquite* grass becomes scorched. Dry and inflammable as tinder, it assumes the appearance and consistency of hay. Only in this point does *mesquite* differ from other wild grasses, that if a heavy shower of rain happens to fall, it will again become green and resume its growth in what seems an impossibly short space of time.

While in the dried-up state it only requires the smallest spark to set it off in a blaze, which if not immediately checked, goes racing along the surface of the ground, licking up everything that comes in its way, and sending up as it goes dense volumes of heavy white smoke. When this cloud lifts or is blown away by the wind, one sees what was a short time before a fine useful range of grazing country, reduced to a charred and blackened wilderness, with here a blazing tree and there a still smouldering tuft of buffalo grass, and now and then, lying half roasted among the ashes, the body of some poor creature that had not been lucky enough to make its escape to the shelter of a creek before it was caught by the fire or suffocated in the smoke.

When the atmosphere is very clear, as it usually is in Western Texas, the columns of smoke from a fire ascend to a great height, and throw themselves against the blue of the sky with marvellous distinctness, so that one gets the impression that the fire is quite near instead of being, as it really is, a long distance off.

I remember one marked example of this, when on a lovely June day two of us were quietly driving a loaded waggon up a long wide valley. On turning the point of a hill, we had a view up one of the smaller side draws, at the head of which we saw the sky was obscured by heavy rolling billows of smoke, showing that a prairie fire of considerable dimensions was in full blast.

The smoke appeared as if the fire were so close that it must be just over the crest of the ridge and therefore approaching very near to our range. As it is the duty of everyone within reach to lend his aid in fighting a fire, we at once unhitched the horses, left the waggon where it was, mounted bareback and galloped off in the direction of the fire. On our climbing to the top of the first ridge of hills the smoke appeared to come from the second line of heights. We crossed this too, and indeed, several others, but never seemed to get any nearer. So, after riding several miles we gave it up and turned back to our waggon. We heard afterwards that the fire was between 35 and 40 miles away.

But the fire was not always at such a safe distance. On one occasion it had burnt off everything up to within a quarter of a mile of our fence when, after thirty hours of hard fighting, we mastered it.

We were one day busily engaged in building a new fence round our house yard, to keep the saddle horses from pushing their heads in at the doors and windows of the house to get a lick of salt or mouthful of bread on their own account. Just about the time we were going to leave off to get dinner, on happening to look up towards the Western sky we saw large masses of smoke rolling up from beyond the line of hills which bounded the horizon. We knew at once that some real hard work was before us.

Leaving the dinner uncooked, we saddled up our horses, and armed with wet sacks rode off to give our help in fighting the fire which was still about eight or nine miles distant, but steadily advancing. On arriving at the scene of the conflagration we found there were several other boys there already, and more arrived later on. One thoughtful fellow, a sheep-man, brought two barrels of water in his waggon in which, until they were burnt away, we were able to wet our sacks; and this was a great help to us in beating out the flames.

The fire was travelling down a broad straight valley, burning up all before it. We soon saw the best means to control it was, if possible, to turn it into one of the side valleys and confine it there. To do this half our number set to work to burn a "fire-guard" in front of the main fire. This is done by going some distance ahead of the fire, setting light to small patches of grass and brush, and beating them out before they can make any headway. If this be done successfully there should be a broad, bare belt of ground, on reaching which the fire dies out for want of fuel.

While some of us were busy at this work the rest of us attacked the advancing line of flames at either end, fighting hard to keep it from spreading.

With much hard work and by the help of a light breeze that favoured us we got the fire headed off from the main valley and turned into a side draw.

Up this the blazes raced with renewed vigour, as a fire always burns most fiercely when it is going uphill. But it got no further than the top, as the grass there was very scanty and the space more limited. So, we were able to get the mastery and finally extinguish the flames.

After this, although the worst of the fight was finished, we had to continue riding over the smouldering ashes for several hours, going from one point to another to extinguish little fires which were constantly breaking out after every puff of wind. Almost every tuft of grass or stick of wood was a glowing mass of embers, and the wind blowing sparks from these into the dried grass was ever threatening to start the whole affair over again. When our sacks got dry, they quickly burnt up, and then we cut branches from the trees and used them to beat out the fire.

All that night, next day, and well into the following night we rode from place to place wherever we saw we were needed, until everything was perfectly safe. Then scorched, dirty, hungry, and tired we rode off to a line-rider's hut which stood at no great distance from where the fire ended, and after picketing out our horses threw ourselves on the ground and slept the sleep of the weary.

The conflagration, which destroyed numbers of sheep and other animals, besides many square miles of fine pasture, was caused by the ignorance of a youngster, who was driving a waggon for a party of surveyors who were passing through the district. On breaking up camp in the morning, after finishing their breakfast, they rode off, telling the boy to put out the camp fire, load the waggon, and follow them. Instead of extinguishing the fire properly by putting water or earth over it, he simply kicked the burning wood about, which at once set fire to the grass. He could have stopped it if he had extinguished the first flames, but he became frightened, lost his head, set the horses to a gallop, and left the fire to spread. He would have had an unpleasant quarter of an hour if any of us had been able to lay hands on him next day.

CHAPTER 18

# Skunks and Other Pests

We already had one ranch house on the place, and that ought to have been all we required. But one of my partners and myself, in order to get an extra grant, made application to the State Land Board, and were each given one section of School land on condition that we became "actual settlers"; that is, that each of us undertook to live on his own section for at least twelve months. We did not wish to have to build separate houses and live like hermits, each by himself, and as the corners of our two sections came together like the red squares on a chess board, we were able to avoid the starting of separate establishments, and still fulfil the conditions of the grant by building a two-roomed house exactly over the point where the corners touched, in such a way that the front room was in one section and the back room in the other.

Fortunately, this point made a pleasant situation for a house, as it was on a gentle slope of ground overlooking a broad, smiling valley, thickly studded with trees, which occupied the best part of my section.

The house was not large, only 16ft. by 16ft., and the second room, which we used as a kitchen, measured just 8ft. by 16ft. Still it was extremely useful and comfortable, and small as it was I have seen, on a stormy night before a "round-up" of cattle, as many as nineteen men sleeping in it. At other times I have lived there all alone for as long as three weeks at a time. But generally, there were two or three of us living together, and our usual sleeping place was in the yard, where one could see the sky and feel every breeze that blew.

We built the house ourselves from cellar to roof, living the while in a small tent made by stretching a waggon sheet on a pole over a shallow trench dug in the ground. The height of this tent was not more than two and a half or three feet, and we had to crawl into it on our hands and knees. Once there, with plenty of blankets over us and the ends of the sheet tied down, we were as snug as could be, no matter how wet or cold the weather might prove.

The building of the house did not proceed very rapidly, as there was a constant run of interruptions from one cause or another. Finally, we got two or three friends to help us, and putting all other work aside for the time being, we rushed the building through, and soon had the roof on, the floor laid, and the stove fixed. Then the house was considered to be in a habitable condition. During the fine weather of the spring, summer, and autumn months we almost invariably slept out of doors, but during the winter when cold nights are the rule, we were very thankful to have the shelter of the house, even though it was by no means wind-tight, there being openings of half an inch or more between the boards of which the walls were built.

One evening in the late autumn, as a cold wind was blowing and

OUR HOME.—THE 9 T 9 RANCH.

the appearance of the sky promised a fall of rain before morning, we thought it wiser to move our blankets into the house. On turning in we left the doors open, and after a quiet read in bed we put out our lights. Shortly after midnight I was awakened by a rattling among the pots and pans near the stove, close to the head of my bed, beside the doorway between the two rooms. On striking a match and lighting the lantern I saw a healthy-looking old skunk busy licking the grease out of the frying pan, which we had left standing on the floor.

The first thought that enters the mind of the Texas skunk is to attack any man immediately he sees him, and this fellow was true to his instinct. No sooner did his eyes become accustomed to the light of the lantern than he ceased his evening meal, disengaged himself from the pots and pans, and charged straight after me as I bolted out through the door. He reached it just in time to have it slammed in his face, my partner at the same time diving out through the window.

A TEXAS SKUNK

The position of affairs was now more comical than pleasant, as we, dressed in the lightest of evening costumes and shivering in the chilly night air, could do nothing but watch through the window the beast inspecting his new quarters. He strolled over our warm blankets, undecided as to which bed he should honour by his occupancy. Before turning in he decided to finish his supper, and with this object returned to the kitchen and was soon foraging among our provisions. He licked the pans, sniffed at the potatoes, nibbled the bacon, and finally coiled himself up for a nap under the stove, where he could enjoy the warmth of the fire. As the pleasure of the position was all on his side and none on ours, he had to be dislodged somehow.

The eviction of a skunk is a delicate matter, as anyone will agree who has had the misfortune to be near one of these vindictive little brutes when his temper is ruffed. The business had to be carried out cautiously and in such a way that it would not rouse his anger.

We could think of no other plan than to gently raise the window and drop little stones all about him. This effectually disturbed his sleep, which otherwise might have lasted till morning. He got up, stretched himself, and looked about. Failing to see us he evidently thought the stones were dropping from the stove and that he had better move his position.

After looking about for a few minutes, he scrambled to the top of a sack of flour, intending to continue his broken nap. As this could not be allowed, we tried another plan, which was crowned with success. I opened the door, seized the lantern, waved it two or three times in front of his face, and bolted out again, with him close at my heels; then making off in an opposite direction, dropped the lantern, which he promptly charged and extinguished. My partner at the same time slipped into the house and got a gun; by which time the skunk had disappeared in the darkness, no damage being done on either side.

This was a lesson to us not to keep our provisions in such an open position. So, we hung the bacon from the roof, and stored the flour, beans, and potatoes in the cellar, which we believed to be safe from outside intruders. What was our astonishment, on descending into the cellar a couple of weeks later, to find a skunk sound asleep on the top of a sack of oats. Now a skunk cannot emit his horrible stench (which is like nothing else on earth) unless his tail is carried at right angles to his body, and if he can be lifted quick enough by the tail, he is harmless (unless anything comes within reach of his teeth), as the weight of his body straightens him out and prevents him from getting his tail into proper position.

We had staying with us at the time a cowboy, who, from his gentle disposition, was known as "Wild Bill." He crept quietly down into the cellar without disturbing the skunk, which he grasped by the tail and handed up to me on the floor above. I carried him out to the open air and slung him off as far as I could throw him, where he was at once pounced upon by the dogs, who quickly made an end of him.

It is a proof of the poisonous nature of a skunk that few dogs will tackle him. Any dog that does kill a skunk, as soon as he has finished the business, rolls on the ground trying to bury his head in the dust, and for some time afterwards foams at the mouth and slobbers all over his sides.

Skunks were not the only night prowlers which disturbed our

peaceful slumbers. Several times we had to get up to slaughter sundry thieving 'possums, which were hard at work trying to steal our chickens from their roosts.

Then we had coyotes galore, which made night hideous as they perched themselves on neighbouring rocks and sang their doleful song. At times these rascals became so bold that they would come into the yard and fight with our dogs over bones or other scraps of food.

They have even gone so far as to walk on to the verandah and stand at the door looking at us rolled in our blankets; but a shout from one of us was enough to scare them away.

It was on a nice warm February night that some much more welcome visitors than these once gave us a call. A bunch of the semi-wild hogs of the country, while roaming over the pasture, were struck by the idea that there might probably be something good to eat in or around our house. With this in view they came up to make investigations, and aroused us with their squeaks and grunts somewhere about one o'clock in the morning.

As soon as we realised who our visitors were, we were out of bed in a trice, and clothed in our shirts and slippers, we gave chase to the fast-retreating pigs. I selected a big old sow for special attention, and after her I went as hard as I could go. A stern chase is proverbially a long chase, and this one was no exception to the rule.

At first, she gained on me rapidly, as she could make much better time than I could through the scrub and prickly pear, which scratched and tore my bare legs. But as she was very fat the pace soon began to tell; she was also considerably flurried by the shots I fired at her as we ran. As I shortened the distance between us, she dodged about from side to side, and finally turning in a large circle arrived back at the house. There placing her back against the wall she stood at bay, gnashing her teeth. I killed her by a ball between the eyes, just as she was about to make her charge. She was the most considerate head of game I ever shot, as by coming back to the house to be killed she saved us the trouble of carrying home her carcase, which would have been no light job, as she weighed over 300 pounds.

While running my pig I had heard M—— fire one or two shots, and as he had not yet returned when I had secured my beast, I set off to look for him.

There was no difficulty in finding where he was, as from a bunch of brush about half a mile off proceeded a series of barks, yelps, and squeals. Round the fight between the pig and dog was M——, dancing in his airy costume, endeavouring to get a shot at the hog without hurting his dog. Altogether it made a striking picture in the bright moonlight. Just as I came up, he fired his shot-gun at precisely the wrong moment, for the charge, instead of hitting the pig, lodged in the dog's shoulder, taking off half its ear.

The next shot finished the hog and so ended the fray. We set off for the house, where we stood the dog on the table and spent the next two hours picking out the shot and bathing and bandaging her wounds. She stood the doctoring splendidly, being highly delighted with the attention she was receiving.

Although this dog, *Queen* by name, ultimately died by poison, having picked up a bait that had been set for a coyote, she seemed for a long time to bear a charmed life. She had been wounded by shot, kicked by a horse, tossed by a cow, chased by wolves, which caught and ate her companion. Worst of all she was run over by a heavy waggon loaded to the full with firewood, which ought to have broken every bone in her body. She was a smooth-haired, brindled, yellow animal, about the size of an average collie.

CHAPTER 19

# Rattlesnakes

Many different kinds of snakes are to be found in North America, but no variety is better known or more feared than the "rattlesnake" (the "moccasin" alone excepted), on account of its aggressive disposition and the poisonous nature of its bite. Yet here the old saying holds good, that *"familiarity breeds contempt,"* for, even in localities where rattlesnakes are known to be numerous the cowboy will at night time calmly roll down his blankets and go peacefully to sleep, although he is well aware that the neighbourhood is infested with these pests, a bite from one of which would mean almost certain death. Seldom is his confidence misplaced. Accidents occur only at rare intervals. If a cowboy happens to be gifted with a careful, prudent disposition, he will, before going into a snake-infested district, provide himself with a rope made of horse hair, which he places in a circle round his bed.

He can then go to sleep with an easy mind, for no snake has ever been known to cross this simple but effective barrier, as it cannot endure the irritation caused by the bristles of the horse-hair getting in between its scales. As this safeguard is often neglected every now and again a case occurs of some unfortunate person being bitten while sleeping on the ground. If the night is at all chilly the snakes, which love warmth, are attracted to the bed of the sleeper on account of the heat to be derived from his body. When they have once coiled themselves up for a snooze, they strongly object to being disturbed in their slumbers, and in their easily aroused anger will probably strike out at the nearest living thing within reach.

One of the most painful occurrences of this kind that I heard of happened to two brothers, cowboys, who had made their beds close together, and were sleeping under the same blankets. As the night air was cool and sharp, they had drawn the covering up over their heads, and slept so soundly that they did not notice that a rattlesnake had crawled to the top of their upper blanket, and settled himself to sleep in the hollow between their bodies.

Towards morning, thinking it was time to get up, the elder brother put his head out from below the bedding. The first thing he saw was their dangerous bedfellow, swollen out with anger, coiling himself up and preparing to strike. Instantly he withdrew his head under the protection of the blankets, at the same time shouting to his brother, "Look out!" His poor brother, taking the words literally, did look out, and was immediately bitten by the snake, once in the face and once in the neck. He quickly died from the effects in spite of all his brother could do to help him.

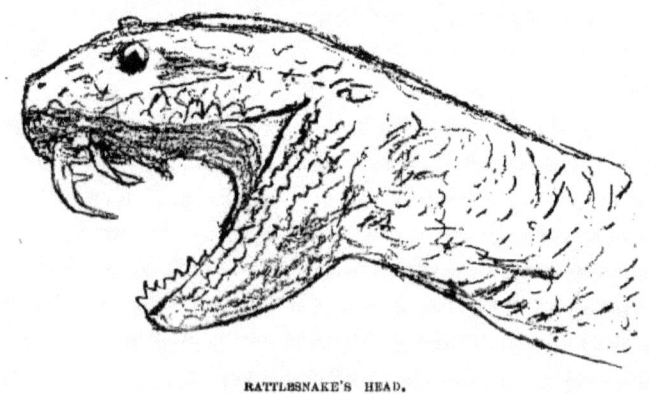

RATTLESNAKE'S HEAD.

As a general rule, the rattlesnake avoids as much as possible all houses and other places frequented by human beings. Once we killed a pretty fair-sized specimen while it was in the act of crawling into our house by the kitchen door. On another occasion, a number of us were gathering at a ranch about 20 miles from our place for a round-up, and we found that we should have to spend the night at the ranch-house, instead of camping on the range. So, we rolled down our blankets in the yard, and after watering and hobbling out our horses, turned into bed. Somewhere in the middle of the night Wild Bill, who has been mentioned before, was awakened by the singing of a rattlesnake at no great distance from where he lay.

On raising his head, he saw, about two feet off, a good-sized snake coiled up on the floor of the verandah, swaying its flattened head gently backwards and forwards, and spinning its rattle for all it was worth. Bill made no rapid movement, but quietly took his heavy quirt from the horn of his saddle, which he was using as a pillow, and with a smart back-handed blow broke the back of the reptile.

Many stories are told as to the extraordinary length of jumps taken by rattlesnakes when in full fighting trim; but out of the large number I have killed, or helped to kill, I have never seen one that was able to strike more than its own length. If a rattlesnake is not coiled up it is unable to strike at all, and, further, if the head is not flattened out, as it is only when they are badly vexed, they cannot lower their poison fangs, and consequently are not dangerous. Were it not so, they might inject poison into the animals which they swallow as food, and in this way introduce it into their own systems, with fatal results. For snake poison is just as deadly to the snake itself as it is to any of its enemies. It used to be a favourite amusement among the cowboys, when they found a rattlesnake, to tease and irritate the reptile until it became mad with passion. After striking out several times unsuccessfully it would turn round, bury its fangs in its own body, and quickly die from the effects.

One morning, as I was following the tracks of a deer along a narrow cow-trail through some long dry grass, I was not watching where I placed my feet, and was unpleasantly startled when I felt my heel turn on the wriggling back of a rattlesnake stretched out across the path, looking for all the world like a piece of dry stick. I made a most energetic spring forward, then turning round, shot his head off before he had time to coil and strike. Of course, the report of the rifle frightened off the deer I had been tracking, but not wishing to return entirely empty-handed, I picked up the snake by his tail, and marched into camp with this as the sole result of the chase.

It was suggested by someone that as the snake was all we had in the form of fresh food, we had better eat him. So, pulling the skin off the still wriggling body, we soon had him cooking in the frying pan.

A very good meal he made, the flesh being white and delicately flavoured, and much resembling the breast of a chicken.

The bite of the rattlesnake is most poisonous during the months of August and September, when he is changing his skin. But as at that time he is almost totally blind, anything he attacks has a good chance of escaping. At other times his bite, though very dangerous, is by no means fatal.

I knew of one boy who for bravado took a snake in his hand, but stupidly caught it by the middle of the body, instead of close behind its head, in which latter position it would have been helpless. The snake, as was to be expected, turned about and bit him on the wrist. The other boys roughly cauterised the wound with the red-hot end of a burning stick, tied a band tightly round his arm above the place where he had been bitten, and setting him on his horse told him to ride hard to the nearest doctor, 50 miles off. This he did, arriving in a marvellously short space of time. Although he was laid up for some months, he ultimately recovered entirely.

Just two more cases of snake bite, both of which happened to favourite saddle horses of my own.

In the first case the pony was badly bitten on the knee, which caused him a great deal of pain and trouble. The knee-joint remained stiff and swollen for some time, but ultimately got quite well again.

The second case was worse by far, and it happened to my pet, "*Little Roan*." He had evidently been bitten while grazing, or seeking a mouthful of the sweet grass which grows among the rocks or close to the roots of the bashes, a favourite lurking place of the rattlesnake. However, that may be, he aroused me early one morning by pushing his nose in at the door so as to draw my attention to the state of his head. The whole of his face and head were so much swollen that his eyes and nostrils were almost closed, and both seeing and breathing must have been a labour of great difficulty. Evidently, he was suffering terrible pain. On examining his face, I found where the snake's fangs had entered, in the soft flesh at the end of the nose. I saw then that if I could not quickly give him relief it would soon be too late to do anything. To reduce the swelling, I held his head fast, and taking my penknife I ran it into the wounds a number of times until it bled freely, and while the wounds were still open rubbed in paraffin and ammonia to counteract the poison.

This treatment, though rough and severe, was quickly successful, and undoubtedly saved the life of my faithful friend. As the swelling caused the upper lip to protrude about four inches beyond the lower one, he was unable to eat or drink in the usual way for several days, and I had to feed him like a baby. He well repaid all the trouble I took by helping me to the best of his ability whenever occasion required, and many a tight place he carried me through safely. But ever after he was bitten, he would be careful to give a wide berth to all snakes or anything that looked like a snake, although it might be only a piece of dry stick lying across the trail.

One summer evening, while riding home about sundown I had the unusual experience of watching a snake take his prey. As I was jogging along, I chanced to notice a rabbit sitting in front of a bush, in a rigid position, but drumming on the ground with his hind feet. This conduct on the part of the timid "cottontail" struck me as being peculiar, especially as he took no notice of my approach. I stopped to watch. After a few minutes I saw first the head and neck and then the whole body of a snake slowly glide out from among the roots and dead leaves, and gently approach the miserable rabbit, which seemed utterly incapable of making any attempt to escape. The snake quietly took hold of the rabbit by the middle of its body, and turned it round so that they were face to face.

His next proceeding was to arrange the rabbit's head and front feet close together, so as to facilitate the swallowing process; then, dislocating his own jaws peculiar power possessed by the snake to enable it to open its mouth to the greatest possible extent) he set himself to enjoy his supper by swallowing the rabbit, which he did slowly and deliberately, taking ten or fifteen minutes over the operation. Having finished his meal, he started back towards his den to sleep off the effects. But he never reached his home, for I killed him on the way, and ripping him up took out the rabbit which was quite dead, although to all appearances uninjured.

Besides the rattlesnake, there are many other kinds of snakes which inhabit Texas. There is the Mocassin, a very treacherous snake, which when angry appears to have its mouth full of cotton wool. The greenish grey of its back makes it almost invisible when lying in wait for its prey on the banks of some little frequented creek or water hole, and as it gives no warning one may easily place an unwary foot within reach of its sharp poisonous fangs. Then there is the whip-snake or prairie-runner, an innocent, harmless creature, which loves the sun and lives upon frogs, lizards, and such like small fry. He is similar in appearance to the chicken snake, which dearly loves to get into a poultry-run and feast on the new laid eggs, and is not averse to a chicken now and again. Neither of these snakes is poisonous, nor is the pretty little thunder-snake, with its red and black diamond markings.

The puff adder, on the other hand, is deadly in its bite, and has a nasty habit of taking up its abode among any lumber that may be stacked for building purposes. There are various opinions as to whether the corral snake is poisonous or not. It grows to five or six feet in length, and is marked in regular bands about an inch wide, alternately creamy-white and brownish-red.

It may be taken as a general rule that all snakes which have pointed heads and long thin tails are harmless, and that those which have blunt heads and thick stubby tails are poisonous.

CHAPTER 20

# A Round-Up and a Stampede

To ride through a real genuine stampede—the headlong flight of a herd of panic-stricken cattle and come out of it unhurt is an experience that, once gone through, a man is never likely to forget. For although the time actually occupied is short, everything is so sharply defined that it is indelibly stamped on his memory.

The worst stampede I ever had the luck to ride in happened during the "Fall round-ups" when we had been working a very large range of unfenced country, and consequently had a big herd of cattle gathered together. They numbered not less than 4,500, and as no corral was big enough to hold them, we had to guard them on the open prairie night and day.

The whole outfit of cowboys was made up of representatives from numbers of different ranches scattered over many miles of country, who had joined the general round-ups to gather their strayed cattle. The camp consisted of three or four waggons for hauling the necessary provisions, bedding, branding irons, etc.; over one hundred cowboys; and an average of five horses for each man. Altogether the camp made a pretty big assembly, and wherever it stopped it brought plenty of noisy healthy life into the usually quiet and deserted districts. The commissariat included a two-year-old heifer *per diem*, besides enormous quantities of flour, coffee, molasses, and canned goods.

We had for several days past been steadily working up the North Fork of the Concho river, and had arrived at a point about 25 miles above the junction of this river with the South Fork.

A ROUND UP.

The valley of the North Concho is some 40 or 50 miles in length, and averages about eight or nine miles wide, between the fairly continuous ridges of hills by which it is bounded on either side. In the course of ages, the river has hollowed out for itself a deep channel almost in the centre line of the valley. From the source of the river to its junction with the South Fork, there is a gentle slope of the land towards the river bed from the surrounding hills, which after any heavy downpour of tropical rain send tributary streams to swell the main current.

As a usual thing most of these creeks are either perfectly dry or at best contain only pools of water here and there along their course, but one or two of them hold running water for the greater part of the year. The face of the country is dotted over with clumps of fine old live oaks, or at odd intervals with single specimens of this handsome tree; and between these there is in many places a dense growth of *mesquite* or wild acacia.

Wherever the ground was open and free enough from trees and brushwood to suit their taste, it had been seized upon by the mischievous little prairie dogs, and by them made use of as a site for one of their so-called "towns."

I give this description of the country to show that riding over it even in broad daylight was not all plain sailing. One can picture to oneself how much worse it was to ride across it at a headlong pace, closely followed by a maddened herd of crazy long-horned cattle, and shut in by a darkness so intense that it was impossible to see your horse's ears in front of you, except when the scene was illuminated by the blinding flashes of forked lightning which at times followed each other so closely that the darkness had hardly time to close down between them.

On the day of which I am writing our camp was pitched about a mile from the river on the opposite side to that on which it was joined by the Big Dry Creek. That morning we had driven a very large tract of country, so large in fact that many of the boys, in order to reach the points where they had to begin their part of the drive, had to start out the night before, and sleep at their posts, so as to be ready to begin their work with the first streaks of daylight.

All the morning we were busy driving the cattle from hundreds of hills and little hidden draws and gulches. And a splendid sight it was, to look down from a rise of ground, over the broad valley, which seemed to be literally alive with cattle of all sizes, ages, and colours, from the little unweaned calf, timid and frightened at the unusual noise and movement, to the lordly old bull, hero of many a hard fight, all drifting steadily along in one direction, towards the spot where the round-up was to be held, on the salting ground of the range.

By eleven or twelve o'clock we got them thrown together, and an immense herd they made, such as is never to be seen nowadays. Probably there were 8,000 or 9,000 head all told. The dust they raised enough almost to turn day into night, so far as seeing was concerned—settled on our hands and faces, and made mud where the perspiration was rolling off us. It choked our throats, it blackened our teeth, and made us almost unrecognisable by our nearest neighbours; it even changed the colour of our horses.

If it was bad at first, it became ten times worse when the "cutting out" began. First the beef steers had to be parted out, then the cows with calves for branding, and lastly the strays.

How we rode, and how we suffered, can only be appreciated by one who has gone through it himself. It is impossible to convey in writing the sensation of being thirsty at every pore in one's body, and instead of being able to slake this thirst getting more and more thoroughly coated with the dry, powdery, pungent dust which makes its way through hat, shirt, and boots alike, till one is thoroughly enveloped in it from head to foot.

Add to all this the fatigue of many consecutive days of hard riding, with insufficient sleep, and a blazing hot sun, with a temperature of not less than 110 degrees in the shade. At such a time, most people would be inclined to say that a cowboy's life was not a happy one. But it is so, for all that; and I venture to say that not one of those present would have been willing to change places with any of the well-fed, well-paid city men of London and New York.

At last, it was over, and turning loose the herd to go back to their favourite haunts, we quietly brought over to the camp those we had cut out. Changing our hard-ridden horses for fresh steeds, we set to work to brand the calves, not by any means an easy task in the open, where men on horseback had to keep guard in the place of the stout walls of a corral. The cattle were wild and excited from the driving and handling they had already gone through. The branding presently came to an end, and we looked forward to an hour or two of rest and something to eat before the night work began. But the fates had ordained otherwise.

While Kearney Mays, the "boss" of the outfit and one of the finest cattlemen in the West, was telling us off into four guards to watch the cattle through the night time, dark clouds began to appear in the sky, and a feeling of electricity in the air became all pervading, giving sure warning of a coming storm. The cattle, instead of quietly settling down and taking their places for the night, became uneasy, moving about in a restless manner and giving their herders much trouble in holding them together. As rapidly as possible we saddled up our "night-horses," and hastily proceeded to swallow a mouthful or two of fried beef, bread, and coffee.

Hardly had we started to feed when the boss gave a shout of "Get to your horses, boys, the cattle are going," and we of the first two guards had to gallop off to help those who were fighting hard to hold the herd in control. To keep the beasts in their places was impossible, as they drifted first in one direction and then in another. Darkness was rapidly closing down, and the temperature of the air was falling so quickly that it made us shiver after the great heat of the day. All Nature was deathly still, and the only sounds to be heard were the distant mutterings of the fast-approaching thunder, mingling with the low, complaining grumbling of the cattle.

For five or ten minutes, silence reigned; then the storm broke. First a dazzling, blinding sheet of lightning seemed to split the heavens in two and strike the ground almost at our very feet. This was accompanied by a crash as of thousands of tons of rocks falling on a sheet iron floor only a few feet above our heads. Again, it came, and again and again almost without a pause. The cattle did not wait for more than the first flash. With one mighty bound they were off like the waters of a bursting dam.

Those of us on the side towards which they broke had only just time to wheel our horses and gallop ahead of them. We rode as we had seldom ridden before, fully conscious that death was *probably* before us, and *certainly* behind us should our horses by any chance slip or fall; for nothing in the shape of flesh and blood could hope to live before the charge of 4,000 furious beasts, crazy with terror.

Onwards they rushed, a living wall of horns, heads, and hoofs, half a mile wide from flank to flank; and on we rode just ahead of them, bending low over our horses' necks where the trees grew thick, to avoid, if possible, being struck by some overhanging branch; and again, where the country was more open, sitting up in our saddles shouting, yelling, and firing off revolvers, trying if by any means we could arrest the mad rush of the cattle. But goaded on by the stinging blows of enormous hailstones which were now pouring down upon us, they seemed as if they would never tire.

We could not tell how far we had travelled, but from the direction in which we were going it seemed as if we must soon be nearing the only fence which crossed the valley, about 5 or 6 miles below our camp. To have struck these four strands of barbed wire at the pace we were going, followed closely by the stampeding cattle, would have meant destruction to some, if not all of us, and we redoubled our efforts to bring the brutes to their senses.

A man's voice can make but a poor impression during such a thunderstorm as was then raging. Once, as the cattle came to a fairly open space of ground, they seemed to hesitate, and we began to pull in our panting horses. But no sooner did we slacken speed than we felt the heads and horns rushing up alongside our horses' flanks, and to save going down before the pressure we had to ride again.

If one glanced along the line by the light from the vivid flashes of lightning one could see the row of boys riding about 20 or 30 paces apart, their faces set hard, and in many cases the spurs working in the flanks of an over-tired pony, goading him on to further exertion. Ever close behind, almost touching the horses' tails, came the mass of cattle thundering along, with heads lowered, and eyes staring out at nothing, all intent on escaping from—they knew not what!

Onward still they rushed, till by one of the most brilliant of flashes, which appeared to strike directly in front of us, I saw the man and horse next to me go down in a heap. The horse had put his foot in a dog hole. In the next instant the cattle would have been over them, and horse and rider trodden out of existence, had not the same flash which showed me the picture, turned the cattle at right angles to the course they had been following, and the whole herd passed within a few feet of where man and horse were struggling to rise.

During the first run my own horse slipped, and came so near to falling that my feet touched the ground, but recovering himself he brought me safely through.

The worst was now over, as the cattle were heading up towards the hills, and this, added to the softness of the ground, which had been rendered heavy by torrents of rain, soon began to tell on them.

Our horses were too much spent to round them up properly, so we were forced to let them break up into small bunches at their own sweet will, each of us staying with a band until the weather cleared and we could get them together again. I had a little herd of about 200 head all to myself, with which I wandered about, up and down hills and draws, until the storm cleared off somewhere in the small hours of the morning.

By this time the clouds were all gone, the moon was shining out brightly, and we were able to see the enormous fire which had been kept up by our friends in camp to act as a guide to us in finding our way back. The weather having now so much improved we were able to push the herd along in the direction of the camp, and it was with real pleasure that on the bedding ground we handed them over to the new guard, and could dismount and stretch our stiffened, aching limbs.

By that time, we had been in the saddle for over 20 hours, almost without a break, had ridden down three horses apiece, and covered many, many miles of country. When we dismounted the water poured out of our top boots as if they had been leather buckets, and so much had they shrunk on our feet from the soaking they had had, that it was impossible to pull them off. So, we had to keep them on till they dried next day.

Just before the stampede my chum and I had been about to make our beds in a slight hollow of the ground so as to be ready for us when we came in off guard; but we had been compelled by the force of circumstances to leave them, and likewise our suppers, and go to help with the cattle. When we returned, we found that this hollow was full of slush, at the bottom of which, covered with mud, lay our blankets. After some groping about in the water we got them out, and spreading them at the root of a tree where the ground was a little higher, we crept into bed, and had a splendid sleep for two or three hours till we heard the morning shout of "Daylight," and the silent camp once more roused into active life.

After changing our night horses and swallowing our breakfasts we rode to relieve the guard that had held the cattle for the second part of the night. It was not till then that we found that one of the men had been lost. He had noticed a bunch of stock on an island in the river, and as the water was rising rapidly, he saw that if left there they would soon be carried away.

So, he set out to swim over to them, but had not gone far before his pony became entangled in a floating tree, and not being able to extricate themselves both pony and man were drowned. We found him the following day and buried him on the prairie, close to the house he had built only a short time before, and to which he had just brought his newly married bride.

She received the deep sympathy of all the cowboys, who, though rough and uncivilized in their ordinary life are, at a time like this, quiet and gentle as any men could be. As they stood uncovered in the evening light listening to the burial service read by the local justice of the peace, one could hardly believe they were the same men who would curse, drink, gamble, or fight for the mere love of excitement.

Another fact, of which we became aware when morning broke and the sun rose, was that the whole herd of saddle horses had stampeded during the storm, and were scattered for miles over the surrounding prairie, each one making for home as fast as his hobbles would permit him. As none of my ponies were to be found, all of them having swum the flooded river in spite of their hobbles, I was lent by the "Boss" of the outfit one of the waggon horses so that I could go on guard. This beast was about 17 hands high, and by no stretch of courtesy could be called a saddle horse. He seemed a regular camel after my own neat little 14 hand ponies.

CHAPTER 21

# A Cattle Drive Under Difficulties

In the following year I had another experience of a stampede. A neighbour of ours, who was owner of some 30,000 acres of land, determined to reduce his numbers on this ranch by picking out a thousand head and sending them up to a tract of land he had leased in the "Indian nation" for fattening, before being shipped to the Chicago market. In making up the herd, which was to consist of steers, dry cows, and a few bulls, he bought about 150 head from us to round off his numbers, part of the bargain being that one of us should help to drive the herd to the shipping point. It fell to my lot to go with them.

By the end of a week's work, we had got together all the stock that was wanted and started out with our herd. It was not an easy one to drive, as it included many old cows cut off from their calves, of which some were as much as one or two years old. These cows were constantly breaking back in the vain endeavours to make their way home to their desolate offspring, so we had constant hard riding to hold the herd together.

The first day of our trip we made a very long drive, hoping that the cattle would be more or less tired out and be glad to rest quietly during the night. But this they would not do. They refused to bed down, and kept restlessly moving about, so that it was deemed advisable instead of making four guards of two hours each to have only two guards, each to stand watch for half the night.

My chum and I were told off to form part of the first guard, and before going out made down our bed on a nice clear spot, from which we picked off all sticks, stones and other inequalities. It was a lovely moonlight night, and after the heat of the previous day the cool evening breeze was most refreshing, taking away to a great extent the weariness and stiffness caused by the long hours spent in the saddle under a broiling sun.

Our camp was pitched on the top of a high divide, where the land flattened out into a broad plateau, from the edge of which one could look down into the lower lands below. There were few trees to break the evenness of the scenery which, spread out in the brilliant moonlight, made a lovely and reposeful picture. All was still and quiet. The only discordant note in the whole range of hearing or vision was to be found in our 1,500 head of restless uneasy cattle, pushing, drifting, and driving, first in one direction and then in another, but always carefully held together and brought back to the camping ground by the efforts of their herders. Although this work necessitated plenty of hard riding, there was not much danger of losing any of the stock, as there was plenty of light, and we could at once thwart their efforts to stray.

They kept up this drifting till shortly before midnight, when they shewed signs of settling down; and we of the first watch began to think our work for the day was nearly over. But suddenly, without the slightest warning, the cattle broke and came along with a rush, right in the direction of the camp. In the fury of their first charge, it was impossible to hold them or even to guide them until we could again get them under control. So pell-mell right through the camp we went, and in the rush, I rode over my own bed. Other beds besides mine were upset, and all the cook's careful preparations for an early breakfast—coffee, beef, bacon, and flour—were scattered far and wide.

Any horses that were staked nearby broke away, and a general commotion was caused by this miniature stampede. The camp had been formed about one-third of a mile from where the cattle were being held, and the boys who were in bed at the time could hear the cattle coming. Knowing by instinct what was happening they reached their horses before the rout arrived in camp, and so escaped without injury.

After running some distance further, we got them to "milling," that is to say we succeeded in heading in the flanking cattle so that they were forced round in front of the centre line, and becoming confused as to their directions the whole herd began turning round and round in a circle. The boys were then able to get them once more under control. When they had quieted down sufficiently, we moved them back to their bed ground (not through the camp this time), and after one or two more little runs they settled down and stayed quietly for the short remainder of the night. We of the first guard rode wearily back to camp and turned thankfully into any blankets we could find, taking the precaution to place them close to the waggon or some tree stump, which would give us protection in case the cattle should again visit the camp.

The next day was hot, hotter than anything I have ever felt before or since—not with the usual clear, bright heat which we were accustomed to, but with a dull, sultry heat, which seemed to sap the very life out of limbs and body. The sun shone down with a bronze, metallic lustre, imparting to the scenery a dull, coppery hue, most trying to the eyes. All around on the prairie one could see the waves of heat shimmering on the ground like ripples on the sea when stirred by a light wind.

The cattle shared in the feeling of oppression in the air, and greatly objected to being driven. We turned them on to an open piece of land, surrounded on three sides by the Wild Horse Creek, which here made a large sweep almost like the letter S; and two of us by turns stood guard on the neck of land. There was not much to do, for with the exception of one old dun-coloured cow, the beasts were willing enough to lie quiet after their exertions of the preceding night.

Towards evening it rapidly grew cooler. So, rounding up our herd, we pushed on for a few miles further, to a spot above the Morgan Creek, which we considered would make a good camping ground for the night. Camp was quickly formed, supper cooked and eaten. Having saddled up our night horses and put on our slickers (the Western name for oilskins), we all took our places with the herd, for we could judge from the appearance of the sky that something unusual was about to happen. Ere long it suddenly became quite dark, and a strong cold wind began to blow from the north. No animals will willingly face a wind. Cattle and horses alike turned their tails towards it and drooped their heads. We had stood thus for a few minutes when I suddenly felt my horse lash out with both heels, which came with a sounding thud on the head or shoulders of the steer immediately behind him.

I took no notice of it, thinking that he was only resenting the forwardness of some beast which had prodded him with its horns. The next minute I knew better, for I felt a blow between my shoulders which almost knocked me off my horse. It was as if someone had struck me with a good-sized stone. I had no time to think about it then, for these first hailstones were quickly followed by more, none of them smaller than hens' eggs, which, acting on the cattle like thousands of whips, stung them to madness—with the natural result that they at once stampeded.

In their mad gallop they were heedless of all ahead of them, and only struggled to get on, on, they knew not whither. Nor did we either, till the "boss" of the outfit, who was familiar with the country, got his bearings by one of the brilliant flashes of lightning. He knew where we were, right on the top of the high bluffs overhanging Morgan Creek, now swollen to a raging torrent. He yelled to us to follow him and let the cattle go, and by good luck we were able to hear him, as just then there was a lull in the almost continuous peals of thunder.

Having gained some distance on the cattle in the uphill race, we were able to make a sweep round to the left in the direction he had taken and so get clear away, a small number of the beasts on the flank of the herd following in our wake. In this way we saved ourselves and some of the cattle; but the rest of them went blindly on and disappeared in the darkness over the edge of the bluff, some of them dashing through a rocky little canon which went winding down to the river. Slowly and sorrowfully, we made our way back to camp with the few beasts we had left. A gloomy party we formed, for the one time in life when the cowboy is in any way dejected or ashamed of himself is when his herd of cattle manages to escape from his charge.

The storm soon blew over, and the night became beautifully clear. We kindled again the fire that had been put out, made our beds on the muddy ground, and prepared for sleep. But it was not to be. Another storm blew up and raged as violently as its predecessor. The boys, disheartened by their previous failure, soon lost the few head that remained to us. Then coming back to camp, we spent the rest of the night standing beside our horses in the pouring rain, ankle deep in water and nodding as we stood, much inclined to subside into the mud. There were not many hours of the night left, but what there were seemed very long. Even our tobacco was soaked and it was impossible to make a cigarette. At last, the first faint streaks of dawn appeared.

Cold and shivering we mounted on our horses, which were dejectedly standing with their heads down and backs hunched up, the rain streaming from their manes and tails, and their poor tired knees trembling with the cold. We rode off in different directions to gather up as many of our scattered cattle as we could find. Within an hour or two we had the majority of them rounded up, and once more formed into a respectable herd. The reason we were so fortunate in getting them together quickly, was that they were both hungry and tired. When, therefore, the fury of the storm abated they were only too glad to stay quiet, and when morning broke, they began to graze as hard as they were able.

They were not all to be found, as some had struck out for home, and stragglers kept on arriving there for the next few weeks. One of ours, an old red and white cow, appeared on our range six months after the stampede. She did not come alone, for she had a dear little calf trotting at her heels. Some of those that had gone over the bluff into the river below were never seen again. Altogether, on making a rough count in the morning, we found we were some 60 or 70 head short.

We were not the only ones who suffered in this storm, one of the most violent of its kind. A sheepman, who had camped near where we tried to hold our cattle, lost many of his fat muttons, killed by the hailstones, besides those trodden upon by our cattle. His tent and camping outfit were entirely wrecked by the storm.

Having got our cattle once more well in hand we travelled on as far as a point on Morgan Creek where it was spanned by a fine new iron bridge, by which we intended to cross the flooded stream. But our obstinate brutes could not be induced to trust their precious lives on a structure such as they had never seen before. We brought them up to it soberly and quietly, but after sniffing and snorting they swerved off to one side or the other, over and over again, always suspicious that it was some dreadful trap planned for their destruction. We finally tried rushing them at it. But it was no good, they would not cross.

Our next plan was to rope several of the gentlest of the cows and tie them at various intervals along the sides of the bridge, hoping thus to give confidence to the others and encourage them to follow. But only a few went across and the rest baulked again. At last, we succeeded in getting the herd over the creek, but only by taking them in small bunches and crowding them into the water to make them swim to the other side. A few of the rearguard we had to rope and throw bodily into the river, which was running very high, much swollen by the rain of the late storm.

This was the end of our trouble for the time being. That evening the weather was perfect, being clear and fresh; and as the cattle were as well-behaved as any herd could be, we had a quiet, peaceful night, which we thoroughly appreciated.

Next day we crossed the Colorado River, without any objection on the part of our now submissive and obedient charges. We expected to be able to deliver them at the Stock yards on the following morning, but on arriving there we found that much of the railroad line had been washed away by the floods, and that we should have to hold the cattle for a week or ten days until the damage could be repaired. So, we moved them out towards Lone Wolf Cañon and held them there.

Not far from the railway line there was a triangular piece of ground about 100 acres in extent, almost enclosed on the three sides by the fences of small pastures, but open at each of the corners, allowing roads to pass through the enclosure. As no objection could be raised by anyone to our making use of this accidentally formed field, we made it serve us as a corral, turning the cattle into it at night and closing the gaps by sleeping therein. The gap where my chum and I made down our beds was perhaps 70 or 80 yards wide, and by tying one of our horses to the fence at either side and sleeping in the middle ourselves we believed we had made it pretty secure. Still, we felt obliged to sleep with both ears wide open.

One night about two or three o'clock in the morning I seemed to feel by instinct that some of the cattle were approaching the spot where I was sleeping. Instantly jumping up and looking towards the field I distinctly saw the dark bodies of several beasts showing up in the bright moonlight against the light-coloured background of the prairie. In my sleep-dazed condition, without waiting to get my horse, I rushed off bare-footed and undressed to head them back to their fellows. But they did not move, though I shouted and gesticulated, enough indeed to rouse all the other boys and awaken the camp. It did not seem to stir these vagrant cattle in the least.

On coming up to them I found they were only the sun-dried hides and bones of some 20 head of steers that had sometime before been killed on the railway and left where I found them. As a reward for my zeal, I got my feet well filled with cactus thorns, and was laughed at by the other boys.

After more than a week's delay, we received notice that the line had been repaired and the railway company were ready to ship our stock.

THE NORTH CONCHO.

We loaded them into the cars and got rid of one of the most troublesome herds it had ever been our lot to handle.

CHAPTER 22

# Blizzards

With the exception of the blizzards, the winter climate of Texas is one of the most delightful in the world. But blizzards are so sudden in their arrival, and so severe when they come, that they form a great drawback to the pleasure of life.

One of the most trying blizzards or "nothers" ever known to sweep the country occurred in the early spring of 1888. There were three of us on our ranch at the time, and in the forenoon two had been out riding the fence line and inspecting the stock, while the third stayed at home to cook the dinner and do some washing.

By the way, it would seem strange to English eyes to see full-grown bearded men, clad in little more than top boots and enormous spurs, bending over the washtub and scrubbing at a woollen shirt or an old pair of breeches, stopping every now and then to stir a pot of beans or to look into the oven, to see if the coffee were roasted or the bread burning.

But to resume. We got back to the ranch about mid-day, and as it was extremely hot, and we did not expect to require our horses after noon, we turned them loose in the horse-pasture, and sat down to dinner.

At that time the sky was beautifully blue and clear and the sun was shining brightly. Ere long, however, everything assumed a duller hue, and we began to feel so chilly that we shut the doors and pulled on our coats. Looking towards the north we could see from the threatening sky that a blizzard of no mean proportions was approaching. As it was sure to last for at least three days we knew that we must at once replenish our wood-pile, then very low.

The waggon horses were in the horse-pasture. We found them quickly, and jumping on them bare-back galloped up to the house. To do this cannot have taken more than half-an-hour, but in that space of time our pump had been frozen so hard that we could not get water to give them a drink. Fortunately, we did not have far to go for the wood. We were able to get a full load in a long canon, where many live oaks grew, only about a mile from the house. We came back at a gallop, running alongside of the horses to keep ourselves warm. After thawing out the pump, we filled every available bucket with water, and set ourselves to endure the cold spell as best we could.

It *was* cold, *frightfully* cold, with a cold more suitable for the Arctic regions than for the sunny south. At 12 o'clock noon the thermometer had stood at 90 deg. in the shade. By midnight it had dropped to 10 deg. below zero, a fall of 100 deg. in 12 hours. Such a rapid change of temperature would be very trying even in the solid well-built houses of England, with every possible appliance for warmth and comfort. Much more then was it felt in a little wooden house standing on the open prairie, fully exposed to the violence of the wind, built of rough boards only one inch thick, not by any means fitting close together at the edges, and warmed only by an open fire, which seemed to throw out the smallest possible degree of heat, no matter how much wood we piled upon it.

It was so cold that as the snow sifted through the shingles of the roof and fell upon the kettle, boiling on the stove, it did not melt, but remained white and pure till brushed off. My friend who was carrying in a bucket of water from the kitchen stumbled and spilled much of the water. It ran across the floor in front of the fire, where it at once froze, and had to be scraped off as ice. We spent that evening and next day trying to stop up the cracks in the walls with old newspapers.

On our return next evening from riding about among the stock the house felt quite warm and cosy—certainly a hundred times better than the freezing we had undergone during the day; and when bed-time came how comfortable it was to creep beneath the blankets, head and all; and curl up under the load of miscellaneous bedding heaped on our respective couches—including saddle-blankets, long leather leggings, top-coats, odd garments, deer and antelope hides, and above all a waggon sheet. In the morning the blankets over our heads were frozen solid, the moisture from our breath having adhered to the woollen surface, and formed a hard cake of ice.

Our horses of course had neither stable nor artificial shelter of any kind. It seemed selfish on our part, after riding a horse all day to pull the saddle and bridle off him and turn him loose to pass the night in the cold pasture with nothing to eat but the frozen grass. But they looked for nothing else, and trotted off to a sheltered hollow in the creek, where a high bank and clump of trees to some extent broke the force of the wind.

On the second morning of this trying "norther," before going out to ride the line I put on two pair of breeches, in hopes of thereby keeping out the cold. If these nether garments had been new, it would have been all right, but like most of our wearing apparel they had seen much hard service, and were somewhat frail. When my horse, objecting to the cold saddle on his back, began cutting capers instead of letting me mount, I was forced to make a lively spring to reach the saddle, with the unfortunate result that both pair of trousers split from top to bottom.

This blizzard was the coldest "nother" we ever had, and did much damage all over the United States and Canada.

The friendly stockman whose herd had given us so much trouble in shipping to the Indian nation, had enclosed a pasture about 20 miles from his home ranch, and decided to stock it with about 200 head of his one- and two-year-old steers, which were to be cut away from their mothers. It was about the end of January or the beginning of February, and we offered to help him, having nothing much going on at our own place.

As the weather was warm and fine, and looked like holding out at the very least for several days to come, we took neither coats nor blankets with us, intending to sleep in our saddle blankets. The day before the cattle drive, we rode down to the little lumber shanty which was the headquarters of the cowboys, and after supper and a pleasant evening lay down on the floor to sleep till morning. It was just our luck that during the night a very sharp frost set in, which gave us plenty of muscular exercise in the form of shivering under our light coverings. By morning the ground was frozen hard as iron, and the air was biting in the intensity of the cold. Nevertheless, we saddled up and were just starting out to our work, when I noticed a fine warm overcoat hanging on the wall.

Although everyone was chattering with the cold no one seemed to wish to put it on. Asking the reason, I was told "Oh! the coat is unlucky; Ben (a cowboy well known to us all) was killed by the sheriff while wearing it only ten days ago, and no one will put it on." It seemed to me better to risk the bad luck and go to the "round-up" warm, than to be half frozen in riding there. So, I pulled it on in spite of the remonstrances of the other boys, who assured me that something would happen to me before the day was over. And they proved right.

Having got the herd together, we began to cut out the old cows, leaving the young stock, that we were going to take away, in a herd by themselves. To this the youngsters strongly objected, making frantic efforts to get back to their mothers. Constant hard riding on our part ensued. After about a couple of hours of this work, the sun shone out in all his splendour, and soon melted half an inch or so of the top surface of the frozen ground, forming a dangerous layer of soft mud above the still unthawed soil. While things were in this condition a fine, spanking two-year-old steer chose to break away. I followed to head him back to the herd. As he had splendid legs and knew how to use them, he gave me a stiff race, and when I reached him, he at once doubled back on his own tracks.

Naturally, my horse and I tried to do the same, without thinking of the state of the ground. It was then that the earth seemed to jump up and hit me. When I came to myself, I was sitting in the mud, with a useless right arm and a badly twisted foot; and I could see in the distance my horse standing in a dejected attitude, with broken reins trailing loose, the saddle hanging mournfully underneath him, and a thick layer of mud plastered over him from head to tail.

One of the boys brought him back, and we patched up things as well as we could. Both my horse and I felt very sore and bruised, besides which he had a hole gouged in his side where he had fallen on my spur, which was almost bent double.

The herd by this time had been all sorted out, and we started off on our drive of 12 or 15 miles to the new feeding grounds. After going a few miles, I found my horse "*Little Roan*" was in great pain, and on examining him discovered a thorn (a species of cactus), fully 1½ | inch long, sticking in his fetlock. When we succeeded in getting this out, he went all right again for several miles, but towards evening he became much worse and finally gave up altogether, unable to go a foot further.

So, I pulled the saddle off him, and he and I had to stay where we were while the rest of the boys and the herd went on. It was not a very joy-inspiring position to either man or beast, sore and crippled as we both were, to be left alone on the open prairie, in the dull grey of a winter's evening, with a cold wind blowing; nothing to either eat or drink, and no prospect of shelter for the night. Some of the boys offered to stay with me, but this I would not have, as already the outfit was too short-handed to manage the herd properly.

After watching the last signs of the herd disappearing among the *mesquite* and brushwood, I looked around for the least uncomfortable corner in which to pass the night. I noticed a thin column of smoke ascending from behind a patch of trees at no great distance. Towards this I made my way as fast as I could hobble, greatly impeded by the pain in my arm and my ankle, both of which were by this time considerably swollen and very stiff.

On reaching the trees, I found there the camp of two men, who were engaged in sinking a well. From them I received a ready welcome to share their blankets and provisions, and I passed the night pretty comfortably, although the pain in my arm made sleeping almost impossible, and it seemed hard to warm the ground we were sleeping on. The unlucky coat did good service here, if nowhere else.

Next day my mate Jack brought me up a fresh horse, on which I rode back to our neighbour's ranch. It luckily happened that a friend of his, a young Irish doctor, was staying with him at the time, and he patched me up in good form. I found my own horse a couple of weeks later almost entirely recovered from his hurts, and ready to go through it all again if called upon.

CHAPTER 23

# A Hunting Trip

By this time, we had been about four years on our ranch, which was ten miles from our nearest neighbour, and nearly 100 miles from the railway. We had come to look upon ourselves, like Robinson Crusoe on his island, as monarchs of all we surveyed. We awoke one morning to find that we had neighbours, and that at no greater distance than five miles from our house.

As might be expected we did not let the grass grow under our feet before we found out who had come to pitch a tent, or rather, build a house almost within sight of the smoke from our chimneys. We soon learnt, not altogether to our satisfaction, that the section of land had been "jumped" (pre-empted he called it) by old "Moustache Jack," so named from the enormous pair of moustaches which adorned his weather-beaten countenance. Besides his wife and son, he had with him his brother-in-law, who like himself had been one of the buffalo-hunting fiends who had wastefully and wantonly butchered and exterminated that splendid monarch of the plains, the American Bison.

This was not the kind of settler that we would have chosen for a neighbour. But the land was not ours; it did not even lie in our range. All we could do was to make the best of a bad business, and try to get along with them as well as we could. One thing we knew for certain from the moment of their appearance in our vicinity—that the deer and antelope, which were pretty plentiful on our property, were doomed; and later events proved this to be the case. Formerly we had only shot one now and again when we were in want of fresh meat; but very soon we found it a rare thing to see a deer, and a much rarer one still to be able to kill one. These men were heard to boast that they had killed and hauled off to market in one winter 360 head of deer, which they had shot in our place alone.

We were very angry and annoyed, but were powerless to prevent their depredations, as it would have been useless to attempt to prosecute them. No jury would convict them on any charge that we could bring against them so long as they did not interfere with our stock, which would have been quite another matter. They were careful not to offend in that way. Moreover, it would have cost us too much to quarrel with them, as a wire fence 18 miles long is very easy to cut in several places without leaving any mark to show by whom it was done. A few breaks in the fence might cost us months of labour in gathering the cattle that would escape thereby. So, all we could do was to grin and bear it, and keep as good a look-out as we could without neglecting our own regular work.

Our new neighbours, despite their deer-destroying proclivities, seemed anxious to settle down peaceably, cultivating a few acres of land, breaking in and training a bunch of horses which they had somehow or other become possessed of, and making occasional journeys to town with a waggon and team of four or six horses, to return loaded with freight for some of the surrounding ranches.

While I was talking with them one day about their mode of hunting, the old man said if I would only make a little expedition of a few days with him, he would show me the wonderful way in which he could load up his waggon with game. I need hardly say that if old "Moustache Jack" could shoot straight, he knew also how to talk big. Taking him at his word I said I would go next day, and matters were quickly arranged. He was to find one horse and harness and half the provisions, while I supplied the other horse and the waggon, also, of course, my own share of the food.

So next day we set off on our hunting trip, and after going 12 or 15 miles we came on a herd of antelope. Out of this old Jack managed to bring down two beasts, after firing a dozen or more shots. As I was only "seeing how it was done," in fact taking a lesson from him, I did not fire, but remained with the horses, neither of which had as yet been trained to stand fire quietly. "Jack" was highly pleased with

ON THE TRAIL.

himself, and took every chance of saying so, yarning away the rest of the afternoon about his fine shooting, and what he had done and what he was going to do.

When the sun went down a cold "nother" blew up and froze everything solid, even to the water in our coffee pot. This was an unpleasant change from the bright warm sunshine of the day before, and was a great disappointment to us. Besides making the rest of our trip a hardship instead of a pleasure, it greatly increased the difficulty of finding game, for during these cold spells all birds and animals seem to disappear mysteriously, no doubt hiding in the most unlooked-for corners to gain a little shelter from the piercing cold of the north wind.

We had pitched our camp in a "mot" of pecan trees, and had spent the evening in trying to get some of the wild turkeys which abound in the neighbourhood. All we got was a fine raccoon, which I shot while he was picking nuts on the topmost branches of a hickory tree.

As we were in a fairly sheltered position, we hesitated some time about breaking up camp next morning, but finally decided that it would be best to push on towards Tepe Creek, which ran through the district we had chosen as our hunting grounds.

We travelled all that day almost due south, and having the wind at our backs did not feel it so keenly as if we had been facing it. Even at the best, however, it was cold enough to force us to walk or run alongside of the waggon in order to keep up the circulation in our half-frozen bodies. By evening we had crossed the South Fork, and made a good distance up the seldom-visited Tepe Creek. Finding a dry hollow in the bed of the river where the perpendicular banks were nearly 30 feet high and completely sheltered from the north, we settled down for the night, knowing it would be difficult to find a more comfortable camping place for miles around. How warm and cosy it felt to be sitting there enjoying our supper of antelope steak and hot coffee, quite protected from the Arctic wind, which was howling far over our heads.

We hobbled out our horses on the prairie, where the grass was in splendid condition. Instead of "hobbling" both horses, we ought to have "hobbled" only one, and "staked" the other to a tree. But this would have prevented them from seeking shelter from the wind, and we could not find it in our hearts to force them to remain in the cold. So, we turned them both loose with their hobbles on to find for themselves some protected nook. When our horses had been attended to, we carried our two antelopes into our hollow and hung them up on the branch of a tree. Then lighting our fire and spreading our blankets we made ourselves comfortable for the night.

The only drawback to our peace and repose during the hours of darkness was caused by the wolves which, attracted by the smell of our supper and the fresh killed antelope, came every few minutes to the top of the bank, and looking over at us set up their melancholy howls. Although in the bright moonlight we could see them clearly defined against the skyline, we were afraid to fire for fear of missing them and hitting one of the horses. So, the brutes were allowed to continue their concert undisturbed (save for a few rocks we heaved at them) till daylight put an end to their music.

Our first care on getting up was to see that the horses were all right. But they were not to be found anywhere in the vicinity of the camp. Swallowing a hasty breakfast, we started out on foot to hunt for them, for without horses, and miles from human habitation, where we could renew our supply of water, we were in an unpleasant position. Leaving our camp in the creek-bed to look after itself we started in different directions to hunt up the trail of the truants. The "old man" was the first to find it, and following up the truants, discovered them busily engaged in grazing their way straight for the position in which they knew by instinct that their home lay. By night-fall he had them back again in camp.

In the meantime, I followed up the tracks of a herd of antelope which I had come across. I had to make a long detour through an open valley in order to place a hill between myself and the game, thus gaining cover from view. The wind being in the right direction I carefully climbed the hill, and scrambling up to the top found a really ideal position. On the very brow of the hill there grew two small bushes, up to which I crawled very carefully over rocks and through cactus, and was rewarded by finding myself within easy range of the antelope.

As yet they were quite unsuspicious of my presence, and within easy rifle shot. Unfortunately, the wind here was blowing so keenly that it filled my eyes with tears, causing me to misjudge the distance and to think the game was much further off than it really was. Besides this I forgot to make clue allowance for shooting downhill, so that when I fired, the bullet went clean over the back of the antelope, and I missed one of the best shots I ever had. Naturally I was very crestfallen on returning to camp, but my failure added immensely to the satisfaction of my old buffalo-hunting comrade.

That night we picketed one of the horses in order that they should not leave us in the lurch again. We drove nearly all next day without seeing anything till just before sundown, when we came across five antelope. "Old Moustache Jack" got down to stalk them. He did a good deal of creeping on his hands and knees and fired a number of shots, without other result than frightening our game, which came tearing past the waggon. I could not resist any longer, and snatching up my Winchester blazed away at the fleeing antelope. I was lucky enough to bring down the last buck, which fell at the head of a little canon some distance off. My companion came running back, and jumping into the waggon we started to drive at full speed to where the buck lay.

But the excitement of the firing and the chase was more than our horses could stand without joining in the sport; and this they did by rearing, buck-jumping, and lashing out with their heels. A little fun would not have mattered, but they did not know when to stop, and carried their sport to such an extent that they soon reduced almost to matchwood the pole, single-trees, and front end of the waggon. Finally, doubling sharp back, they broke the front wheels short off from the running gear of the waggon. Not till they had wrought all this mischief did they tire of their amusement and stand quiet. Even in the midst of the excitement I could not help laughing, to hear "old Jack" howling that he was being killed, as the splinters were sent flying past his head.

We were now in a very awkward predicament, utterly wrecked, on the top of a high, bare divide, all the sides and approaches to which were covered with rocks and boulders, which, at the best of times, made it difficult for a waggon to get either up or down. Of course, the first thing to do was to clear the horses of the broken remains of the harness, pole, and neckyoke, and stake them out for the night. To repair the damage, we only had by way of tools one axe, two pocket knives, and a few bits of rope.

The most serious part of the business was the breaking of the waggon "reach" and "stay irons," for without these, although the waggon could go straight ahead, it was impossible to make the slightest turn either to the right or the left without running a great risk that it would swing off in exactly the opposite direction.

Making use of the horses' hobbles and stake ropes, strips of our own bedding, and thongs cut from the antelope hide, we managed, by the light of the camp fire, to splice one place here, and patch another break there, till we had most of the wreckage looking shipshape again. But then came the "reach," a piece of the hardest of well-seasoned oak, through which we had to bore a number of holes. As we could make little or no impression upon it with our knives, we managed it by making the "king-bolt" of the waggon red-hot, and with it burning the holes through the "reach." This plan answered capitally, but it took a very long time to do it, and morning had nearly come before we had finished our work.

In travelling next day, we were forced to go along very carefully and gently. One of us led the horses, while the other walked ahead to pick out the easiest places for our crippled waggon to make its way up or down the various ridges we had to cross in heading towards the nearest ranch-house, where we could get some tools and materials to mend up breakages.

It was all right on any fairly level piece of ground, where we could go straight forward; but let one of the wheels strike a tuft of buffalo grass, an old root, or a rock, and then our uncertain course would suddenly veer round to this side or that, as the case might be, but always in the opposite direction to the one in which we expected it to go. Then again in going downhill, as there was nothing to hold it back, the tail end of the waggon showed a decided objection to always having to remain in the rear, and therefore made strenuous efforts to get round in front of the horses. There was no extreme hurry about the speed of our journey, for we were constantly forced to call a halt in order to retie knots or tighten up our ropes and thongs, which were for ever stretching more and more, thereby loosening our numerous tyings and bandages.

A couple of days of this sort of work brought us to the ranch-house of a friendly sheepman, who supplied us with saw, hammers, nails, and other tools and materials necessary to effect an efficient repair. When we had finished, we found our work was successful enough to allow us to venture trotting for a good part of the way home. We had no means of repairing the ironwork, and the waggon had to go to the blacksmith's shop to have this done.

Although the trip was rather an expensive one, and had not turned out as profitable as we had expected, I was not much disappointed, and had gained some insight into the methods adopted by these professional hunters.

From all I had seen and picked up from the remarks of "old Moustache Jack," I came to the conclusion that although they can when necessity demands it make some very accurate shooting, yet since the introduction of the repeating rifle, they trust not so much to the accuracy of their aim as to the amount of lead they can, as they say themselves, "pump into" a herd of game. In the time of the short-ranged, slow, muzzle-loading rifle, one shot was as much as they could expect to get while the quarry was within range; and it behoved them to take every care that this one shot was successful.

But nowadays with long range, quick-firing rifles, they take less care and fire as many shots as they can while the animal is still in sight, hoping that one of the bullets may bring it down. The result of this is the rapid extinction of all big game on the American continent.

## Chapter 24
# Caught by a "Norther"

Although my first hunting expedition had not proved an unqualified success, I was not to be discouraged, and when invited by the sheepman at whose house we had repaired our waggon to join him for a week or so and try what we could do, I readily consented, and with my rifle, bedding, and a good supply of cartridges climbed into his waggon, which was waiting at our door.

As the weather at the time was threatening, and a "norther" was to be expected at any time, we intended to make his ranch our headquarters and venture on only short expeditions during the day time. The first day we drove through a number of valleys where game was usually very plentiful, and running across a herd of antelope my friend managed to get one of them. We dressed it and hung it on a tree, intending to pick it up on our way back in the evening. But as events turned out it had to hang there for nearly four days before we were able to bring it in.

Hoping to get some more out of this herd, we followed them up, but they always kept well ahead of us without getting so far away that we could consider them lost. As we always expected that the next time, they stopped we should be able to get up to them we continued the pursuit till we found that night was falling, and that we were many miles from home or anywhere else where a meal or a bed could be obtained.

Having by this time wandered into country that was unknown to either of us, with tired horses and no light to guide us, we thought it wisest to stay where we were till morning came, and the sun would once more give us our directions.

We had not intended to be gone from the ranch for more than a few hours, and we had brought neither blankets nor provisions with us. As the night was warm the want of bedding did not trouble us much, but we should have liked something to eat, and much regretted that we had not brought our antelope with us, instead of leaving it on a tree. A nice steak, fried on the embers of our wood fire, would have been most acceptable.

When daylight came, we looked round eagerly for the sun, by which we knew we could find our position. But no sun appeared. All was dull and grey, and the sky was heavily covered with masses of black threatening clouds, hurrying along before the impetuous force of a coming "norther." The country was new and unknown to us, but we remembered having heard a week or two before that a well-boring outfit had set out to sink for water somewhere in the direction where we then found ourselves.

We decided that instead of trying to find our way back to the ranch-house our wisest plan was to hunt for this camp, which might be quite close to us. But we had no luck in our search, and we wandered about all day with no other result than finding ourselves still more miles from home than on the previous evening.

Fortunately, we came across a pond of fairly clean water, and both we and the horses were able to have a good drink, after breaking the already thickly formed ice. This, to a certain extent, made up for the want of food, but it was cold comfort, and a cup of hot coffee with a bite of bread and bacon would have been better. We had not even our jackets with us, and the piercingly cold wind blew through our flannel shirts with the keenness of knives, chilling us to the bone. Many times, during the day we were forced to seek the shelter of some rock or bush where the force of the wind was broken, and there rub our frozen limbs into circulation again.

When night overtook us, we were in a dreary open waste covered with sand and scrub. The few trees to be seen were either dead or leafless, and the wind howled across this open prairie. The dead trees served us well in one way, as we were able to get from them plenty of dried wood to make a roaring fire, which we kept up all night. The fire was absolutely necessary to keep us from being entirely frozen, but it did not do all we could have wished, for it absolutely refused to warm more than one side of us at a time. The result was that if we turned our faces to the fire the freezing wind blew through the thin backs of our well-worn shirts, quickly forcing us to turn round and toast that part of our bodies. And no sooner were our backs well thawed out and just beginning to feel comfortable than the cold compelled us to turn some other portion to the fire.

We spent most of the evening and part of the night practising this "turn-spit" business in hopes that the wind would fall, but it did not moderate in the least. Occasionally we would try placing ourselves so that the fire was between us and the wind, but it was no good, because when we got close enough to the fire to derive any benefit from the warmth, we became smothered with smoke, and, worse still, covered with the sparks and bits of burning wood which were constantly being carried out of the fire by the force of the wind. After one or two attempts, and having our clothing set on fire in several places, we retired, growling, to the windward size of the blaze.

We were not totally destitute of bedding, for we had with us one very thin and very old cotton quilt which someone had thrown on the seat of the waggon by chance before we left the ranch house. It was but scanty covering for one, and almost useless for two. With this and nothing else for bed and bedding we stretched ourselves on the frozen ground, agreeing that we should change places every hour, so that the one next the fire for the first hour should act as "windbreak" or shelter to his companion during the next. I don't think we did much sleeping, though I believe we did not feel the want of food while lying down quite so much as while standing up. Almost worse than the wind was the horrid cold of the frozen ground, which was hard as iron, and every little projection from the surface felt like an icy gimlet boring its way into one's very bones.

Towards morning I felt drowsy and less uncomfortable. I must have slept for some time; for when I awoke the sky was beginning to show a slight greyness in the east. I soon found out how it was that I had passed the latter part of the night so much more comfortably than the first part. My friend noticing that I was beginning to doze had cautiously crept from under our light covering and carefully doubled his share of the quilt over me. Moreover, he piled round me and over me everything he could think of that might possibly serve in the slightest degree to keep off the wind.

He even divested himself of the waistcoat he had been wearing. He kept up his circulation as well as he could by alternately crouching over the fire and running up and down at his best speed. Poor fellow, he was almost frozen; but he would accept no thanks for his self-denial, saying that he knew I would have done the same for him had he fallen asleep before I did.

Finding from the position of the sun that we had been travelling in a wrong direction, we set off again at an angle to the course we had been pursuing the day before, in order to strike, if possible, the well-borer's camp. As the cold wind continued, we did not meet with any game to supply us with food, and the horses, which were nearly as hungry as ourselves, could not be expected to travel fast or far.

Night again found us in a position of lonely isolation. Fortunately, we had come across a pool of good water, so that we did not suffer from thirst, which is much more difficult to withstand than hunger. There was nothing for it but to camp as we had done before and make the best of it. The blizzard had now blown itself out, and gradually died away as the sun went down. During the night, therefore, we had only a very keen frost and no wind to contend with, and it seemed almost like summer warmth after what we had gone through.

When morning came, we were gladdened by seeing the sun arise in all his wonted splendour. On again resuming our journey we soon fell in with tolerably fresh waggon tracks, and following these up for a few miles were rejoiced by coming in sight of the well-borer's camp.

Needless to say, we got a most hospitable reception and the first "square meal" we had had since leaving my friend's ranch three days before.

On our way back we got several shots at antelope, but missed them all. I managed to shoot a wolf, and this, with the antelope, not to speak of a frozen heel and two frost-bitten fingers, was all we had to show for our long trip and many privations.

Chapter 25

# Some Stalking

Although bad luck of the worst kind seemed to pursue us through the two expeditions I have just described, there were many others in which we were as successful as we could wish. But taking it altogether, I believe that I got the most enjoyable form of sport, not when we went out on a regular hunting trip, but by making a point of always carrying my rifle with me when it was possible to do so, and stalking any deer or antelope I might chance to run across during my numerous rides about the country.

It happened, for instance, one bright afternoon in the late autumn that my way lay along a deep, rocky *cañon*, with steep, though not precipitous, sides, the bottom well covered with underbrush. On turning a corner, I saw some distance ahead of me two fine bucks quietly grazing on the side of the "draw," just above the line where the brushwood gave place to the low scrub which covered the slopes on either side. Cautiously dismounting, and throwing the reins over the horse's head, I drew the Winchester out of its scabbard, and began to crawl on hands and knees towards the game.

The underbrush gave excellent cover, but had the great drawback of making it necessary to use extreme care in passing through it, as any unusual disturbance among the branches or cracking of dry twigs would be enough to frighten off the deer. Added to this I found it necessary to make a halt every few yards to clear my hands and knees of the prickly pear, catsclaw, and cactus thorns which seemed to take immense pleasure in burying themselves in my skin. Arrived about the spot where I expected to find the deer, I slowly raised my head, and was astonished to see the two bucks within a few feet of me, gazing intently into my face. It was only for a second, however, and before I could clear my rifle of the bushes, they had bounded off 80 or 100 yards. Then they again turned round to see who or what I was.

In turning the larger of the two exposed his shoulder, and I at once fired. Feeling certain from the sound of the bullet that he was hard hit, I was surprised to see both of the beasts go up the steep side of the canon at a fast gallop. On reaching the top the buck I had fired at again turned round, and seeing me standing in the open lowered his head and came down at the charge. As he thundered down the steep slope, bringing with him a small torrent of loose rocks and flints, I fired twice at him, but dazzled by the rays of the setting sun and flurried by the excitement of the moment, I missed the first shot and hit him only on the hindquarters with the second, not severely enough to check his charge.

On attempting to fire again I found, to my consternation, that I had expended my last cartridge, and although I hurriedly searched all my pockets there was not a shot left. However, it was not necessary. The first bullet had done its work. In his downward rush the buck had reached the spot where I first fired at him, when he suddenly stopped, looked about him in a dazed sort of manner, then shaking his head, gave two or three leaps like a jumping broncho, and subsided on the ground stone-dead. When skinning and cutting him up I found that the bullet had passed through both shoulders, injuring the heart in its passage, and having mushroomed out, had failed to penetrate the elastic hide on the off side. It now has its own place among the treasures of my younger days.

On another occasion I had been working all day at one of our windmills, and had taken my shot gun with me, intending to shoot some quail or prairie chicken on my way home in the evening.

With this object I was strolling along a fairly broad valley, where the underbrush, although plentiful, was not very dense, and should have made good cover for small game. While searching quietly about for some sport, I saw not very far off two fine antelope, busy feeding a short distance up the hill side. As it was some time since I had shot any big game, it struck me that this would make an excellent opportunity to practise my powers of stalking. I seemed to have luck with it that evening, and succeeded in getting up to between 40 and 50 yards of the antelope before they noticed me. Great was my regret that instead of a rifle I had only a shot gun, loaded with very fine bird shot. Search as I would I could find nothing that would in any way act as a bullet, and could be trusted to go with any accuracy for 50 yards or so.

As they would not allow me to stalk them any closer, the question now arose, should I leave them alone, or should I jump up, make a run as close as I could and fire both barrels in hope of killing or at least disabling one of them. In doing this there would be a great chance of only wounding the poor beast, which would then crawl away and die in some remote corner, and I should have taken his life uselessly. I have always looked on this more as murder than sport, and have abhorred doing it; I therefore chose the former alternative and getting up walked past them, evidently much to their astonishment.

But I had not finished with them yet, for no sooner was I out of sight than I started off home at a run to change my shot gun for a rifle. Arrived at the ranch I quickly pulled off my heavy boots and donning a pair of light, noiseless *moccasin* slippers, seized my rifle and a goodly supply of cartridges. I started out for a hunt, leaving instructions for one of the boys to saddle up a pair of horses and follow on my trail as soon as he was ready. On getting back to the place where I had done my previous stalking, I found the antelope had crossed over to the other side of the valley and were moving about in an uneasy restless manner, evidently a good deal upset by my former actions.

For half an hour or more I manoeuvred up and down the valley, hiding behind trees, creeping under bushes, or crawling across the open patches in vain endeavours to reach some position from which I could make a certain shot at the game. But as the light grew more and more feeble, I saw my prospects of success gradually fading away, and very reluctantly I gave up the chase.

Just as I was turning my steps homewards, however, I had the good fortune to descry something most soothing to my disappointed spirits. Far up the *cañon*, and showing clearly against the light in the western sky, there was a big bunch of wild hogs or *peccaries*. A minute's inspection showed me that they were coming down to water at some of our artificial tanks, where I had been working during the day. Although one or two of them would stop every now and then to squabble over some fallen acorns or other tit-bits, the majority kept steadily on their way, and I saw I had no time to lose if I wanted to cut them off. Setting off at a trot I soon crossed the valley, and climbed half of the opposite slope, but not before the hogs had reached the spot I was making for.

I dropped one before they were aware of my approach, but before I could shoot again, they broke cover, and dashed headlong down the steep side of the canon. After them I went, making a spurt of the best speed I could put forth. In this first rush I gained considerably, owing I suppose to the greater length of stride. But it was not for long, for the ground, broken up with scrub and loose stones, was more suitable to the hogs than to my light slippers, and I soon began to fall behind. Dropping on my knee I took a flying shot at the last of the *peccaries*, and was greatly rejoiced to see him turn a somersault and roll down the hill, along with a stream of rocks, flints, and leaves.

The horses and dogs had now come up, and my friend and I set to work to prepare the two beasts, having previously set the dogs on the tracks of the fleeing herd. Having carefully hung up our two hogs so that they would be safely out of reach of any prowling coyotes, we mounted our horses and galloped down the valley, guided by the yelping of the dogs which had evidently, from the noise they were making, brought at least one or more of the hogs to bay.

Night had now completely closed down, but a bright moon gave us light enough to see a big old tusker busily engaged in repelling the attacks of our two dogs. In the fight he was more than able to hold his own, but no sooner did he attempt to escape than one of the dogs would seize him by a hind leg, and on turning to fight his first assailant he would be caught by the other. A rifle shot soon finished the struggle, and having now got as much fresh meat as we could use for some time to come, we called off the dogs and rode home well loaded and highly pleased with our evening's sport.

A friend of mine owned a Martini-Henry sporting rifle, of which he was very proud, but unfortunately, he had never been able, from one cause or another, to test its killing powers on anything larger than a jack-rabbit. So, he asked me to make use of it for a time and report to him on its merits. I had only been carrying it for a few days when one morning while riding the fence line, on coming over a rather steep rise of ground, I saw a single antelope standing by itself with the whole of its left side turned towards me. It was the work of only a second or two to dismount, load, and fire; and the next instant the antelope galloped off on three legs, with the fourth one hanging useless.

As deer and antelope can run almost as fast on three legs as on four, provided the injured member is a front leg, I was afraid I was going to lose him, but on following up the chase round the shoulder of the hill, I found him standing examining his wound. My second shot knocked him over, but he again rose and ran a hundred yards; then stopped, with his tail towards me. I fired for the third time, and he fell to rise no more.

The bullets I had been using were hollow, plugged with soft wood, and I found on cutting up the antelope that the first ball on striking the shoulder had expanded to such an extent that, after smashing the shoulder-blade and surrounding flesh for a couple of inches on each side of the point of impact, it had broken into minute fragments, and so failed to penetrate to any of the vital parts. The second shot had acted on the ribs in the same way as the first had done on the shoulder. The third bullet, striking only the soft flesh and meeting no bones in its passage had not expanded, and had passed through the animal transversely, causing instantaneous death.

I never used the so-called "explosive bullet" again, but always preferred one made of soft lead, which, although it mushrooms out, does not break up, and therefore retains its power of penetration. If it does not show so much damage for its hit, it is, I consider, much more fatal, and therefore more merciful. With it I have killed many deer, antelope, wolves, cattle, badgers, and numerous other animals, and in only a very few of these cases has it been necessary to fire a second shot.

But to return to my antelope. While preparing it for bringing back to the ranch I found embedded in the ribs a small leaden bullet, showing that it must have been wounded at some previous period of its existence, although from this it had perfectly recovered. It was not a large animal, and I easily lifted it on to my saddle, intending to carry it home in front of me. Just when I had got it well settled, the pony happened to turn his head to bite at a fly on his shoulder. Instead of catching the fly his nose came in contact with the head of the antelope, which gave him such a start that he immediately made the biggest' buck jump of which he was capable, sending the carcase of the antelope flying through the air to land with a dull thud many feet ahead. Not till I had cut it up into pieces could I induce him to allow me to fasten it on to the saddle.

There is an old story one often comes across in reading accounts of hunting in the far West, to the effect that deer, but more especially antelope, are of such an inquisitive disposition that on seeing anything new or unusual they cannot resist the temptation to come up to it and thoroughly examine the novelty. This trait in their character is frequently made use of by hunters, it is said, to lure them to their own destruction. The hunters, we are told, hoist a piece of red cloth on the end of a stick, or lying on their backs fasten a coloured rag to one of their feet, which they gently wave in the air. Thus, they attract the game, which on coming up to examine the curious looking object, afford the hunter an easy mark to fire at.

Wishing to prove the truth of this by my own experience, I hunted out of one of my trunks an old dressing gown, the one side of which was red and the other blue. Armed with this and my rifle I set off to a spot where I knew a small bunch of antelope was likely to be found. As I expected, on rounding the base of a hill I saw four or five head quietly grazing in the evening light. This was just what I had wished for, and seemed to be an excellent opportunity to practise the delusive form of hunting, the merits of which I had often heard extolled.

Finding a favourable position for seeing and being seen I lay down on my back and covering my feet with the old dressing-gown so that the red side would show, I gently waved them about in the air, giving at the same time a low cough to attract the notice of the game. My heart beat high in hopes of getting at least one good shot. But the plan did not act as it was intended, for either my antelope were destitute of all instincts of inquisitiveness, or else they had at some former period of their existence had all their desires in that line so fully satisfied that, believing there was nothing new under the sun, they did not feel called upon to make any further enquires.

With only one glance at the ludicrous-looking sight which I must have presented they set to work to put the greatest possible distance between themselves and me in the shortest possible space of time. So well did they succeed, that by the time I had cleared my feet of the useless old dressing-gown and straightened myself up they were already disappearing over the head of the valley as if on the wings of a whirlwind. They had been frightened so badly that they never came back to their favourite haunts again.

CHAPTER 26

# A Suprise Visit

Living as we did far away from civilised society, and ten or twelve miles from the county road, we were not at all prepared to receive any visitors save those who could be content with a hearty welcome and the roughest of rough fare and accommodation. True we were constantly entertaining neighbouring cattlemen or wandering cowboys riding through the country in search of work or making enquiries for stock which had strayed from their own particular range. But all these men and boys, accustomed to a rough life, were glad to take us as they found us.

A few years of this solitary and uncivilised existence and the original savage which seems to be lying dormant in every human being began to assert itself in one shape or another. As was to be expected, the first steps in this retrograde movement were noticeable in the matter of dress and personal appearance. This was soon followed by carelessness of bodily comforts, which at the best of times never would have reached a very high standard from an English point of view.

As time wore on the feeling gradually grew upon us that everything was as it should be, and, further still, that as everything now was so it would continue to be through the indefinite future. The natural result of all this was that on the ranch itself during the quiet season of the year, when our time was not occupied in cattle work or other pursuits in which we should be likely to come in contact with people from the outside world, we felt little or no restraint as regards our dress or customs; our own inclinations being the only rule we were disposed to follow.

Things were in this happy condition one day in the height of summer when somewhere about ten or eleven o'clock in the forenoon my partner and I were busily engaged in routing a snake out from the roots of a prickly pear bush a little over two hundred yards or so from the house. While intent on our sport we suddenly became aware of the unusual sound of wheels. Instantly we dropped our sticks and stretching upon tip-toe surveyed the approaching vehicle. It was a buggy, and a smart one, too. And, horror of horrors, there was a lady in it!

I believe that both our unshaven faces paled as they had not done during the most terrific stampedes. The shock we received was not without a cause, for to tell the truth we stood there very nearly in the garb in which we entered this vale of woe. One instant we stood aghast, and the next we were off to the house as if Old Nick himself were after us. If we did not then break the record, we at least tried very hard to do so; for it was a neck and neck race as to whether we or our visitors should reach the house first. Certainly, novelty and excitement were not lacking to add zest to the contest.

Luckily, we were the winners, but not by more than a fraction, for as we bolted in by the back door our uninvited guests pulled up in front of the porch. Without waiting to answer their knock we quickly dived through the trap door into the cellar below, and pulling the door down after us hastily began to pull on such articles of respectable attire as we could fish out of our trunks in the semi-darkness. As we struggled frantically with buttons, studs, and such like obstinate but necessary adjuncts to our apparel, we could hear our visitors above, after repeated knockings, open the door and walk into the silent and apparently empty house. We could also hear their remarks of astonishment at finding no one there. They felt certain they had seen, while approaching, at least two flying figures disappear in the direction of the house.

No sooner had we huddled on our clothes, more rapidly than elegantly, than one of us seized a piece of bacon and the other a sack of flour, and armed with these, to act as an excuse for our presence in the cellar, we raised the trap door and climbing up the ladder tried to appear as if nothing unusual had happened. But our efforts in this direction were signally unsuccessful, and after the surprise caused by our sudden appearance from below had passed, and mutual greetings had been exchanged, we had to join in a hearty laugh at our own expense.

The new arrivals proved to be a Mr. S—— and his wife. We had known him some time previously, when he had been part owner of a very large herd of cattle, whose range lay not very many miles from our pasture. Having married a charming lady from the North he had sold out his interests in Texas and had entered into business in Chicago, but before finally settling down in that city he was, with his bride, making a tour of visits to his former acquaintances.

Everything in the Wild West was new and enchanting to this lady, and she most thoroughly enjoyed entering into the minutest detail of Texas ranch life. Before leaving she kindly told that the visit to our "Stag Ranch," *i.e.*, Bachelors' Hall, was one of the most interesting experiences she had had.

As this was the first occasion on which we had ever had the honour of a visit from a lady, we were naturally extremely anxious to make the best show of hospitality in our power, and also to set before her the most appetising fare we could provide. But our resources were very meagre, accustomed as we were to living on fried bacon, bread, and molasses, with a choice of black coffee or cold water as a beverage. Forgetting that our visitors had quite lately come from living in the best hotels and other places where every delicacy was easily obtainable, we quickly decided that fresh meat was the greatest treat we could give them, as it always was to us after one of our periods of scarcity. To provide the required luxury I shouldered my rifle, and, asking to be excused for a short time, hurried off to a long canon down which I knew many of our cattle would be proceeding towards the watering troughs.

My partner, who was a better conversationalist than I, was left to entertain our guests, and at the same time to go on with the cooking of the rest of the dinner. A fine fat yearling dropped to a lucky shot behind the head. As quickly as I could, I pulled him into the shade of a bunch of oak trees, up which I had to scramble to avoid the charge of the angry companions of the slaughtered beast. Fortunately, they soon dispersed, and went on their way with much growling and threatening, allowing me to come down from my refuge among the branches.

Once on the ground again I lost no time in cutting out the tit-bits, and with these in my hand hurried back to the ranch. Within a very short space of time, they appeared on the table nicely fried with bread crumbs, as the *chef d'oeuvre* of the homely feast. In the evening, after our guests had departed on their further round of visits, we returned to where I had killed the yearling. Finding it all in good order we skinned it, and after dressing the carcase, brought it back to the ranch to be used as provisions, partly as fresh beef, but principally in the form of "jerked" (that is sun-dried and salted) meat.

I think that after this lady's visit we were always more careful in our attire, so that we were never so nearly "caught" again.

But we were once caught in another way, during the early spring of the year following the episode I have just described. There were four or five of us living on the ranch at the time, and as there was nothing very pressing to be done in the way of cattle work, we were repairing fences, making up the standing ground around the troughs, and seeing that the windmills were kept in good running order. Although this work kept us all pretty busy, there was no very great "rush" to get it done, and some of the boys seemed to think that there was not much need for them to exert themselves beyond what was absolutely necessary.

The first duty they began to shirk was the taking of their share of the unavoidable household drudgery, such as cooking the meals, chopping wood, or sweeping the house. They would quietly lie in bed until the breakfast was on the table, then at once jump up, and just as they were join us in doing their full share of consuming the viands. It may have been very nice and comfortable for them, but was hardly fair or agreeable to the rest of us.

So, one day we struck work saying that it was their turn to cook breakfast next morning and our turn to lie in bed. To this they objected, telling us that if we waited for them to cook the breakfast there would not be any breakfast for us.

In the evening before going to bed we left everything ready in the usual way for lighting the fire and boiling the coffee, and they fondly believed we had forgotten our threats of the morning. But they were not aware that we had taken to bed along with us a goodly supply of books, bread and cold bacon. Next morning dawned, dull, cold and cheerless, a very uninviting day for turning out of one's warm blankets; and our long stay in bed was all the more enjoyable. When the light became strong enough for reading, we got out our books and quietly munched our bread and bacon, feeling no little satisfaction at the uneasy movements we could notice now and again in the beds of the hostile camp on the other side of the room, where the pangs of hunger were beginning to make themselves felt.

It was already pretty late when a head was raised from under the blankets, and we heard the inquiry made in an anxious tone of voice, "Say! when are you fellows going to get breakfast ready?" We were able to give the cheery answer: "Oh thanks, we have had breakfast some time ago." Down popped the head, and we knew that the struggle had begun—with the advantage on our side, that we were satisfied and comfortable while they were not. For a long time no other sound was to be heard in the silent house but the occasional turning of the leaves of our books or a smothered grumble from one of the hungry boys.

Ten o'clock came; eleven o'clock came; twelve o'clock passed, and still, no one would give in. There is no saying to what length this struggle of endurance might have been protracted, if we had not heard just as one o'clock was about to strike the jingle of spurs and bits and the tap, tap, tap of approaching horses' feet. Ashamed of being caught in our childish dispute we all with one accord jumped out of bed, hauled on our breeches and boots, and rolled up our blankets.

By the time our visitors reached the door we were busily engaged, some with pots and pans near the stove, some with plates or knives and forks, just beginning to get *dinner* ready as we told our guests, omitting to mention that as yet there had been no breakfast. Had either of the two new arrivals touched the icy cold stove they would at once have suspected that there was something unusual on the cards. But fortunately for us, neither of them approached it until we had a good fire in full blast, which speedily cooked a welcome meal. They fully appreciated it, remarking that it was very lucky we chanced to be so late that day as it had allowed them to be in time for a warm dinner, which they had hardly expected.

After they had gone there was no further dispute among ourselves as to everyone doing his fair share of work. From that time onwards each seemed to be willing to do his part of anything that had to be done.

CHAPTER 27

# *Al Fresco* Cooking

Cooking is always more or less of a trouble, and is, worse luck, one that cannot possibly be avoided. But when men are living alone on a ranch as we were, the culinary art is reduced to its finest (by this I do not mean the most perfect) point. That is to say, they do as little of it as they possibly can get along with, and would be very glad indeed if someone else would do that little instead of themselves. Many various and curious expedients are adopted in the endeavour to relieve the monotonous routine of boiling, frying and washing up.

There were a number of men living together on a ranch on equal terms as to work, wages, etc., and as no one was specially engaged to do the cooking this very essential duty became anybody's and everybody's work. Now each and all of them felt that they had within their breasts a soul above pots and pans, and no one wanted to be harnessed down to this most unpopular job. Still, it had to be done somehow.

CAMPING OUT.

Lots were drawn among them as to who should be the first to fill the uncoveted position. The unlucky loser was installed as "chef" to the establishment, and had to do the cooking for the whole outfit.

But after all, his position was not altogether without hope, for at the time of drawing the lots, it had also been agreed that the first man was only required to do the cooking as long as no one complained of anything that he had cooked. Immediately anyone began to find fault, the cook was relieved of his post and the grumbler had to take his place, until someone else became dissatisfied, when another change was made. With the beginning of each new turn everything was usually well up to the required standard, but as time went on and the cook became gradually tired of his job, the cooking became worse and worse, till some horrible messes were served up and the food was hardly eatable.

Then someone would be bound to grumble, saying that he would be hanged if he could not cook better with his eyes shut, or some such remark; and he would at once be requested to take the work in hand and show what he could do. So, it went on, until the busy season came round again, and the boys had to separate for the cattle work on the range.

On our ranch we generally worked on a different plan. When four of us were living in the house together two would do the cooking and the other two the washing up of the dishes and cleaning the pots, changing duties week and week about. At other times we would divide the work up, one of us seeing to coffee, tea and potatoes, another doing the baking while the third boiled the rice and chopped the firewood. Each one then cleaned up the utensils he had used.

It was while this order of things was in existence and I was at the time chief baker to the establishment that routing about among our stock of provisions I came upon a bag of currants, and determined to try my hand at baking a batch of fancy biscuits. To this end I mixed up a good supply of dough, and adding a liberal amount of lard, currants, sugar, and molasses I worked it up in proper order. Then cutting out the biscuits by means of the lid of the coffee pot, I placed them in the largest of our bread pans and put them in the oven to bake. As there was a fine fire in the stove they were soon thoroughly done; and I placed them on the end of the table to cool.

While I was busy baking the biscuits a long lanky cowboy who hailed from "back East" came in. He was a perfect stranger to us, but following the custom of the country we set before him our own dinner of which we were about to partake. This he polished off without loss of time, and then reaching out his hand to where my pan of biscuits was cooling at the end of the table, he picked up a couple and stuffed them in his mouth.

A minute after, when his mouth cooled off a little, he spoke for almost the first time during the meal, and his remark was forcible if not very elegant. What he said was "Durned if this truck don't eat mighty slick," and with that he went straight forward without a halt till he had finished all that was in the pan. He then said "Goodbye," got on his horse, and rode off, leaving us greatly astonished and highly amused at his extraordinary behaviour. We never saw him again.

On one occasion, in the middle of summer, when we were gathering a herd of beef steers to drive up to the railroad for shipping to the Chicago market, the man who had been engaged to do the cooking for the outfit disappointed us at the last moment. It was impossible to fill his place at such short notice, and there would have been a serious hitch in our arrangements had not one of us taken the job in hand. As no one else was willing to do the work, I volunteered for the post.

Never again. One experience of the kind was enough.

I had not held the position for many days (I had almost said "hours") before I fully sympathised with the persistent grumbling and complaining in which the cooks of cow-outfits usually indulge, and I had no trouble in seeing how a good cook fully earned the high-priced wages he always demanded.

To begin with, the cook's work usually commences somewhere about 2 o'clock in the morning, when he has to begin getting breakfast ready, in order that the boys can eat it and get to their work by the time daylight appears. If the meal were all finished at one time it would not be so bad, but this is not the case. No sooner has the first lot of boys breakfasted and ridden off, and the cook started to wash up the dishes, than those who have been on night-guard come clattering up, all as hungry as hunters, after their four- or five-hours' riding in the keen morning air. Their wants have to be satisfied, and if these wants are few in number, they are very large in quantity. It is astonishing the amount of bread, steak, and coffee that a hungry cowboy can devour in a remarkably short space of time.

After these have finished and gone, the cook has to clean out all his pots, pans, and dishes, see the fire safely extinguished, fill his water-keg, load up his provisions, and stow the boss' bedding away in the waggon. He must see that his coffee-pot is empty and his molasses-can securely

A Prairie Thanksgiving Dinner.

fastened; for, strange as it may appear, some of the boys are inclined to get very hot and rusty if they find at the next camping ground that either the coffee or molasses has upset or leaked out and run over their blankets. Another thing they do not take kindly is to find a lump of fat bacon has rolled out of its box and got sandwiched in among their bedding. So, it behoves the cook to be somewhat careful in the manner in which he packs things away.

Having got through these preliminaries, he hitches up his team and trots off as fast as he can to the next camping ground, perhaps ten or twelve miles distant, where he at once sets to, lighting his fire and preparing dinner. While on the road between the two halts, he must keep his eyes open for dry sticks and wood to make his fire, for fuel may be scarce at the next stopping-place, especially when it happens to be on a line of travel much used by passing herds. This wood he picks up and throws into a raw-hide slung under the body of the waggon. inner has to be got ready with the shortest possible delay, as the boys do not care to be kept waiting. If they do not let him hear of it, should it chance to be late, the "boss" certainly will do so, and the language of the prairie is very expressive and has a varied and powerful vocabulary.

When the different sets of boys have dined, and also any strangers that happen to be in the neighbourhood at the time (the smell of dinner seems to attract them, and they appear mysteriously from what at other times appears to be an uninhabited waste), the cook again loads up his waggon and proceeds to the night camp. There all the same duties have to be gone through again, with the addition probably of roasting a supply of coffee for the next day's use. By the time that is finished and everything cleaned up, there will remain to him perhaps three- or four-hours' sleep before beginning the same round of labour on the following day.

Of course, from the nature of the employment all the work has to be done in the open, and it is no pleasant thing to spend hours stooping over a roaring hot fire, with a blazing sun pouring down its unbroken rays on to one's back and shoulders till one feels as if the very last drop of moisture were being drawn out of one's flesh and bones. What splendid visions one has at a time like this of cool draughts of beer or ice-cold lemonade.

I fear I did not make a very satisfactory cook; still I did the best I could, and nothing very exceptional happened during my term of office. In fact, I cannot recall any incident worthy of being recorded except the following. One morning, just as I thought I had nearly finished washing up the dishes, and was about to clear up all the odds and ends scattered about the camping ground, one of the boys, who had been sent back to me with a message from the "boss" as to which road I was to take, came tearing along at full gallop, and only pulled up short when he had arrived so exactly in the middle of the camp that his horse's front feet were almost in the fire. Whether some of the burning sticks touched his hoofs, or whether it was that the thought passed through his equine mind that he had done enough work for one day, I do not know.

Anyhow the result was the same, for he instantly resolved to get rid of his rider with all possible speed, and to this end began to pitch and buck-jump all over my nice clean cups and plates. He entered into the operation with such hearty good will that his rider, though more than an average horseman, was soon sent sprawling among the flour, bacon, and other provisions, which had not yet been packed in the waggon. Had our dishes been made of china or other delicate ware, the result would have been disastrous. But since they were all manufactured out of good substantial tin, with the aid of a hammer and the tyre of the waggon wheel for an anvil, we soon managed to effect the necessary repairs. The dishes became once more as good as ever, and all trace of the upset, except in the cowboy's own injured feelings, was effectually wiped out.

On the last day of the trip one of my waggon horses, *Paddy* by name, fell sick, so sick in fact that we feared he was going to die. He lay down on the ground and groaned; every now and again stretching out his limbs and rolling back his eyes till only the white of the eyeballs was to be seen. Beyond pulling the harness off him and pouring a bucket of water over his head we could do nothing in the way of alleviating his pain. Fortunately, he was not far from a waterhole when he was attacked with the sickness, so harnessing up one of the cow ponies which had at one time done a little work in a waggon we pulled out and left him where he was. Two days after this, when we had delivered the cattle, one of the boys provided with the necessary medicine rode out to look for him. He found the old horse, although still weak and shaky, very nearly recovered from his attack; well enough, that is to say, to trot up whinnying when he recognised the comrade which had come out to find him.

It often happened that the boys, if they saw a chance, thought it good fun to play a practical joke on the cook of the establishment. But I remember one instance where the cook turned the tables on the boys and had the laugh entirely to his own credit. This is how it came about. One of the neighbouring ranches belonged to a syndicate with a very large number of stock, for the proper working of which they had to employ more than the average number of cowboys, as the country ranged over by their cattle was one hundred miles or more in extent.

To provide for these cowboys and keep them comfortable, a resident cook was employed at the home ranch. The man who held this position at the time of which I am writing was a clever old fellow, who had served his time during the Crimean War with the 11th Hussars, and prided himself on his smartness and punctuality, and also on his early rising. He was, therefore, very much hurt and offended when the "boss" said to him one December evening, "Now then, Uncle Johnny, tomorrow I am taking the 'outfit' down to Devil's River, and as it is a long ride, I want to make an early start. So, mind you give us breakfast in time as I don't want to be late."

In recounting the affair to us afterwards "Uncle" Johnny said, "I had never once been late, so the boss need not have spoken to me in the way he did; but as he had done so I determined to give them a really early breakfast for once in a way." About half-past eight or nine o'clock in the evening they all turned into bed, "Uncle" Johnny among the number. After waiting half an hour or so till he knew by the heavy breathing of the boys that they were all fast asleep, he quietly got out of bed, and betaking himself to his own particular province in the kitchen, set to work to cook breakfast.

In little more than an hour he had everything ready, and bringing it into the dining room he set it on the table, and lighting the lamp he called to the boys that breakfast was ready. Everyone at once got out of bed, rolled up his blankets, had a wash and, sitting down to table, ate his meal without the slightest suspicion that everything was not as usual on one of the mornings of "an early start."

Some, indeed, remarked on the darkness of the morning, but as there was not a watch among the whole "crowd," and no one thought of going to consult the tin-cased clock, which alone kept the time of the establishment, the trick remained undiscovered.

After the breakfast was finished, the "horse-rustler" went off to drive up the cow-ponies, and the other boys gathered round the fire, to wait for daylight. But the daylight seemed very long in coming. One cigarette after another was consumed, and still no morning star arose. The horse-rustler came back saying it was too dark to find any of the horses. Thinking the joke had gone far enough, Uncle Johnny brought in the clock, and pointing out that it was nearly 12 o'clock (midnight) asked them, rather sarcastically I fear, if they would soon like dinner.

Then he had to flee for his life, with all the boys after him, and it is to the credit of the old man that he gave them a long run and a good chase in the dark before they caught him, and brought him back in triumph to the ranch. Everyone enjoyed the joke immensely, and he said that never again was he told to remember not to be late in the morning.

CHAPTER 28

# A Fighting Parson

A good long ride separated us from our nearest neighbours, and a still longer ride was required to take us to the nearest town. Even when there we were only half as far as we should have to travel if we wished to see that great sign of civilisation, a railway train. Still in spite of all this we were not entirely out of the world. The United States Government (familiarly known as "Uncle Sam"), ever mindful of the educational requirements of its youthful citizens, had generously employed some of the taxes which it squeezed out of us in erecting a building which it was intended should be used as a school-house.

It was beautifully situated near the river's bank, and surrounded by a luxuriant grove of live oak and pecan trees. Had there been children in the neighbourhood no doubt the schoolhouse would have been very useful for the purpose for which it was built, but though there were many people in the country who could have received much advantage from going to school they had rather passed the age at which one generally begins to learn to read or write. The consequence was that the schoolhouse was a schoolhouse only in name and not in practice.

Nevertheless, the building was very useful for other purposes. It made, for instance, an excellent polling station during the somewhat frequent elections, and the surrounding grove of trees provided a nice cool shady place where the voters were free to air their political views while imbibing freely of the cheap but powerful whisky, which was always supplied *gratis* by the opposing candidates. If the discussion should at any time wax a little too warm, the stout trunks of the trees made excellent cover for the more peaceably inclined members of the audience.

When occasions offered, we made the schoolhouse serve also as a church. If a clergyman or minister, no matter of what denomination, so long as he could be described as what they call in America a "preacher," chanced to be staying in the neighbourhood or even passing through the district, someone would hear of it and at once pass the word round that there would be service in the schoolhouse on the Sunday following. Many nice quiet little services we had—perhaps on an average two or three in a year.

As was to be expected, the congregations were not large, but any want in numbers was fully made up for by the enthusiasm with which the singing of the hymns was conducted, only such hymns being chosen as were fairly well-known to a majority of those present. There were always a few ladies at these gatherings—wives or sisters of neighbouring ranchmen; but the majority of the congregation was, of course, composed of stockmen and cow-boys who gathered together, some to worship, some to chat, and some merely "for the fun of the thing."

Some of the last-mentioned class, were fond of playing innocent tricks of thoughtlessness which they considered would tend to enliven any tediousness of the service. They derived an immense amount of pleasure one Sunday morning from a half-broken broncho pony which one of the boys had ridden up to the meeting-house and tied to the limb of a tree within a few feet of the walls of the building.

For some time, the young horse, tired out with his gallop across the prairie was glad to stand still and rest his weary limbs. But no sooner was this accomplished than rousing himself up and finding no one near he determined to make yet one more struggle for his liberty. This he did by rearing and throwing himself backwards against the walls of the meeting house, just when the "preacher" had arrived at the most serious portion of his address. Finding that the stout plank walls were strong enough to resist his first onslaught, and deeming that it was some obstacle in the way of his obtaining his liberty he set to work at the barrier with his heels, and hammered away with such right good-will on the resounding boards of the building that it was impossible for the clergyman to make his voice heard over the horrible din and clatter.

Without exception all the various preachers who at different times held services among us were zealous, worthy, hard-working men who made every effort to leave some trace of good behind when they passed through this rough and sparsely inhabited district. These good men were preachers of the Gospel and therefore ministers of peace. Yet one at least among their number proved when the occasion arose that he had lived long enough In the Far West to have found out that the soft answer which turneth away wrath comes more forcibly from the man behind a loaded rifle than from him whose hands are empty. For if the man in the latter position begins to talk, he is likely to get beaten over the head with his opponent's six-shooter, just to shut his "darned impudence."

On the occasion referred to a friend of ours, who was engaged in the sheep-business, was acting as host to one of these ministers, who was going to hold a service the next day in our local schoolhouse. Besides the minister, there were two or three more of us who stayed at our friend's ranch for the Saturday night, intending to ride home on Sunday afternoon after the service, of course partaking of our host's dinner before setting out. Having finished our Saturday evening's supper of roast mutton and warm bread, we turned to the natural topic of conversation, the all-absorbing subject of sheep.

Our host graphically described how a man from "down South" had laid claim to some of his legally purchased stock, and had threatened to come up and "clean him out" before long. The preacher got quite excited over the question of the ownership of the sheep, and said he hoped this fellow would just try to do anything of the sort while he was there.

Strange to say, the preacher had his wish fully gratified, for next day when the service was drawing to a close, we saw at the door of the church an excited Mexican shepherd, making frantic efforts to attract the attention of our last night's host. On being asked what he wanted, he spluttered out the information, accompanied with many grimaces and much waving of the hands, and more than a few expletives that the "dam man from down South" had come with his herders and driven off the entire flock of sheep, those of the disputed ownership being only a small proportion of the herd.

The Benediction was given without loss of time, and the congregation dispersed. Some of the boys who wanted to see the fun, besides our host and those of us who had stayed with him and knew the merits of the case, at once got to their horses, to take up and follow up the trail of the raider.

As we were on the point of starting, we came across the parson busily engaged in hurriedly buckling a broken-down old saddle on to his buggy horse. He besought us to wait a moment for him till he could get out his rifle, which he said with gusto was "sure fine for long distances." With this rifle and a pocketful of cartridges, and mounted on his high lean horse, his own tall gaunt figure arrayed in clerical garb "of sorts," he made a striking figure leading our motley party as we took up the trail and galloped off over the prairie to rescue the stolen sheep.

The Mexican had told us in what locality he was grazing his flock at the time they had been pounced upon, so we had no trouble in finding where they had been rounded up and started off. The tracks on the prairie showed that they were being driven at their best speed, but we knew that as the day was a fairly hot one, the poor brutes would not be able to travel very far at the rate at which they began their journey. We counted that they could not be a very great distance ahead, in spite of the long start they had had—for it must have taken the Mexican a good while to walk in and give us warning of the raid.

We were not surprised, therefore, when after galloping some miles along the track of the fleeing flock, we saw in the distance clouds of dust rising high over the *mesquite* brush, showing where the sheep were being pushed along over the dry ground in the direction of the nearest pass in the hills towards the head of the valley.

We rode on, but now more cautiously than at first, and holding ourselves all prepared for the miniature battle which we fully expected would follow on our making our appearance on the scene. But there was no fight after all. Our enemy at once recognised the fact that our force was so much superior to himself and his Mexican supporters that he did not stand the remotest chance of success if he attempted to make a fight of it. He also saw that the sheep were played out and could go no further, suffering as they were from the effects of the rapid drive during the heat of the day.

These were probably the real causes of his retreat, but we did not fail to assure the parson that it was his warlike appearance which had put the robber to flight. Whatever the cause may have been, the result was the same, *viz.*, the man from "down South" thought that discretion was the better part of valour, and that if he ran away, he might live to steal sheep some other day.

He very quickly acted on the principle of running away, for as we came up, long before we could make him hear our shout of "hands up," we saw him and his followers abandon the flock of sheep and bolt into the low scrub, where they at once scattered and made off in different directions. We let them go, because if they had not the courage to show fight, they were not the sort of game that was worth following up, and we felt sure that badly frightened as they were they would make no further attempt to raid our friend's flocks.

Nor did they. There was never any further question as to the ownership of the disputed sheep. We allowed the poor driven thirsty beasts to rest where they were till the cool of the evening, and then slowly brought them back by moonlight to their own range, from which they had been so roughly carried off. Not one of us, not even the owner of the sheep, was more pleased with the little adventure than was our parson. The only thing he seemed to regret was that there had been no opportunity for him to show how fine his rifle was at long distances.

CHAPTER 29

# Road-Making

In the United States there is a very just and equitable law which compels every able-bodied man between the ages of 16 and 60 to pay annually what is called the poll-tax, a sum of from $2 to $4, according to the regulations of the state in which he may be, on the 1st of March of each year. The money derived from this tax is used for the up-keep of the public hospital and the maintenance of the roads in the county in which the money has been collected. If any man objects to pay the tax in cash, or is unable to do so, he can if he wishes it put in a certain number of days' work on the roads, equivalent to the money value of the tax.

In the district in which our ranch was situated we one and all made a point of "working-out" our poll tax, instead of paying over so many dollars to the collector. We usually had a very good time of it, because it was the only occasion in the year when many of the boys could meet together without having any troublesome herd of cattle to hold, or weary night-guards spent in riding round a lot of fidgety beasts.

There was always a "road-boss" appointed, one who was a man of some standing in the district. He was responsible for a certain section of the road, say fifteen to twenty miles in length, and his duty it was to allot to each man, or party of men, the portion of work which he or they were expected to do. He had, moreover, to see that the work was properly done, and this was the hardest part of his duty; for men

STAGE ROAD CROSSING THE DIVIDE.

performing forced labour of this kind are remarkably clever at doing the smallest possible amount of work in the greatest possible length of time.

One year in particular I remember when this was carried to the extreme. The road-boss for that season was an energetic little Scotchman, "Jimmy" by name, who, though a universal favourite, was not by nature a leader of men. Consequently, in getting through whatever work he might wish to have done he had to trust more to example than to precept or command, and of this failing the "boys" took full advantage.

On being appointed "road-boss" he at once became inspired with the noble ambition of making his section of the road superior to any of the other divisions between the two termini of San Angelo at the one end and Colorado City at the other. When he took the work in hand, the road for most of the way consisted merely of a number of rough waggon tracks, which wound in and out among the trees. For the teamsters had always tried to find the most open spots, least encumbered by stumps and brushwood. Our first piece of work was to straighten the road, and by cutting out these useless curves and bends shorten the distance between the two given points.

With this object in view, we set to work, armed with knives and axes, and before the season's turn of work had ended we had a fine clear road of 40ft. in width stretching in a straight line from one end of the section to the other. This was all correctly done according to the county regulations. But these regulations required only that trees should be cut to within six inches of the ground, and the remaining stumps were apt to make the travelling somewhat rough, especially if any high rate of speed were attempted.

Now our boss resolved that the very next piece of work to be done was the removal of these obnoxious roots and stamps. This ambition of his met with anything but a kindly response from us, his unwilling and rather mutinous subordinates in so far as the road working was concerned. For although a cowboy can handle an axe pretty well when occasion arises for him to do so, there is nothing that he hates more than to come down to the spade and shovel line of work, especially under the orders of a "sheep-man," which was the calling of our worthy section boss. But the boss had made his mind up to it, so it had to be done; and on the appointed day we gathered together, a sorry looking crew, carrying spades, shovels, mattocks or crow-bars.

We all pleaded utter ignorance as to the best means of getting the stumps out of the ground, so our boss after a little expostulation would seize a pick or a shovel and exert his best energy to show us how it ought to be done.

The rest would stand looking on till the work was nearly finished, when he would pass on to go through the same performance with the next group of workers (?). Then he would be called back to the first gang to show them how the stump should be finished off or the hole filled up, or on some other trivial excuse. He never really lost his temper, although he had good cause to do so a hundred times or more during the first day, and he certainly did more work than any five other men put together.

By the use of his utmost powers in the way of coaxing, begging and threatening his unwilling workers the most of the work was got through somehow or other, and all the very obtrusive roots and stumps, and even some of the smaller ones were dug up and moved out of the road.

The boss had then to look about for some other marked improvement to effect on his section of the highway. He was not long in deciding that the greatest benefit he could confer upon the travelling public would be the erection of mile-stones to inform travellers how far they were from anywhere. We were, therefore, divided up into numerous working parties. One set of men were sent off into the hills to get out slabs of fairly smooth rock to act as mile-stones; others were put to work cutting on these stones the names and distances of the towns to which the road led.

It was the duty of others again to haul these rocks from the hills down to the county road. Two men marked the miles along the line, while two more distributed the stones. Last of all my partner and I came along and planted the stones some three feet in the ground. They were well and firmly set, and should remain there for many a long day to come.

To measure the miles along the road the man whose duty it was took the exact circumference of the hind wheel of his waggon, which was, for example, say 12 feet, and divided that into the number of feet in a mile, *viz.*, 5,280. By the answer, which is 440, he knew that when his hind wheel had made 440 revolutions travelling on level ground, he had gone one mile. So, he tied a coloured rag to one of the spokes of his wheel and his mate sat behind counting every time that this mark turned up, and at the end of each mile, dropped a stone.

CHAPTER 30

# A City Man's Holiday

As time went on and months and years slipped past, filled with episodes and adventures such as I have attempted to describe, the longing to see my friends and home in the "Old Country" became stronger and stronger. At last, one moonlight night, lying beside a log fire, far up a lonely canon, I made up my mind to accept the pressing invitations contained in every letter from home and to come back to England on a visit.

Talking it over with Leslie, my closest friend, I found that he felt as I did, and I was rejoiced when he decided to join me in my trip to the Old Country.

We took with us no baggage worth speaking about, so our preparations were soon made, and we were quickly off on our 5,000-mile journey. The clothes we had brought with us were long since worn out, we therefore travelled in our western outfits. We found them no drawback, for our broad-brimmed *sombreros*, flannel shirts, high-heeled boots, and tanned faces gained for us all through the eastern States a great deal of respect, which would not have been our lot had we been dressed in every-day clothes. It was only on landing in Liverpool that we invested some of our dollars in a more civilised form of attire.

We spent six very happy months of holiday, although during all this time we could feel the West tugging at our heart-strings. And except for the pain of parting with our friends, we were delighted to be once more outward-bound.

On our return journey we had two more companions with us. One of them was a young Englishman who had heard some of our glowing accounts of life in the far West and felt that he also would like to take a share in it. Our other companion was considerably older, and was a man of much influence in business circles in the city of London, who, finding that his health required a complete rest from business, had determined to pay us a visit in our Texas home, and see with his own eyes what sort of life we were leading.

During the four days' rail from New York to the town where we left the train Mr. N——, our senior friend, naturally travelled in the Pulman sleeping coach. But Leslie and I, accustomed as we were to "roughing it," were satisfied to sleep as we were in our seats in the ordinary day coach, and in doing this our younger friend joined us. He came through the first night somehow or other, but the second night he was tired out, and about midnight hunted up the conductor and got a berth in the sleeper. Unfortunately for him he forgot to say where he was bound for, and so got into the wrong sleeper, and was turned out of bed about 2 a.m. to change trains, having obtained for his five dollars only about two hours' sleep.

On leaving the train we found that the ranch waggon had come into town to meet us and also to bring back a supply of provisions. The waggon was in charge of a dear old fellow, who was acting as cook for the time being on our ranch. In nearly all respects he was a fine old man, but he had this failing—that he loved the whisky bottle more than almost anything else on earth, and he always made a point of indulging his failing whenever he had an opportunity to do so. When he met us, he was gloriously drunk; indeed, he had reached such a stage that in trying to mix some toddy for himself he actually forgot to put in the whisky. And we were hard-hearted enough not to draw his attention to the omission.

We started out from town, three of us in a buggy and the fourth in the waggon to look after Uncle Johnny, who was hardly in the right condition to look after himself, let alone the team of horses. The first day out we only went about 25 miles to a ranch where we were most hospitably received. After supper, the cowboy who happened to be the only one on the place at the time of our visit, was recounting to us the different events that had happened on the range during the last few months—who had been killed, whose steers had been sold, which outfits had been rounding up and so on.

In doing this he made full use of the many very expressive idioms of the western cattle country, which were almost like a foreign language to our two new companions. There was one expression in particular of which he so frequently made use that Mr. N—— at last asked him for an explanation of the term. McClinton simply stared and a broad smile of pity for the stranger's ignorance overspread his good-tempered countenance as he explained the term in other idioms, which were not much more intelligible than the one originally made use of.

As our waggon was heavily loaded, we could travel but slowly, and the second night found us only about 50 miles on our way, but not far from where a newly arrived settler had started what he was pleased to call a hotel. Night had fallen before we reached this haven, and Mr. N—— was looking forward to a comfortable night's lodgings in the hotel.

But it was hardly what he expected. The only supper the hotel could provide was a dish of eggs boiled in bacon fat. He also complained that after climbing a ladder to reach his bed he found his rest considerably disturbed by the uneasy movements of numbers of fowls, which were roosting on the rafters directly over his head. My chum Leslie and I had elected to sleep on the ground beside the waggon, and we, at least, had a splendid night's rest.

Next day we arrived at the ranch. Our one trestle bedstead was taken in from resting against the side of the house, which was its usual position, and we fixed it up for Mr. N———'s use; for we wanted to do him the honours of the place and make him comfortable during his visit. We took him to see a round-up of cattle on Dry Creek, and also brought him to where he could have a shot at a bunch of antelope. Then we fetched up a yearling steer and killed it at the front door, that there might be an abundance of fresh meat during his visit.

But this did not prove altogether a success, because as it turned out we were too hasty in our methods. Before the body of the animal had become cool, we had what were considered the tit-bits already cooked and served on the table for dinner. This was too much for Mr. N———, and caused him an attack of illness which was very unpleasant so far from medical assistance. We therefore decided the best thing we could do would be to get him to town as soon as possible, so I brought up two of my cow-ponies, harnessed them into the waggon, and then we trotted off to town, nearly 40 miles away, arriving there safely about 10 p.m.

The nearer we drew to town the less unwell our patient felt, till by the time he was comfortably in bed in the hotel (a real one this time), and a cheery old army surgeon was talking and joking beside him, he did not require more than one bottle of physic to put him all right again. A few days in town and then we were able to begin our return journey, which we made very leisurely, staying at several of our friends' ranches on the way.

While staying at one of these hospitable country houses, we went to the corral where the boys were at the time branding calves. While watching us throwing and holding the calves on the ground Mr. N——— felt himself left out in the cold, and not wishing to be merely an idle spectator he came into the corral to join in the fun. He was not there many minutes before a good stout calf was roped by one of the boys and came past Mr. N———, bawling and jumping. Mr. N——— at once seized the calf and attempted to throw it, an operation in which much knack and dexterity has to be exercised.

A novice is more often upset by the calf than the calf is thrown by the novice. Mr. N—— had caught hold of the tail, and to this he held on manfully; but the calf was the stronger of the two, and soon we were all laughing heartily to see a sober, highly-respected and influential city man, no longer in the first flower of his youth, careering round a dusty old log-built Texas corral, holding might and main to the tail of a bucking bawling calf. How long the struggle would have lasted I do not know had not some of the boys come to the assistance and brought the calf to a proper state of submission. Freed from the calf Mr. N—— joined heartily in the laugh.

A few more days on the ranch and Mr. N——'s visit came to an end. We were one and all sorry to say goodbye to him. Two of our friends were going home on a visit to England and accompanied him on the journey. The whole luggage taken by one of them consisted of a collar and tie in his jacket pocket.

CHAPTER 31

# Farewell

My own time in Texas was now drawing to a close, for while I was in England I had become engaged to a very dear little girl, whom I was not willing to subject to the hard life and the privations one has to endure in a newly-settled country, where a man can "rough it" in ways almost impossible for a lady of gentle birth.

In less than a year after the end of my holiday I had sold out my interests in the ranch and returned to settle down quietly in England. But even now, after years in the Old Country, on every bright sunny day that comes along there rises up in me a great yearning to be once more on the free open prairies of the West.

# Cowboy Life

Rufe O'Keefe

# Contents

Cowboy Life                                        175

MAY AND JO HAL
MAY RYAN, MY DAUGHTER,
JO HAL WOFFORD, MY GRAND-DAUGHTER,
TO THESE
I DEDICATE THIS BOOK

# Cowboy Life

### Chapter 1

I was born on a farm in Randolph County, Alabama, January 19, 1857. I was the youngest of four boys who were James E., Christopher A., David A., and Rufus W. O'Keefe.

My father, Thomas O'Keefe, died when I was only three months old. Mother was left a widow with four boys and the oldest, James, was nine years old, and, of course, we had a hard time. The Civil War came on in 1861 and lasted until 1865. I, of course, don't remember much that happened during the war.

One thing that I do remember was what was called the "Home Guards," which resembled our Texas Rangers. When they used to pass our house there was one in particular that rode a very beautiful fat horse, had a gun in front of him and pistol belted on. Of course, I thought when I grew up to be a man, I would be a home guard and have a nice horse; but the real thing was to carry the gun and pistol. There were lots of squirrels in that country and other wild game. I used to go with my brothers to kill squirrels and they would let me carry them. I thought that was the next thing to being a home guard.

We lived near a small stream and mother used to let me go fishing. I remember how she would caution me to look out for snakes as all the children went barefooted in the summer. Mother used to tell me to keep on the bridge so the snakes could not bite me.

We used to go three miles to school to a log schoolhouse. They had split logs for seats, and had no backs. The legs were made by boring two holes in each end of the round side of the split log.

My first book was the *Blue Back Speller* with which we had pieces of card board called thumb paper to place under our fingers to save the paper. Later I had McGuffy's *First and Second Readers* and *Arithmetic*, in which my hardest part was to learn the multiplication table. Next, we had to cipher problems, we called it, and when we got that far along, we thought we were doing great things. We had slates, slate pencils, and sponges. The latter was used to rub out mistakes, and I think that I used it more than anything else.

The road to school led by grandmother's house half a mile from our house, and I always liked to go there because the apples tasted better than ours, even though they were the same kind as ours. We almost always had cornbread at home, but when we went to grandmother's we got biscuits. Grandmother had forty-two negro slaves, and one, Aunt Melia, cooked the biscuits. Soon after the Civil War times got better, so to speak, and people had more and better things to eat. We had homemade shoes and clothes.

Mother would send my brother Dave and me to the woods to gather Shoemake Berries to dye the cloth. Mother would sit up till late at night spinning and weaving cloth. Another kind of dye was Walnut Leaves. As well as I remember, walnut made dark brown and shoemake berries made light brown colour. We would call this kind of clothes "Brown Jeans," which we wore in the winter. They were very warm; but how they would scratch your wrist or neck! For summer wear we had cotton clothes; the pants were blue in colour and the shirt was white.

This is what we wore to school, and when I was dressed in this manner, I thought I was dressed up indeed. The small boys, up until they were about ten years old, wore shirts that came down below their knees about half way, resembling a modern dress or night shirt. They wore these about the house, but did not go to school in them. They would sleep and eat in these, which were called shirts and were white and made of cotton.

When we would go to school, we would carry our lunch with us and take milk along. We would put the milk in the spring branch to keep it cool, but before long some other kids found it and we had to keep it in the school house.

It was a timber country and I remember how I would stump my toes on the stumps and roots, as well as the rocks in the road. We would sometimes bruise our heels on sharp rocks and this kind of bruise we called stone bruise. This kind of bruise would make your heel sore for a considerable length of time, and to see a boy with a stone bruise and a toe nail stumped off was not unusual. My older brothers would carry me on their backs when I would stump my toe, or get a stone bruise. I don't remember how long this lasted, but if I counted the number of times I had a stone bruise, or stumped toe it would be a considerable time.

I was eight years old when mother was married, the second time, to James H. Bell of Cleburne, Alabama. We moved up there; it was twenty-five miles. We moved in a wagon; had four mules to the wagon. Brothers Gus and Dave drove the milk cows. Brother Jim being at work in Georgia did not go up with us, but came later. Mr. Bell let me drive the team and ride the mule. The lead mule had a long stick tied to its hames and the other end tied to the bridle bit of its mate. Jerk lines were used then instead of check lines, as we use now. The lead mule or horse had to be well trained so as to know the different pulls and jerks. When one pulled on the single line that was attached to the left side of the bit of the lead mule, the mule went to the left and pulled his partner with him because the stick would pull him over.

If one jerked on the line the lead mule would go to the right, and the stick would push on the bridle of his mate and cause the mate to go to the right also, therefore leading the others. The mules would stay in the road all right until they came to a mud hole, and then Mr. Bell would have to take the line. Everyone knows how shy mules are of mud, and because of this, I noticed that Mr. Bell would have to jerk pretty hard sometimes to make the mules walk through the mud holes. I had no trouble in driving the mules except when they came to a mud hole. I thought I was doing a whole lot anyway, as that was my first experience with mules. However, until this day I had rather ride a good cow-pony than do most anything.

After the family was settled in Cleburne County, my stepsister and myself started to school at Chulafenne. She was four years older than I. It was some four miles to the school house and we rode one horse, with me riding behind her side saddle. I remember how I would have to hold on tight to the back of the saddle when we would gallop because I was afraid I would fall off, but I never did. Mr. Bell would tell us not to run the horse, but we did when we were out of sight in the woods between the house and the school. That was fun for me and Izora enjoyed it also. There really was no harm to gallop the horse, but my stepfather feared we would be running the horse before the school was out, which we did. We did not get a whipping, but we got several scoldings. I think that was a three months school.

Wheat harvest came on and my job there was to carry water for the harvest hands. They cut wheat with cradles fixed like a mowing blade, but had a frame with prongs to hold the wheat. When they would swing the cradle into the standing grain and cut a handful, they would lay that in a pile. Every time they made a stroke they would lay down another pile, and one man would follow each cradler and bind the wheat in bundles tied with wheat straw. It was all very hard work and they did drink lots of water. I carried water in jugs from the spring which was in the field. As they progressed, they got further from the spring, then Mr. Bell would help me carry water.

There were twelve men whom I thought drank entirely too much water. I saw some of the men take off their shirts and ring water out of them from perspiration. They would run races they called it, to see which one could cut the most wheat, and I learned when they had a race on that it called for more water. In a few weeks, harvest was over; then came the threshing. They had a different set of men, but I thought they drank just as much water as the harvest hands.

The next year we went to school, we had to walk two miles to Green's Chapel. By this time, we got to wearing shoes and I did not have so much trouble with sore toes. We would have to stop school because of the harvest, or crops, and when we would get the crops cleaned out, we would go back to school again.

In 1869, my stepfather sold his farm expecting to go to Minnesota. Before he got off, he had information from his son and some friends who were there, that the country was not satisfactory. He bought another farm fifteen miles up the Tallapoosa River and moved there. My two oldest brothers had gone to Minnesota, but they did not like it, so left and came to Texas. They were just boys and said the trip was hard. I have heard them tell some of their experiences. They came down the Mississippi River on boats to St. Louis, and from there went through the country to Texas, walking quite a bit of the way. They told about getting in with a man and helping with a herd of cattle to Little Rock, Arkansas, and finally made their way into Texas at Clarksville, Red River County. They wrote such favourable letters that brother Dave went to Texas in 1872.

In 1873, the Panic struck the country. People compared it with the Civil War times. Some said it was even worse than the Civil War panic. Others said it was just a continuation of the war panic, and it took it that long to spread all over the country, which seemed plausible. Hard times remained with us for several years.

## Chapter 2

I came to Texas in December, 1874, in my seventeenth year. I had never been away from home before and thought it was pretty rough going for a kid. I first landed in Texas at Calvert, Robertson County.

My three brothers had drifted there that fall to pick cotton. The cotton crop was good there that year. There was lot of work during the picking season, but I got there too late. The fine cotton had been well advertised and people just flocked to that country to pick cotton. The country was full of negroes and Chinamen. That was the first time I had ever seen any Chinamen. Most of them had long hair plaited in three plaits. The Texas folks called them Pig Tails. I had been used to negroes all of my life and knew how to get along with them, but I did not like the looks of the Chinamen, or Pig Tails.

Brother Dave went up to Ellis County and wrote back to us at Calvert. He thought Ellis was good country and was developing fast into a farming country. He thought it would be easier to find work and a little more healthier. The Brazos River was bad on a person with chills and fever. In a few weeks we started for Ellis County.

Jim, my oldest brother, and myself rode not horses, but mules. My brothers had a wagon and two mules, but sold the wagon and tried to trade the mules for horses, but could not. Brother Jim and I rode the mules and brother Gus was to meet us in Waxahachie the twenty-fourth of December. He was to remain at Calvert to see Major Hanna on whose farm the boys had worked that fall for a settlement. We were four days on the road. Nothing unusual happened on the trip, only the weather was unusual to me, for we had a cold norther to meet us. It was cold, with cold rain, then snow and sleet. We spent one night at Mount Calm and it was an awfully cold night. We did not get in till late at night; because the country was not settled much, we could not find a place to stay overnight.

It was a prairie country, and I thought we were going uphill all the time, but Jim laughed at me and said it always seemed that way until one got used to it. I remember how the *mesquite* trees reminded me of peach trees back home. He said they used to remind him of peach trees until he got accustomed to them. We passed a place that had a tread mill that ground wheat. The thing had a great big wheel with one side much higher than the other.

When steers would try to climb it, that would turn the wheel. I did not get to see it in operation, but Jim explained how it worked. (I always wanted to see that thing work.) I never did, much to my regret. They seemed to change, or abandon them about that time, as the country began to settle and they began to improve their methods.

We spent one night near Milford, and next day we rode in to Waxahachie and found brother Gus. It was the day before Christmas and of course everybody was making preparation for Christmas. They were to have a christmas tree at the schoolhouse north of town (now Trinity College). We could see them collecting the presents, and I saw one boy with a red and white striped candy walking stick, which I supposed was for his best girl. We three, brother Jim, Gus, and I had a conference as to what would be best to do, for none of us was very flush with money. It was decided for me to go out where brother Dave was located and see if I could get in to work there. Jim and Gus were to go up to Red Oak, a small town on the head of Red Oak Creek.

After dinner I started out to find Dave and was told that Mr. Hill, the man Dave was with, lived near Farrar's Mill, on Red Oak Creek, six miles east of Waxahachie. I got my saddle bags (that was what I carried my clothes in) and bade my brothers goodbye, and started for Farrar's Mill. They mounted their mules and were off the other direction, but would see me in a few days, as they did. I had to walk most of the six miles and got there about sundown. The weather had warmed up some and the snow was melting and that black mud was just as sticky as wheat dough. It just seemed to crawl up my boot legs.

On the way I saw my first prairie chickens and the fields were full of them. They would fly up in front of me in droves; their habits are very much like quail in that they fly a short distance and light again. I thought of the old double barrel, muzzle loading shot gun at home; the one I killed a wild turkey with. That was too far away, but I was hunting a job and not turkeys, nor prairie chickens. The sad part of it was it was my first job that I was hunting. As I plodded along through that black mud, I thought of how I would approach a man to get work, for I had never worked a day for anybody but my stepfather.

I did not know any more about that kind of business than a child. I was only seventeen years old, but I remembered stepfather used to say some boys were good workers and others were no good for they would not work, and told me not to be afraid of work. I thought if I could just find the job, I'd do the work. While I was thinking over things, I came in sight of Farrar's Mill. I had wondered if it was a tread mill, but it was a steam mill and had a saw mill attachment. It sawed cotton-wood lumber and it was the most crooked lumber I ever saw.

I inquired for Mr. Hill's place, the man said Mr. Hill's place was just one mile farther on down the road. I got to Mr. Hill's just before sunset and found my brother Dave. He seemed well satisfied and had made a trade with Mr. Hill to clear up some timbered land for a part of the crop. Mr. Hill and his wife were fine people. I told them I wanted to board with them a while and see if I could find work; he said for me to just make myself at home and he would help me find work. He said he liked Dave so well, that he knew he and I could get along. I was there just a few days when Mr. Hill said his brother-in-law might want a man and advised me to go see him. His name was Bryant.

So, I lost no time in going to see Mr. Bryant. I told him that Mr. Hill had told me about his putting in some timbered land and might need help. He asked me if I was used to chopping wood and said it was pretty hard work. He wanted the wood cut into cord wood length and asked if I could do that. I told him I had not corded any wood, but I had split lots of rails. He laughed and said if I had split rails, I could put up cord wood. He then asked me when I wanted to commence work.

I said "right now."

He said he liked the way I talked, and asked what would I work for. I told him just whatever was customary. He said he would give me fifteen dollars per month.

I said, "all right."

He asked if I had any clothes. I told him I had left them over at Mr. Hill's, and said I could get my things this evening and go to work next morning. They were good people, so I found it was not so bad to be away from home as I had found good people to work for; however, I did get homesick to see my mother. I was only with Mr. Bryant two months. Brother Jim was trying to rent a farm for us to make a cotton crop. He thought he could find something nearby and came to see me soon after I went to work for Mr. Bryant. He asked if it would suit me and I told him I much rather do that than work for anyone else. He asked if the Bryant's were good to me and I told him they were good as could be, but I did not like the idea of working for somebody else. I wanted to work for myself. He laughed and told me not to get discouraged and said that he would be back soon.

In a few weeks he came and told me he had found a farm that we could get the first of March, which was two weeks off. He told me I had better tell Mr. Bryant so he could get someone to take my place. Mr. Bryant said he was in hopes I would stay on with him, but said he did not blame me for going. Jim was fixing up the house and getting things ready for us. First of March he came after me, and told me it was not much house, but thought we could make out with it. We rented this farm from Dr. Hendley on Grove Creek.

He let us have a young team of horses for the breaking of them. We did very well, made twenty bales of cotton and received nine to ten cents per pound for it. We had only about fifteen or twenty acres in corn. I had my first experience at batching and brother Jim was a good bachelor for he had been in a saw mill country in Minnesota and learned all about camp life.

We had neighbours by name of Bass. We bought butter from Mrs. Bass and she would give us buttermilk. They lived less than half a mile just across the field and were good Texas people. They told us if we boys needed anything to just call on them and they would help us. We got along all right batching until in the fall of the year. I had a spell of chills and fever, and when I would lay in that little old shack of a house and almost burn up with fever, I'd get homesick for mother. I would not say much about it, at first. I would have a chill in the forenoon, then have fever for an hour after that. I would feel pretty good sometimes and would go over and visit with Mr. and Mrs. Bass and get some buttermilk. Other times when my fever was not so bad, I'd pick cotton in the afternoon.

After taking a lot of quinine I got better. I did not get well of homesickness though. So, in December of that year, 1875, I sold my interest to Brother Gus, and went back home to Alabama. My brothers all laughed at me and teased me quite a bit about going back to Alabama. I soon got used to that and told them Alabama was better than Texas. I did not dislike Texas, I just wanted to go home and so I did.

I got home a few days before Christmas. I had been gone a little over one year. Of course, I was glad to get back home again to mother and my three half-sisters who were just children. Nusie, the oldest, was nine years old; Lou, the second, was seven; Dussie, youngest, was five years old. It seemed to me that they all had grown more in that one year than they had grown in all their lives. I was glad to see my stepfather for he was always good to me; he did joke me some about getting homesick and coming back to my mother, but said he did not blame me much. That last part fixed it up some, but still I felt a little ashamed for coming back to my mamma. I considered it a kind of a baby act.

Things never did look just right to me and I don't believe they ever do look right to anyone going back to the old place they moved from. I believe it's best to move forward, not backward. The only excuse I had to tell them why I came back, was that I had bought my brothers' interest in some land our father had left us when he died. The fact was, I did not trade with them until after I had made up my mind to go home. The folks back home did not know that and so I got by with it. After I was there a while, I could see plain enough I had made a mistake, for Texas was a new country and just coming in, and Alabama was wearing out. Stepfather said he would rent me some land to farm; so, I went right to work fixing to make a crop.

One thing I did not like; we had to haul fertilizer from the lots and even haul leaves and fine straw and mix with it and then scatter that and plough it under, to enrich the land to make a crop. I would say I would not have to do that out in Texas, but stepfather would encourage me as he always did to try and make what I could. I knew I'd have to do all of that before I went back, but for him to talk that way would give me new courage.

I remember back when I was twelve or thirteen years old, we had a lot of black walnuts. I asked my stepfather if I could hull some of them and have them for my own. He said I could have them, and as I would get time, I would carry a basket full and put them in a pile in the yard. I remember one particular time when I went out after supper and built a fire of pine knots which were plentiful in that country. I was busy hulling my walnuts; stepfather looked out the window and saw me and told mother I was hulling walnuts and would be trying to sell them next thing. He told her to not bother me but let me sell them if I wanted to.

Brother Dave was three years older than I, and he came down and told me what he had heard. He looked so funny with his nose all turned up and mad. He said if he were I he would not do that, but it did not discourage me for I was enjoying hulling the walnuts. It was fun for me, so I got a few bushels. I don't remember just the exact number of bushels, but I do remember I got one dollar per bushel for them. That was the most money I had ever had up to that time.

Two other incidents that I well remember. One concerned an old house nearby that had been a negro house (it was later a chicken house). It had a small yardfence around it. I suppose perhaps one eighth of an acre of ground was in it. I asked stepfather if I could have that for a tobacco patch. He asked if I wanted to chew tobacco. I told him I wanted to make some money out of it, I told him that Bob Story said it would make a good tobacco patch.

Bob Story was a tenant on our farm and raised his own tobacco. Bob had told me he would give me the plants and show me how to set them out. Stepfather said I could have the patch and he even helped me break the ground, which had been trampled very hard by the negroes. I made pretty good with my tobacco and got about twelve or fifteen dollars for it. The other incident that I never will forget, happened when I bought a steer yearling from stepfather. I did the feeding at that time of the horses, cattle and hogs. This steer had grown up about the place and was a pet; I was very much attached to it.

I asked stepfather what would he take for this yearling; he said about five dollars. I said right off the bat that I'd give five dollars. I got my money out that I kept in a small slate pencil box; counted out five dollars and took it to him. He said wait a minute; the calf is not worth five dollars, but you promised to pay five dollars, now you must pay it. I did not try to "Jew" him, and he told me to always buy anything as cheap as I could. He was not going to give me back any of the money; he did not want me to forget to buy things as cheap as I could. I thought at first, he was going to give me back some of the money. I learned in after years it was worth more to me that he kept it than to have given me back twice that amount.

It taught me to always look out for my own interest, because the other fellow would be looking out for his interest. He said if I wanted to buy anything that I did not know the value of, to ask some disinterested party the value he thought it was worth, and not to take the other fellow's word that was selling it. I have not always followed that advice and sometimes have gotten the worst of a deal by not doing so.

When I got back home I did not like ploughing with a Georgia stock, one furrow at a time, and have to go over one row five times to get it sufficiently cultivated. Now it takes just about one half the work that it used to take. I said I would stick to it for a while, but I only stayed there little over two years and came back to Ellis County, Texas. During my first year back in Alabama, I sold the land for five hundred dollars that I had bought from my brothers. Times were pretty hard, money scarce, but I managed to accumulate a little. My mother told me when I got home that I might not make as much as I would have made in Texas. She said there was more in taking care of things than in making it.

She, like all mothers, was glad that I was back; but if it had not been for the looks of things I would have come right back. In little over two years, I was back in Ellis County. My brothers wrote such interesting letters that I just had to come back.

## Chapter 3

My two brothers, Jim and Dave, were farming together and had made a dandy good crop of corn and cotton. I got there just at the beginning of cotton-picking season. I went to picking soon after landing there. Mother and stepfather had taught me not to be idle and I have always found it best to keep busy. They said it would keep me out of mischief; well, whether there was much to that or not I helped them gather their crop. Brother Dave went out west where Gus was located on a cow ranch in Mitchell County with Waddell and Byler. I thought of going with him, but decided to stay in Ellis County. From what they told me about the cattle business, I wanted to go; but it always seemed like too big a thing. I made up my mind I wanted in the business, but thought best to go in with a small bunch and grow into something larger. I bought about one hundred head; it was the very wrong thing for me to do, but of course I had to learn.

One thing I did not like was to go on a ranch and work for somebody else which was the very thing that I should have done. Brother Jim told me if I wanted to get a small bunch of cattle, he thought they would make me some money in Ellis County. I could make my home with them and attend to my cattle and he would help me get work among the neighbours when I was not busy. So, I decided to stay with them. While I worked for other people, I most always went to Jim's and spent Sundays; then went back to work either Sunday evening or Monday morning.

I worked for a man named James Smith; he was an old gentleman and his wife was just a few years younger than himself. They had a grown son and daughter that lived with them; they were all fine people. They would insist on me staying with them over Sunday, but I would tell them I wanted to go see about my cattle. The truth was it was not so much the cattle as it was, I wanted to be with the home folks. I have thought of those times often, and I guess Jim and Mollie kept me from really getting home sick to see mother.

One time while I was buying some cattle, I found a man down on Onion Creek who had a small bunch of cattle and also had two work steers. I had heard Jim say he was short one team. I told the man I would go home and talk it over with my brother to see if he could use the oxen, and if he could I would be back. Really I wanted to get Jim's advice about the oxen.

I told Jim I could drive his mule team and he could drive the steers, since I did not know how to handle the oxen. In that way, we could get up with his ploughing. He asked what price the man had on the oxen. I told him the price was fourteen dollars apiece, or twenty-eight dollars for the pair. He said that was cheap for the two because oxen were usually higher.

I said, "We can plough your land with them then sell them and come out even."

He then asked if they were in good shape. I said, "Yes, they were fat."

He asked how old they were. I replied that I didn't know, but I did not believe they were old enough to hurt or they would not be so fat. That was a good thing to go by, according to Jim.

I said, "If you say so, I will go buy them and we will try it."

Next morning, I went and bought the cattle, oxen, and all. The man helped drive them home, and helped brand them. Brother Jim looked at the oxen and said they looked all right. He asked the man all about them, and we ploughed some with them that evening. The oxen proved to be all they were said to be. The man seemed to be honest for he had not misrepresented anything. For the next few weeks after that I ploughed with brother's team and he used the oxen. We got up with the ploughing, then Jim found a buyer for the oxen for thirty-five dollars. During the time we were ploughing Jim found the job for me with Mr. Smith that I have just told about. Mollie used to tease me about Miss Kate Smith, Mr. Smith's daughter. That might have had something to do with me not wanting to stay there during Sundays. I was young then and rather bashful, and pretty green also.

About the latter part of May I left Mr. Smith, and went, as we said, a way out west to Mitchell County. Two brothers were out west, Gus and Dave, and two reasons I wanted to go were to visit with the boys and to learn something about the ranch business, which I wanted to learn more about. I had the time of my life. I was there about three months and while I was there Mr. Waddell wanted to send a wagon and outfit up the Colorado River about fifty miles north of their ranch on Champion Creek. I heard Mr. Waddell tell Gus if he had enough men, he would send him up on Deep Creek, and work that country and brand up the calves.

I heard Gus tell him he could get what cattle there was with four men and a cook. Mr. Waddell said he ought to have six men. That scared me; I was afraid they might not go then. They counted up how many men they had. Waddell said that he had to keep two boys to ride the south line, Frank Vaughn and Wes Slaughter.

Gus said he could take the balance of the boys, then laughed and said, "We will make Rufe help us."

Mr. Waddell spoke up and said, "If your brother will help, I will pay him wages for the time he helped."

I said that I didn't want any wages.

Gus said "We will make him work and pay for his grub."

I could see it looked like a good chance to get to go and I did not want to miss it. That was the first big ranch I had seen or been on; and when I had been there about a week, I saw Mr. Waddell drive in one herd from the south. There were about two thousand head; they had branded the calves and turned them up the river north. That was the reason Waddell wanted these other cattle rounded up, to get the unbranded calves before they mixed. I did not exactly understand it then, but I soon caught on to what they meant. They did not want to work the same cattle twice.

Gus suggested to Mr. Waddell to send one boy to the NUN outfit, which was a ranch on the head of double mountain, to come help round up and gather their cattle. This boy was to get the stray men and meet us at a certain place. It took about three days to get there. The country certainly did look good, the grass was fine and there was not many cattle in the county. We got to the appointed place early one evening and by the time we got through hobbling the horses and had supper, the boy with two stray men came into camp. I had learned that hobbles were to tie the horses' feet together to keep them from running of for traveling so fast.

I also learned on this trip what a rope corral was. They made the rope corral by tying ropes to *mesquite* trees, making a square. First, they would enclose three sides then drive the horses in, and close the gate. I expected to see the horses jump out, and once in a while one would jump out, but it worked very well. A very good substitution for a corral.

The next morning, when we started out, my two brothers, Gus and Dave, both told me to be careful and not get very far out of sight of some of the other boys or I might get lost. They told me to be careful and not to be afraid to run my horse. I thought to myself, that was what I came for, to run my horse. They had given me five horses; it was the first time I ever had all the horses I wanted to ride. I saw fifteen deer in one bunch that morning. That was the biggest bunch of deer I ever saw, before or after. I have seen lots of deer, but never that many in one bunch. I have seen antelope as many as a hundred in a bunch in the winter time. They bunch up in the fall of the year. On that first trip I did not get to see any buffalo as bad as I wanted to.

There was a big rough fellow named Peir Lagrange that worked for NUN outfit. He had the first Winchester rifle that I ever saw. I got well acquainted with him and liked him very much and he seemed to take to me. Of course, he saw I was a tenderfoot. We stood nightguard together, he took great interest in telling me what he knew about working cattle. One morning after we made the roundup, just as the last bunches of cattle came in, I saw old Peir leave the two boys, he came running around the herd looking for me. He handed me his gun and said he had seen three buffalo just over the ridge.

I took the gun and went where he told me to go, but did not find any buffalo. I guess something scared them after he saw them and he thought so too, but he said they were grazing when he saw them. After that I tried to stay as close to Peir as I could, but we did not find any buffalo. I saw several small bunches of deer and lots of antelope, but they were too small game for me. I wanted buffalo. We were about two weeks on that trip and we did lots of hard riding. I got pretty tired some days. We stood guard every night, for the country was all open then and did not have a small pasture to drop them in at night like we had later. We turned the cattle loose about where Colorado City now stands, as the railroad did not get there until about two years later. Just a few days after, we came in from that trip with the wagon and outfit.

Waddell had word from John Hulum at the mouth of Bull Creek that he would start rounding up and branding. Mr. Waddell decided to send Gus O'Keefe and one boy to represent Waddell's interest. Gus told Waddell that I made a good helper and I could take the place of one of the regular boys and have more line drivers. The cattle had just been driven into the country from southeast and they would drift back if they did not ride a close line. We started out early next morning with six horses apiece, that was one horse more per man than we had before, so I figured I was being promoted. We went over the same route we had just been over on the other trip, but forty miles further up the river northwest from where we were.

Mr. Hulum and C. C. Slaughter were partners in this herd. They had five thousand cattle branded HS and it certainly was a nice herd of cattle, fat and fine. The grass was fine, it seemed like the further up the river we went, the better the grass was. That was because there were fewer cattle up there. I remember we ran on to some bear tracks where he had been down to the river for water. We followed a cattle trail that was very sandy; we could see every track that the bear made but never did find the bear. He left the trail, and the tracks were too dim to follow. While we were rounding up and working Hulum's range, Mr. John Scarbro and two other men came over to get their cattle and help roundup.

Mr. Scarbro was also a partner with C. C. Slaughter at that time. They had about three thousand cattle branded OS. Scarbro lived on the ranch and was manager, same as Hulum was manager for Hulum and Slaughter. Slaughter lived in Dallas and came out occasionally. The two ranches joined and they worked together, but was twenty miles from one ranch to the other.

When we got through working the Hulum ranch, we boys started over to Scarbro's ranch. We got in early in the evening, being on the nearest side of the Hulum range. The distance was not very far, but Hulum and Scarbro did not start from the Hulum ranch until after noon. They said they were talking and did not pay attention to the time of day it was, and the first thing they knew it began to get dark. They had no road and got lost. They had to lay out all night, but it was warm weather and it did not hurt them to lay out. The funny part of it, they did not want the boys to know they got lost on their own range.

The boys laughed at them and teased them so much they finally acknowledged that they struck Deep Creek about two miles below the ranch and they did not know whether they were below the ranch or above it. They decided to stake their horses out and lay down on their saddle blankets until daylight. They said at daylight they saw some hills nearby that they knew and found the ranch by them. We worked through the Scarbro range the next few days.

The cook caught a fine mess of trout from the creek, the creek at that time had nice deep holes of clear water. It was nice to see a dry herd of cattle go in to get a drink and slack their thirst. I think we gathered about ninety of Waddell's cattle. We cut the cattle and shaped them up one evening, penned them that night so we could get an early start next morning. Scarbro's cook gave us enough bread and meat to camp on, while on the way. The last day at noon our chuck was running very low.

Gus knew where a fellow named Chock Morgan had a hog ranch and we would go by there and get dinner. We were traveling on a very dim road, but when we got near Chock s camp we pushed the cattle off the road for about one mile, Gus went on ahead to see about getting something to eat. I let the cattle graze up near the dugout and went up to see what luck Gus had. There was no one else there. Gus was very busy baking some bread, frying meat, and told me to look around and find some coffee and grind it; we would soon have some dinner. I soon found a package of Arbuckle coffee. He had the water all ready hot and I fixed the coffee. I told him I would see about the cattle again. He said to just bed them down. I looked out and reported about half of them are already bedded down, because we had driven them pretty hard and they were pretty tired. When I got back, he had dinner ready and it surely did taste good. He had a can of stewed peaches to eat with the bacon and coffee.

I said to Gus, "What you going to do about eating up this fellow's grub?"

He replied, "That is the way we do out here."

When we got ready to start, we found a piece of paper and Gus wrote on it;

Dear Chock, We came by hungry, and if you miss anything lay it on Gus O'Keefe. Come to see us.

That ended the dinner party. We drove the cattle to the next water a mile or so ahead and turned them loose. We went on in to the Waddell ranch. They called it twenty miles from Chock's camp. The folks and Mr. and Mrs. Waddell and the boys laughed when Gus told them I did not want to eat Chock Morgan's food since Chock was away from home. I told them I thought Mr. Chock's grub was mighty good, even if it was stolen. Mr. Waddell said old Chock would be mad if we had not had our dinner.

Brother Dave and one other boy were on the south side of the Waddell range in a line camp. I waited a few days to see Dave before I left for home. While I was waiting for Dave to come in, I washed my clothes. I had one extra suit of underclothes, extra pair of pants and two shirts. I surely did need the shirts for those big calves of John Hulum's and Scarbro's had just about kicked my shirts all off of me. But I had one shirt left that was good. I had not worn it in the branding pen, and I figured if I did not get into any more branding pens, it would run me until I got back to Buffalo Gap where I could buy a new one. I carried my clothes in a pair of saddle bags. It was a leather outfit with pockets in each end and lay across the back part of your saddle. Some of the cowboys said I looked like a Methodist preacher circuit rider. Well, I enjoyed my trip and the work on Hulum and Scarbro's ranches even if I did get my clothes torn up a little.

When we started work, my brother told me to be careful and kinda go slow at the start; not tackle the big calves. In those days they roped big calves by the head and drug them up near the fire and the boys would have to flank them. Now we rope them by the hind feet and drag them down and the boys on the ground jump on him and hold him. That is easy compared to flanking. I stood around and watched the other boys. When they would get them down, I would help to hold them while the brander put the 'Hot Stuff" on him. After we branded a dozen or so, I began to tackle the smaller calves, then I got to the larger ones.

Finally, I got to where I would take them as they came, that is, we took them in relays. Two boys would work together, my partner and I take a calf, then two other boys take the next one and so on. About every hour we would stop and rest a while. They laughed at me some at first for I got skinned up a little. Gus especially would laugh when the calf would kick me. Then old man Scarbro showed me how to put my right knee in the calf's flank as I threw him, then jerk up the calf's front foot; in that way they can't kick you. I soon caught on to that and I seldom ever got kicked after that.

Mr. Scarbro seemed to take a liking to me, he told the boys the last day we branded that I was the best hand in the pen. I thought he just wanted to flatter me a little; I was not silly enough to think I was the best; but I knew I was just about as good. I made up my mind if I did get kicked it would soon get well, though sometimes it would hurt pretty bad. I did not say much, but would be a little more careful next time. It was the first branding on the big scale I had ever seen. I branded my little bunch back in Ellis County, but we roped them by the neck and tied them to the fence post, then put another rope on their hind feet.

All the time I was with these men I was planning, might say building air castles. I made up my mind then and there someday I would have a ranch of my own. I would watch these men work, that is the owners. Hulum and Scarbro were just as different as could be. I thought Scarbro much the best cowman; he was just a little on the rough order, but when he went to do anything, he went at it like he meant to do it. When he went in the herd to cut cattle and found one he wanted, he was not long in letting them know he was after them. I would look and admire him when he was working in a herd.

He was not reckless and many times he would just ride his horse in a common walk. If the cow would walk out that suited him all right, but if one wanted to be unruly, then look out Mr. Cow! He rode good horses and seldom ever let a cow get back in the herd on him. Mr. Scarbro was tall and sat straight as an Indian in his saddle and had very long legs. Some of the boys told him no wonder a horse could not throw him for he could wrap his legs around the horse. Now the other man John Hulum was just the opposite to Scarbro. Hulum would poke around in the herd and if they did not walk out but started running, he sometimes would let that one go and hunt one that was easy to cut. While if it had been old Scarbro, he would have made him get out of there. While building air castles about my future ranch, I did not want to be a cowman like Hulum, I wanted to be more like Scarbro.

Brother Gus worked very much like Scarbro; both were very determined when they got after a cow. The cow soon learned she had to go where they wanted her. But neither of them was very much of an expert with a rope, but for any other work they were hard to beat. I decided if I could get to be as good a cowman as Gus or Mr. Scarbro, I could get along with my ranch when I got one. I had fully made up my mind I would have a ranch. I did not just want to manage a ranch, I was going to own one. If I had been very smart, I would have remained right there. Mr. Scarbro told Gus that his brother Rufe would make a good cow hand someday. He said if he had a place, he would put me to work, that I was not afraid of a horse, that I had the energy and that I did not go poking around like John Hulum.

"He is the best hand we have in the branding pen right now," Mr. Scarbro said, adding that I had all the qualities to make a good hand.

Gus told me all this after we had left Scarbro's ranch while on the way to Waddell s. He wanted me to stay, but I already had a little bunch of cattle in Ellis County. I decided I would look at Coleman County as I went back. While I was waiting for Brother Dave to come in, I was with Mr. Waddell and Gus quite a bit. Waddell asked Gus lots of questions about Hulum and Scarbro and their range, as he knew C. C. Slaughter started out in cow business with just a small bunch and had gotten to be very wealthy.

Slaughter had been an old trail man, bought and sold steers. George Waddell was in the same business and drove from the coast country to northern markets. He asked what kind of cowmen Hulum and Scarbro were. Gus told him to ask me, and I said that Scarbro was the best cowman. He thought so too. Waddell laughed and said that if they came down there, he would know which one to put in the herd, which was all a joke.

I later got acquainted with Mr. John Davidson in Coleman County who I thought was another ideal cowman. Being young as I was, I would watch men work about the roundups and it looked to me that

John Davidson did everything just right at the right time, in the right place. He was manager and part owner of OH Triangle ranch. This ranch was located at the mouth of Concho River. He also was made general roundup boss for all of that district. He told me he was raised on a farm in Georgia and came to Texas to be a cowboy. He made a good one.

## Chapter 4

When Dave came in from the camp and spent the night with us, I bade them goodbye and started early next morning for Buffalo Gap. First night I spent at the Carter and Grounds ranch, which was forty miles from Waddells. Next night I spent in Buffalo Gap. I spent the next night with some settlers and from there I reached Coleman City. I liked that country, it was somewhat like Ellis County. It had lots of water running in streams. I inquired at the hotel about the country. The manager, Mr. John Good, had a ranch in Runnells County and he told me there were many small ranches up on Hord's Creek. I decided it might suit me. I put in several days on Hord's Creek and the people were nice to me.

All of them had small bunches of cattle. They had had good rains that summer; the grass was fine, and cattle were fat. I had heard a great deal about Brown County and thought I would look at it as I went through. I spent the first night at Brownwood, after leaving Coleman next day. I had dinner at a farm house with Mr. Tipton. I asked him about the country; he liked it very much. He was in the weeds and wanted a man to help him clean his crop. I asked him about wages he paid. Fifty cents a day, I was told.

As my pony was getting tired, I decided to work a few days and learn more about the country. I worked about a week. Then Mr. Tipton found me another job. I worked for the other fellow a week and by that time my pony was pretty well rested. I went from there to Iredell. I had folks living there, N. B. (Pole) Ross. I spent two days there, then I headed for Waxahachie in Ellis County.

I spent one night with a farmer named Simpson in Johnson County. He was just getting ready to thresh wheat and wanted some help. So, I decided my horse needed more rest. I worked for him ten days. He gave me seventy-five cents per day. They were nice people and he wanted me to stay longer. They invited me to come by and see them if I ever passed that way again. I had told them I had a little bunch of cattle and might move them to Coleman County. I did not like Brown

County. I think I was two days going from Mr. Simpson's to Brother Jim's. I found them all well. I had been gone about three months and Jim said my yearlings had not done so well.

He had been looking after them for me and had but little rain while I was gone. I looked around, counted my cattle and found I had lost some. The water was scarce and made the cattle scatter. I made a trip over to Kaufman County when I heard they had some open country there on Trinity River. I did not like the looks of it for cattle, but I did like the country for a farming country. I found some friends that had moved there from Ellis County and enjoyed my visit with them very much. When I got back to Brother Jim's, he had commenced to pick cotton. In that fall, I decided to move with my cattle. I had made a trip to west Texas. I spent some time in Brown and Coleman Counties and other parts of the range country. I liked Coleman best because of its having good grass and plenty of water and protection.

I hired a boy to help me and in September we rigged up a pack horse and started out. I had seen pack horse outfits and had learned how to do that; but that was about all I did know about the cow business. I soon learned there was another side to it, as well as a funny side. One warm day we were watering the cattle and the pack horse lay down in the tank of water. We had never seen anything like that and, of course, we thought our grub was all ruined.

We rushed in and got the pony out and unpacked and spread the blankets out in the sun. We thought our flour would be ruined, but we found the flour was just wet next to the sack. I learned since flour forms a paste and does not get wet on the inside, so we were not damaged as much as we thought we were. I think we were about four weeks on the road. We got through all right and did not lose any cattle.

Nothing unusual happened on the way. We heard that a child had been lost in Comanche County. He had wandered away from home, they supposed, into the woods. If he was ever found, I never heard of it. We got on the prairie, or open country, at Santa Anna Mountain in Coleman County. It looked much better than the timber country. We came through Brown and Comanche counties.

Near Santa Anna Bill saw his first prairie dog. I located ten miles west of Coleman City on Hord's Creek; we found a vacant log house and camped there for the winter. The country was all open and free. There were a good many settlers along Hord's Creek and they had begun to farm some. Settlers from the east and south drove cattle in by the thousands. Of course, it over-stocked the country and made it hard on everybody. Lots of cattle died that winter.

I worked the country the next spring and gathered what I could and sold them. I made arrangements with a friend to gather the remainder and sell them for me. Cattle prices had advanced considerably and that helped me out. Still, it was a losing game for me. I decided to go back to Ellis County. I took what money I had and went in with Brother Jim. We bought a two-hundred-acre farm. We figured that we could make eight or nine cents per pound raising cotton. Things looked pretty good for a while. We raised good crops, but prices began to drop. Cotton dropped as low as five cents per pound. We found we could not make any money at that, so we sold the farm at a small profit and I went west again.

I went to work for C. C. Slaughter on the Long S ranch in Mitchell and Howard Counties. Brother Gus at that time owned one sixth interest in that ranch and was manager. They were then moving their headquarters from the mouth of Bull Creek on the Colorado River to a spring called German Springs which was near Gunsite Mountain in Howard County, twenty miles north of Big Springs. It was a better place and was more convenient to the railroad and post office. The old headquarters were thirty-five miles from Colorado City. The moving was an easy job; all we had was the cooking outfit, a few rolls of bedding and a few head of horses. We camped on the outside of the range and turned the cattle back into the range. I thought it funny for two of us to move for a ranch that had forty thousand cattle. Of course, the cattle were scattered all over the country because that was before the day of fences.

My first job was to put a fence around two sections of land for a horse pasture. We moved into an old dugout ten by twelve feet. Gus was gone most of the time, but he would drop in and spend a day or two then be gone again. I really did get lonesome. He told me it would not be long until I would have lots of company. Sure enough, as the cowboys began to break winter camps, they came riding in and it was anything but lonesome then.

Sometimes there were twenty cowboys there. Later on, Henry Mason brought his outfit in from Sulphur Springs and brought a cook. Soon Gus came in. Gus asked me how I was getting along. I told him we were a little crowded. He laughed and said while the boys were there, we would build a house.

We had talked about building a house for the ranch for some time. We soon had the lumber on the ground and a carpenter to build the house. The house was a long box house with a wide hall in the middle and a gallery full length of the house. It had a loft, or attic, and we felt that we had quite a fine house. I felt we would get away from the snakes, for there was more rattlers in that country than I ever saw before. There was a creek they called Rattle Snake Creek. German Spring was a tributary to Rattle Snake Creek which certainly had the right name. I suppose buffalo hunters or perhaps the soldiers or rangers saw so many snakes that they just named the creek after them. It was said that the creeks and mountains took their names from incidents that happened. There was Wolf Branch, Skunk Bend, Bullhollow, Sand Creek and Gunsight Mountain which looked like a gun sight and barrel from a distance.

When we first built this pasture fence, I gathered saddle horses and put them in there for spring work. After we put about one hundred in one night, we had a hail storm. The horses stampeded and ran into the fence, broke the wires; but strange to say it did not hurt any of them much. The reason was, they ran straight against the fence and, of course, they broke the wires and went over. I could trail them well enough by their tracks as the ground was wet. Some of them were cut on their breast and front legs; none seriously hurt. I got a lot of empty cans and tied to the wire fence, whether that did any good or not, I don't know. The horses, however, did not run into the fence anymore. Screw worms were bad then and I had quite a job doctoring some of the horses. Some of them were young and had never been handled very much, but we soon got them ready for the spring round-up. Each man would have to doctor his own mount.

I was glad to see the roundup start because I was tired of staying at headquarters. Anything for a change was agreeable to me. Branding calves was hard work in those days. We often had no pens. They roped calves around their necks and dragged them, bawling, pitching and fighting up near the fire to brand. Some of them were almost a year old. A cowboy would go down the line to meet one of these big rascals and the calf would look almost as big as a cow. We would usually take hold of the rope with the left hand and hold the rope until we got to the calf's neck. Then grab him in the flank, put our knee against his body just behind his front legs, lift him off the ground and give him a sudden jerk, or flip. Grab his top front leg and then we had him.

That was not as easily done as it is to tell about it. Sometimes we would aim to get him down, but our plans would not work out just as we planned it. Sometimes these big calves would not stand for that kind of a game and as soon as he saw you coming down the line toward him he would make a run at you for a fight. He may run right into you, may hit you in the breast or face, then you have to fight it out with him the best you can. Sometimes you can grab him by one ear with one hand and by the nose with the other. Twist his head and keep twisting until it cuts his breath off. This is called "bulldogging."

When his breath is cut off, he will fall. Not every time could you get this hold on him. Sometimes when he was jumping and fighting you could get his front leg and throw him. At times, all this would fail, then we would get a rope and rope him by his hind feet. Of course, the other roper already had his rope around his neck and the two would string him out. If some cowboy read this, he would say everybody knew how to brand calves. But they didn't until they learned. After the spring and early branding was over, they put most of the boys in line camps. They gave each camp some saddle horses to care for, also instructions to brand up the big calves, doctor the calves for screw worms and look after the cattle in general.

Charlie Coe and myself went to Sulphur Springs, a Catholic settlement on Sulphur Draw about twenty miles north of Stanton, Martin County. We went over there quite often to see if any of our cattle were there. The people treated us nice and invited us back. They seemed to take pleasure in getting water for us when we needed it. Charlie wanted to see the priest, as he had seen him before and talked so much about it. I wanted to see one. He said they wore their shirt collar buttoned behind and always wore a long tail frock coat.

Next time we went to Stanton we went on a Sunday and I saw a priest for the first time at a well. We did not attempt to go to church because we were not dressed to go. I think they only had one well at that time, for they had been there only a short time. Charlie said we better watch them, they might be killing our beef; but we did not find any evidence of it. We spent about two months at Sulphur, as we called it.

We had a very small box house, and it would really get warm in July and August in the middle of the day. One day a buffalo hunter came and camped with us. His name was George Bell. I had not seen any buffalo yet; he asked me to go out to his camp and we might find some. I went and spent two days, but we did not see any buffalo. He said there were some in the country that the surface water on the plains was drying up and they would have to come in to get water. If we would watch the spring close, we would get to see them. As I had never seen one, I was anxious to kill one. Charlie had killed some before that, but he was just as anxious as I was. We picked out some of the best horses and did not ride them much but kept them handy to use to kill buffalo.

Charlie said we should look for hair on bushes for they would be apt to leave their sign. One morning we saw some hair and lots of tracks though we could not tell much about their tracks, as they were so much like cattle tracks. Anyway, we got our best horses and had them saddled. While we were cooking dinner six buffalo came down the trail and passed within one hundred yards of the house. We waited until they got to the water, which was some three or four hundred yards, then we slipped along through the bushes and got our horses. As we neared the creek the bushes were larger and tall enough to hide one from view. I went down on one side of the creek and Charlie on the other side.

I selected one nearest to me and kept a tree between the buffalo and myself until I was near enough to shoot. I had been told to never dismount, so I sat in my saddle and shot him behind the shoulder. Instead of him falling, as I planned, he whirled almost like he was on a pivot. When he got from behind that tree, he was in plain view of me and here he came towards me. My horse wheeled, and away we went through the brush. I think my horse was scared even worse than I. I circled around and got my horse under control again. The buffalo was still on his feet but he had advanced only a short distance toward us and stopped. It was all I could do to get that horse near the buffalo.

As I got nearer, I could tell he was badly wounded. I got straight in front of him, shot him in the head and killed him. When the smoke cleared away, I looked around and Charlie had killed two. He said he killed the first one in his tracks, and shot the second one as he ran off. Well, we had no reason for killing the poor buffalo, only just to say we killed a buffalo. I felt kind of ashamed of it.

A few weeks after we killed these, I was riding out and saw a buffalo calf following some cattle. I thought now was my time to catch a buffalo calf. I had heard cowboys tell their big stories about marking buffalo calves, so I got my rope and made a run at him; caught him first throw. I have thought about it, often since, how pretty the rope went over his head. It's a wonder I did not get excited and miss him. Getting the rope on him was easy compared to getting it off. I did not know I was getting up against such a mess. He must have been one year old or more, but I did not think of that before I caught him.

I soon saw I was in for it; I would make a run on the rope and jerk him down. He would roll over and land on his feet and come at my horse for a fight. Then I noticed he had horns long enough to hurt a horse and from then on, I kept busy keeping my horse clear. I would jerk the calf down and drag him further each time. I noticed after a while he did not get up so quick. I decided I had him about conquered and decided to make a big run and finish him. I must have run a hundred yards, just as fast as my horse could drag him.

Before I stopped running, I threw my bridle reins over my horse's head so if he attempted to run off my horse would stop by stepping on the bridle reins. I was off my horse almost before he stopped running. I aimed to get to the buffalo before he could get up, but to my surprise he was on his feet and ready for a fight before I could get to him. He must have met me half way down the thirty-foot rope. I had to be careful and not get tangled in the rope for I could see the danger.

I tried every hold I had practiced on other calves, but it looked to me as if they might all fail. I grabbed his front foot and raised his front parts clear off the ground and, of course, he fell on his side. I lost no time getting down on him, for I thought when I got him down, I could sit on him and rest just as I had done many times with domestic calves. There was another surprise coming, for that buffalo never did quit kicking, but I could hold him easier than when I was wrestling with him on his feet. He just kicked me all over. I was sore for a week afterwards. I wondered what to do now; I'd been so smart and got into this buffalo trouble.

I had already given up marking him, and that was what I caught him for. I knew he would fight if I turned him loose. I thought I could kill him and end it all, but I did not want to do that for I had already done enough to him by putting sand in his eyes. I got my rope off and turned his head away from my horse. I figured I could beat him to my horse, but when I got to my horse he was there fighting again. After a little trouble to mount, I ran off and left him.

Then and there I promised myself to never rope another buffalo as big as that one. It reminds me of the old saying, "that fools are not all dead yet." I learned a lesson, and I guess the experience was worth the trouble. So that ended my buffalo troubles at Sulphur.

My next fun was with wild horses and there were great number of them at that time. On my ride one day, I saw a bunch of stock at a distance. I headed my horse towards them thinking it might be some of our cattle, but when I got near them, I could see it was mustangs, or wild horses. I decided to rope a colt and mark him. As they ran away from the water, I noticed a very beautiful mare and a rather small colt. This time I was careful to size things up, for I did not want to have any more experiences like I had had with the buffalo.

I roped this colt; I supposed it was about three months old, and the mother quit the herd, bunch of horses, and came right back to protect her colt. I had heard buffalo hunters tell about creasing horses, that is, they would shoot them through the top of their shoulders. They said they would fall and you could tie them down before they could get up. I thought of all that I had heard. I grabbed my Winchester, which I always carried, and dismounted.

I shot the mare in the top of her shoulder, she fell and I supposed she lay there some five minutes. I did not have any intention of tying her for I had had too much trouble with that buffalo. I began to fear I had killed the mare, but after a while I saw her begin to kick and finally get up and run off. I felt relieved, it had proved that the hunter had told the truth about creasing a horse, but I left off the tying. I proceeded to throw the colt and mark it for that was what I intended to do.

Well, that just about winds up my experiences at the Sulphur, except about branding the big calves. That did not seem so exciting. We rode separately because of the big country. We only rode together on special occasions, such as going to the Catholic settlement. I supposed we thought if the priest was not nice, we would both tackle him. We both laughed about it afterwards.

## Chapter 5

About the first of September that year, we moved back to headquarters at German Springs and began to get ready for the fall roundups. That is always an interesting time, the horses that had been scattered out at the different camps for the last two months, had rested and fattened up. Some of them young, and might say, half-broken would give the boys some fun for the first few weeks. Especially, if we had some green boys that had not ridden much, as some of them would get pitched off.

At German Springs we had a horse pasture. Sometimes there would be several horses loose with saddle on and no rider. Then we would round-up the entire bunch of horses to catch the one that had pitched off the boys. We had lots of fun for they seldom got hurt; but once in a great while one would get a broken collar bone, sometimes an arm would be broken, but nothing very serious. This work that year lasted until about the middle of October.

Then I went to the head of Tobacco Creek about forty miles northwest from the German Spring headquarters. John Holloway was my partner at this camp.

Holloway was married but had no children. We had a very good small house to live in and Mrs. Holloway was a good cook. We had milk and butter, and I remember we found some late plums. John and I gathered them and his wife made a lot of jelly. Mrs. Holloway milked the cow and fed her slop. She would not let us throw away any scraps of bread for she saved it all for the cow. We had plenty to eat and lots of riding to do for we were at the foot of the plains and we had as long rides to make as Charlie Coe and I had from Sulphur. I liked the new camp better than Sulphur for we had a lady to cook and keep house for us.

Of course, we did quite a bit of the work and often cooked breakfast for her, for she was in poor health. I was glad to do that, for we had had to do all the cooking at Sulphur. The outfit came up to start work to gather a herd of beef cattle. Henry Mason was in charge of this outfit. He had about ten of Slaughter's men and six or eight men from other neighbouring ranches; near twenty men in all. They came early in the evening aiming to roundup Tobacco Creek next morning; but late in the evening there came up a north wind and rain and we made room for as many as we could in the two-room house.

Mrs. Holloway had been sick several days; we did not think she was so seriously sick, but about twelve o'clock she died. Of course, John was heartbroken, and as all the rest of us were young men and boys we hardly knew what to do. Henry Mason and I went to headquarters and got a light hack and went on to Big Springs, sixty miles, and ordered a coffin and the grave to be dug. We got back to Tobacco Creek camp the next day and had not had any sleep. Henry and I started for the coffin, while two other boys went to Uncle Willis Holloway's about twenty miles away where Gail now stands, to get some ladies to take charge of the body. They started at once to Big Spring with the corpse. It was sad that she had to die that far out from civilization.

My brother Gus had told me that he wanted John Holloway and me to stay at this Tobacco Creek camp that winter. I was wondering what effect this would have on John. He said he thought he could get his mother to come and keep house for us. I went with Mason's outfit to help gather the beef herd. I got back to camp in December. John and his mother were there and seemed glad that I had come.

His mother was a fine old lady and she sympathized very much with John in the loss of his wife. She was a good housekeeper and always wanting to do something for us. Every few days we would brand some big calves and, of course, we would get skinned up some. Any little scratch on our hands she would doctor up for us. John and I called her the Doctor, but we noticed we were glad to have her there during the winter.

John and I had some experience with buffalo. Several bunches came in for water and we killed quite a few, but this time we saved the hides and best part of the meat. It did not seem so cruel as it did when Charlie Coe and I killed them just for fun. We killed some that were pretty fat, but most of the old ones were poor. Of course, we did not eat the poor ones. I remember we got after one bunch late one evening and killed four. We just let them lay where they fell and kept after the bunch trying to kill some more. We must have gone ten miles when it began to get dark. We stopped and got off our horses, took the saddles off and let the horses cool and rest half an hour.

By that time, it was dark and there was no road. It was cloudy, misting rain and not a star to be seen. We had stopped on Sulphur Draw, but before we left the Draw, we got our bearings. It was the only guide we had, so we started off as near opposite the Draw as we could tell. We travelled a long time until we thought we must be near the breaks of Tobacco Creek, for we were on the plains. We stopped and planned what we might do.

John said his mother would be uneasy about us. We knew if the horses took us to their range, we could recognise the range by the trails at the foot of the round mountain or hill. We did not want to be out all night, so we decided to let the horses have loose rein and go where they would thinking they would go to their range which was three or five miles north our camp. By this time, it was raining hard and when we could tell we were in the valley, we dismounted and looked and waited for it to clear up so we could skylight the mountains. The rain stopped after a while and as walked along we could see the mountain. We knew if we were right there should be a small creek about a quarter mile south of this mountain. We soon found the creek, as we had hoped, and we were glad for this was the first time that we knew where we were.

We had one more problem to solve; there was a dim road half mile south of the creek leading to the camp. We walked and led our bourses until we found it, then two miles to camp. When we were near the house, we saw the light Mrs. Holloway had sitting by the window so we could see it. To our surprise it was only one o'clock when we thought it must almost be daylight, but distance always seems longer at night. Next morning, we took the wagon and gathered up the hides and meat. We found four buffalo, we shot others, but failed to kill them. We did not start out late in the evening after buffalo any more.

We went on several trips on the plains to see if there were any cattle. We had a pack horse and camp outfit so we could stay as long as we wanted. We usually spent one night. I remember on one trip we went to Ward's Wells and found very little water, but we had enough to camp on. We went one route and came back a different one. We killed a young antelope late one evening and that night we had a feast on broiled antelope. The greatest trouble we had was to find wood to burn. We found very small *mesquite* bushes. We did not sit up very late that night as we had a long ride next day that took us down near where Midland now is located.

Then we came back to Tobacco Creek, where we rested up next day. After that we were kept pretty busy branding big calves. Some of them almost ready to wean. I remember getting my foot hurt one very warm evening. We would rope four calves and tie them down. We called that hog tying by tying all four feet together, and when we got two calves tied, we would make a fire and mark and brand them. Each of us would catch and tie two more. Their heads were loose and as I walked up to brand one, I intended to put my foot on his head to hold him still while I branded him.

The calf jerked his head up and being unbalanced, my foot fell to the ground and before I could jerk it up again the calf's head came down full force. His horns were two inches long, and went down through my boot and stocking between the roots of two toes. That ended that evening's branding. I was laid up for a few days, but Mother Holloway soon had me doctored up again.

We would find calves at the watering places and would work the different watering places till we got all, then move on to the next place. The latter part of March in that year, 1883, we began to get ready for spring work. The Slaughter ranch was planning to move a big lot of steers to the Indian Territory (now Oklahoma) on Comanche and Arapaho Reservation. Slaughter, Hunt and Evans leased a lot of that, country and stocked it with steers. Slaughter put four herds there, about ten thousand head. About April first, we broke camp at Tobacco Creek and John and I went with the roundup outfit. Henry

Mason was wagon boss and he was a good one. Mrs. Holloway, went down to headquarters at German Spring.

I felt kind of sad about breaking that camp, for we had such a pleasant time all winter, although there had been lots of work. Brother Gus asked how would it do to get Mrs. Holloway to keep house and cook for headquarters. I told him that she would be all right. She would save more stuff for that ranch than anybody on it.

We made first roundup at Tobacco Creek; gathered about six hundred first day. There came up a cold rain that night and many of the steers, yearlings and some not weaned, ran half of the night. One thing that was in our favour, we had the moon while it was cloudy, but we could see the cattle well. Next day we gathered about the same number, they were not so bad the second night. We boys said the reason was, we ran them to death the first night. Anyway, they seemed to sleep pretty well the second night. It usually takes one or two nights to break a herd into being herded. About the fifth day we decided we had 2,500. Mr. Slaughter and Gus O'Keefe came to the outfit and camped with us. They wanted to shape the herd and start us on the trail for the Indian territory. Next day we counted and had 2,700. I went with the first herd. Rube Hulbert was trail boss. John Holloway went with one herd and Wash Wolf was his boss.

Our herd started from near Snyder, Scurry County. We went by the Double Mountains; 2,700 was the biggest herd I had ever been on the trail with and they kept us busy. We had cold rains and the herd stampeded several times. Sometimes it would take all day to gather what we had lost the night before. For several nights in succession, they ran. On Duck Creek there was lots of dead wood. Our boss decided to try a new scheme. We gathered a lot of wood, had some great big logs that took five boys on horses to drag them up to the fire.

As it began to get dark, we rounded the cattle up within one hundred yards of this big fire, and kept that fire burning all night. They did not get up off the bed ground all night. So, we all got a very good night's sleep. First, we had for several nights. After that we got along very well although we had lost some cattle. Our boss left one man with the Matador outfit to gather what we had lost, as they went to work in a few days after we passed through their range.

We went down Peas River quite a way, went within few miles of Vernon, Texas. I left the herd and went to Vernon to get some medicine. My horse had fallen with me before we left the ranch and hurt my ankle and Vernon was the first place, I could get medicine. Vernon was a very small place then, in 1883. Had a drug store and I suppose a dozen other business houses. We crossed Red River at Doan's Store about fifteen or twenty miles above Vernon. Then we were in Indian Territory where I saw my first Comanche Indians; but from then on, we saw them plenty, for they came to our wagon every day. They were a hungry bunch.

We stayed near Doan's Store three days as we were ahead of time. The grass was fine from there on. When we got to our destination, sixty miles west of Fort Reno, we were out of provisions and had to send the cook to Ft. Reno to get something to eat. He had to cross the Canadian River and it was up, and poor old McIntosh, who was our cook, had to wait for the river to go down. Mac said his mother was a Choctaw Indian and his father a white man. Anyway, he was half white. He was a good wagon cook, and he could stop his team at noon and cook dinner for twelve men as quick as any cook I ever saw. Rube Hulbert, the boss, used to tell me to take Mac and go on ahead of the herd far enough to camp and get dinner ready by the time the herd would get there.

At first, I would take him too far and his dinner would get cold before the herd got there. I soon learned that it did not take old Mac long to get dinner, so I did not get very far ahead. I told Rube old Mac did not need a guide. Just tell him to camp at front end of the herd and by the time the drags got there, Mac would be ready to hollar chuck. He was a good Indian. I never saw him after he left the herd to go to Reno to get us something to eat.

When he left, we had flour, coffee and some syrup. Mac said he could go in two days and come back in three days. I was to stay with Rube until he got the herd divided, then I was to come back to Texas. We had one year olds and two and three year olds which we had to put in three herds. That was to put each age in a herd to themselves. It took lots of hard work, these cattle had to be put in different pastures. We had three herds to hold at night. The bad part of it was, we did not have anything to eat.

Oh, I did get hungry, but when we got time to butcher, we killed one of the smallest yearlings. He was so poor we could hardly eat it, but that was better than nothing. I used to wish for old Mac when we would start to camp to get dinner. We just made the best of it. We would cook that poor beef and put lots of salt in it and try to make gravy, but you can't make gravy without grease.

About the sixth day after Mac left, we got the herds shaped up and the man came to our outfit and received them. I was glad for we had a week's very hard work. Rube told me, of course in a joking way, that he guessed he would fire me as we had got all the work done. He told me to take Dick Malone with me to Reno to bring my horse back. I sold my saddle and bed; so, had nothing but some clothes in a flour sack to carry with me.

Dick and I started next morning at daylight for Reno where I would take the stage for Henrietta, Texas. After we had ridden ten or fifteen miles, we came in sight of a camp. I told Dick we would go by and get something to eat, but when I went in there was no one there. I investigated and found some raw bacon and some good biscuits made with grease. I offered Dick some of it, but he would not eat a bit of the meat. He ate the bread. We did not lose any time arguing about eating hog meat on Friday for we had to make sixty miles if we got to Ft. Reno that day. We had no road but were told to go southeast until we found a road leading due east that would take us to Ft. Reno.

Late in the evening we came to a very dim road. We followed it a few miles and came to a river, the Canadian. It was up and looked risky, but we decided to cross. We went in where the wagon tracks went in. We did not get far until we bogged down in quick sand. I jumped off my horse and led him back to the bank where I had started from. I had trouble keeping my horse from striking me with his front feet because he was struggling in the quick sand. Finally, I got out on dry ground where I could stop. When I stopped, I looked to see what had become of Dick. I saw he was going through the same trouble I had. But he was making it to dry ground all right.

It was dangerous for a horse gets excited same as a man and he will try to get to you; seems as if he thinks man can help him. In trying to free himself from quick sand as he jumps forward, there is danger that he may jump on you. There is another danger, he may get his feet in the bridle reins and if he did it might drown him. I had been in swimming water before, but this quick sand was just about the worst mess I had been into. The water was not more than four or five feet deep. After we got out on safe ground, we took off our clothes and wrung them as dry as we could.

Of course, we had to put the same ones back on. We hardly knew what to do. Dick was just out from New York City and did not know anything about quick sand rivers, and I did not know much. I did know we could take our clothes off and swim the river, but I was not sure we could do that and lead our horses. Then I thought we could take bridles off and tie rope on their neck and it would be less dangerous.

While we were planning what to do, we walked up on a high bank and saw six Indians sitting on a sand hill about a quarter or half mile away. I told Dick they might know of a better crossing. We went to them, but Dick did not like the idea much. I told him I did not think there was any danger. When we got to them, we found they were children. I asked them the best I could where they lived. They shook their heads. I asked where was *tepee*. They pointed a certain direction. I asked how far it was. They held up one finger and I thought that meant one mile. I asked the largest one if they would go with us to *tepee*. He nodded and got on his pony and lead the way, about a half mile to their camp.

One big fine looking Indian came out and smiled and said something, I didn't know what. I told him we wanted him to lead us across the river and I'd give him one dollar. He understood me for he nodded his head and jumped on the pony the boy had ridden to the camp and motioned us to follow. I noticed when he went down the bank of the river, he got a switch from a willow tree. I looked back and told Dick that the Indian meant to ride fast over the quick sand and for us to keep up with him. About the middle of the stream, we stopped on an island, the Indian held out his hand to me and asked for money. I shook my head and pointed across and said when we got over, I'd give him the dollar. He grunted and started; in a few moments we were across the last part of the river. It seemed to have been pretty solid the last part of the way. I asked him the best I could the direction to Ft. Reno. He pointed east. I tried to tell about a road, but he no *sabe*.

We travelled about a mile and it began to get dark. I told Dick we had better stake our horses out and spend the night for the grass was fine. Our horses were tired and so were we. Dick said how could we sleep. I said we would probably get little sleep, but we could rest. We had good saddle blankets, but they were just as wet as could be. We wrung them as dry as we could and spread some on the ground and covered with others. We both had slickers, or gum coats. I slept some and Dick said next morning he fared better than he thought he would.

At daylight, our horses rested, we headed as near as we could tell northeast for we were south of the road we left the evening before. We had not gone very far when we found a dim road that led near an eastern course. We felt that we were on the right road. In a few miles we came to a fresh wagon track intersecting our road. I told Dick we would soon find something. A little later another fresh track came into the road. Pretty soon we saw a small camp house and I told Dick we would get something to eat. We found it was a wood camp getting out wood for the government post at Ft. Reno, ten miles down the road. The cook was the only man there and at first did not want to give us breakfast. I told him how long we had gone without food and that we would pay for the breakfast. He said all right and then gave us a fine breakfast. He did not want to take anything, but I gave him a dollar. I thought that was the best breakfast I ever ate.

We got in to Reno just before noon. I went direct to the stage stand to find what time I could get out for Henrietta, Texas. I was told the stage was due from Ft. Dodge at four p. m., but streams were all up and might be late. I told Dick he had better stake his horses on the best grass he could find and stay till next morning; let his horses rest and get some sleep himself. We found good grass nearby. We had dinner together and took in the sights, which was not a big job for it was a small place.

We saw the negro soldiers in uniform drilling, which was new to me, but Dick said it was old stuff to him. My stage came on time. I bade Dick goodbye not knowing then but what I would see him again on my next trip up. I had been told to hurry back to Big Springs, Texas to drive a herd through myself. I never saw old Dick again, but he was a good Irishman. He could tell lots of funny stories, things about the city life all new to me. He did not know much about that quicksand river but seemed to be posted about the city.

We started out in just a few minutes after the stage arrived, which had two mules. While they called it a stage, it was just an old hack. We came in sight of Canadian River in about five miles. I wondered if we were going to have the same experience that Dick and I had. The manager of the stage line went with us to see that the driver handled it right. This manager told me that a few years before that he ran a freight outfit and he got the whole outfit bogged down in Canadian River. Most of the load was flour and he had to leave it in the river until it ran down. He expected to have to pay for the flour, but to his surprise the flour was not damaged very much. The water formed a thin paste next to the sacks and the balance was good. All this happened at the crossing where we were going to cross.

I asked, "How are you going to get this outfit across?"

He said he would put on two extra mules so we could drive fast.

I was very much interested in all this talk. A man met us at the river with a good pair of mules and put them in front. They let the team rest half an hour before we started across. The driver had a good whip and he never did let the team slow down at all, but I imagined, whether it was so or not, that I could feel the back end of that hack sinking in the sand as we passed over it. We travelled ten miles from the river to the stage stand where we had supper and changed teams. As it was getting dark, we started for Ft. Sill. The driver said we would drive all night and would change teams about every twelve or fifteen miles. He said we should get in soon after daylight, which we did.

I changed to another hack and the driver was not as good as the other fellow. He had a lady and me for passengers. We came to Red River about ten o'clock and it had been up. The boy said they told him they thought it had run down but if it had not, to leave his team in a pasture and go across in a skiff and get another team on the other side. The boy asked me what I thought about it, and I told him I thought the skiff was safest. He left the team and we went in the little boat as we called it. Had some trouble getting over sand bars, and one place the boy and myself took off our boots and pulled the thing across. A short distance from the river was Taylor's store where we had dinner and changed teams again. We arrived in Henrietta in the evening. Henrietta was a small town the railroad had built out there from Wichita Falls.

## Chapter 6

I left Henrietta next morning for Big Springs by way of Ft. Worth. I stopped off at Colorado and bought another saddle and camp bed. I bought wool blankets so I would have them for the next winter. We were having lots of rain at that time and blankets, of course, would get wet. I came in one day and found fly blows all over my new wool blankets that I had spread out to dry. I took my knife and raked them off in great bunches, then I scaled those that I could not get off with my knife, I was so put out at getting my new bedding ruined for I had sold my other bedding when I left Oklahoma. I got Greybacks (body lice) on me while going up with Rube Hulbert, and now to think I'd bought a new bed and now the flies had blowed it.

The older men that had seen all this before, laughed at me, especially Gus O'Keefe, and it just tickled him for he knew it was the first time I had ever experienced a thing like that. They said if we could keep flies from blowing us, we would be in luck. I decided if they did not care, I need not to for I found they all had the same trouble. One thing, I found the hot sun soon kills the fly blows, then you can shake them off. I was not as bad off as I thought I was.

Brother Gus asked all about my trip up the trail and I told him everything as near as I could. We lost some cattle on the head of Peas River and Rube thought it best to leave a man there to gather them and try to meet one of the other Slaughter herds that was to follow us and deliver them. He asked if the Indians bothered us much; I told him the last week I was there we lived on flour and poor beef because they ate up everything. He asked if the streams and high water gave us much trouble. I told him yes, everything was up; then I told him about myself, along with Dick Malone, getting into trouble. He laughed and said he had had the same experience many times.

He told me to never let my horse stop in quick sand, just keep crowding, for if the horse stops, he will bog right down. He asked me if Rube got drunk anywhere on the way for old Rube did like his whiskey. I told him no, for there was no place he could get whiskey. He asked how near we went to Vernon. I told him eight or ten miles and that I went to Vernon to get some medicine for my ankle. He asked if I bought Rube some whiskey and I told him no, he did not even mention it. Rube Hulbert was an old experienced trail man and one among the best when he did not get whiskey.

Then he asked how I liked that country, if I thought cattle would do well there. I told him it was the finest grass I ever saw. It was the first blue stem grass I had ever seen, it was about six to eight inches high. It looked almost like green corn and I told Gus if good grass would fatten cattle, they certainly had it. He told me Henry Mason was gathering a herd for me to drive, and asked if I thought I could handle it through all right. I told him yes, I could, but I wanted my old friend John Holloway to assist me. He said all right that John had just come in from the territory a few days before I did. He came back as soon as he got up there; did not stay to separate the cattle. In that way he got back ahead of me. Anyway, I knew John was a good cowhand and I wanted him to help me to boss my first trail herd.

In about three days we counted out the cattle, eight hundred cows and calves, that was sixteen hundred in all. We started near the head of Deep Creek near Snyder and not far from where we started with Rube Hulbert's herd near the Double Mountains. We got along fine, only we had to travel much slower than we did with the steer herd, but we did not have any stampedes. The main trouble we had, was to get them to go along. We only travelled eight to twelve miles a day and sometimes if we had to make a very long drive to get water, we would lay over one day in order to rest the calves. John knew the route. He or I would go ahead of the herd and find water for next day; in that way he was lots of help to me. I had a good man to cook and drive the wagon; he was much older than John or I and had lots of experience.

One time we got into some rough country on Croton Creek, and there was no road. We had to go in there to get water. I asked Mr. Walker, the cook, if he could take the horse rustler and get through the rough hill. He said he could go anywhere you could with that herd of cattle. I told him we were having plenty trouble and wanted to get out to some open country before night. Just a few miles we got out on open smooth country. I told John I could take care of the herd and for him to go back and help Mr. Walker and the horse rustler get out of the hills. They had a hard time getting across canyons and gulches.

One place they had to take everything out of the wagon and carry it across a creek, then reload again. Just before sundown, I saw old man Walker's wagon come in sight and it made me feel mighty good for I was glad to get the outfit all together again. We boys already had a lot of wood ready and it did not take Mr. Walker long to get supper. We had missed our route and got into that rough country. Mr. Walker said he had been in rougher places than that. I asked John how Mr. Walker was taking it when he got to them. He said he was no more excited than he was now cooking supper yonder. He was not a very good cook, but he was good help on the trail, for he could help you do anything that came up.

In a few days after this trouble in the rough hills, John went ahead of the herd to look for the next water, while I would drive the herd on north until he would come back and meet us. John hurried on for we were making a long drive. He found a pretty running stream and, of course did not stop to taste it and just headed back to meet the herd. After a while, I was up with the lead cattle, for they were getting dry. I had to ride in front of them and hold them back. I rode up on a high point to see if I could see John coming. After so long a time I saw his head bobbing up and down. I knew it was he. I remained on high ground so he could see me. I could tell he was riding fast as he could. I thought he was a long time seeing me, but when he was half mile away, he saw me and waved his hand.

I answered him by waving my hat to him. He signalled to come on, then he got off his horse and took the saddle off to let the horse cool and rest. I soon had the cattle pointed towards him, then I loped to where he was laying down. His horse was dripping with sweat. He said he found a pretty running stream of clear water, but it would be a hard drive to get there and water before night. After he showed me how to go, I told him to rest there until the horse rustler came up with the horses and get a fresh horse and come on up to the front and pilot us into the water.

We got there a little before sunset, but we soon noticed the cattle were not drinking the water; we got off our horses to drink some and found it was salt water. It was just too bad. There we were with a dry herd of cattle and almost dark; but we found a small spring next to the foot hills. We then let the cattle, a few at a time, drift there and drink and by just loose herding and remaining there all the next day we got them all watered very well. I told John the next morning I would hold the herd there until he could locate the next water, so we would know before we left this water where we would find the next.

I said, "You, had better drink some water next time before you turn back."

He said, "I will know what it is next time."

So by noon next day old John was back and said he found plenty of drinkable water about six or seven miles. So, we grazed about two or three miles that evening. I laughed at John about the salt water, but John did just about what the average man might have done under the circumstances. He knew he had to rush back to the herd and thought a pretty running stream like that would be drinkable water. Anyone would have thought so. John hated it worse than any of us for he was responsible for the mistake, but old John knew the water after that. We had lot of fun about it. I told John after that I would not have to hunt any more water, for he had got to be such an expert, but I took time about with him, for it was a job no one liked any too well. Some ranchmen would misrepresent facts to keep you from watering in their range, thereby causing you to make long drives.

After we had that salt water trouble, we were very careful to know where we would water next time. That kept John or myself ahead of the herd most of the time, but found that was the safest way, though it took some hard riding. The Indians did not bother at all this trip; we kept further west than Hulbert did with his herd. We did not see any Indians until we got to the point where we delivered the cattle. There were some there at the headquarters place and, as usual, were waiting to get something to eat. We remained there three or four days, or long enough to brand the cattle. John and I were lucky enough to sell our bedding to some boys that were going to stay and work on that ranch. The only thing we brought back was our saddles and pistols.

We took the stage at Ft. Reno and went over the same route that I took earlier in the year by Ft. Sill, Taylor's store, Henrietta, and Fort Worth. A funny thing happened at Fort Worth. When we left the ranch, we drew enough money to spend on the road and carry us back to Big Springs. I think it was sixty dollars for each of us. We had to lay over in Fort Worth from noon till about eight o'clock that evening and we both bought some clothes. John went to visit some friends and we were to meet before train time at the hotel and get our tickets for Big Springs. I saw my money was running short and I quit spending and just had enough to buy my ticket and get something to eat.

Along in the evening John came to the hotel broke. He had spent all his money but about two dollars. He thought I would have enough to get our tickets. I told him I had enough to pay my own fare. I joked him about it and told him I could go on home and send him the money to come on, which I had no thought of doing for I would stay if he had to. We wired to Bressie Brothers, Big Springs; they were merchants and Big Springs had no bank then. We went to the telegraph office several times, but nothing came. It began to look pretty serious as the time was drawing near for the train to leave. The agent found out that the merchants in Big Springs were having a holiday and business was all closed. We then found the train conductor, but neither of us knew him. We told him our troubles. We told him we had two saddles and two pistols.

He said, "Oh, hell, he had more pistols now than he had any use for."

He asked our names and I spoke first and told him my name was O'Keefe. He asked if I was related to Gus O'Keefe. I told him I was a brother. He was well acquainted with Gus.

He said, "Yes, he would take my friend and me, and we could pay him in Big Springs. We were two proud boys, for it looked for a while like we would have to stay over until we could get some money from home. Next day at Colorado City, Brother Gus got on the train and he let John have money to pay his fare. It worked out just right, Gus had a rig and took us and baggage right out to the ranch. He asked all about our trip; if we got through all right, and how the country looked. I told him it did not look as good as it did in the spring when I was up there with Rube Hulbert. It was getting dry. He said it was getting dry here too, and they don't know how to manage for next winter.

He told me they were on a trade for the Running Water ranch about one hundred and fifty miles north of there and that he was going up in a few days to look at it. They still had too many cattle on the ranch for a dry year, and told John and me to rest up a few days and clear up and get the bugs off of us. I told him we did not get bugs this time. We slept together that night; we did not sleep much for we talked most of the night. He had just ridden most of the range in the last few days and it looked bad. A lot of new cattle had been brought in there from Central Texas and crowded the country full of cattle. One of the owners of the Running Water Ranch would be there in a few days and he would go up with him and look it over.

I think about the third day Mr. Nerot Morrison came to the ranch and took Gus in his buggy to see the outfit. They were gone about a week. They said things looked good at Running Water. I noticed Gus did not say a great deal about the ranch in the presence of Mr. Morrison, but when we got to ourselves, he said he was well pleased with it. He was going to recommend it to Mr. Slaughter to trade, if he could get good enough trade. He said it was the best grass he had seen lately, but he did say it was mighty bleak open country and not much protection, a little of it was in sand hills. He asked me if I would go up there and run the ranch if they bought it. I told him I would.

He and Mr. Morrison went to Dallas and met Mr. Slaughter. They wired Tom Morrison and W. D. Johnson the other two partners and made the trade. They traded ten thousand head of cattle of the Slaughter Ranch for half interest in Running Water Ranch and cattle. Gus O'Keefe at that time owned one interest in the Slaughter ranch. When the trade was made, they formed a company and called it Running Water Cattle and Land Company, Slaughter and O'Keefe owning one-half and the two Morrisons and Johnson owning the other half interest. Gus came back from Dallas about the twentieth of August and told me they had traded and told me to get ready. If I needed any clothes for the next winter. Big Springs was nearest railroad and I had better go prepared for the winter. He said someone would come by soon and go with me to turn the ranch over, as we were to take possession September the first, 1883.

About the twenty-fifth of August, Mr. Tom Morrison and his wife and son, Jimmie, came by in a buggy, leading a horse for me to ride. I tried to persuade them to stay overnight, but Mr. Morrison said he was in a hurry to get up there and get back to Ft. Scott, Kansas, to attend to some business. I asked if he could haul my bed; he could. I got my bed and tied it on top of theirs. Everybody carried their bedding when traveling in those days. I went in the house and bade John and his mother, Mrs. Holloway, goodbye. Mother Holloway said she wished they were going with me. I told her it was too far.

We left the ranch about three o'clock in the evening. We went some fifteen or twenty miles that evening and camped just on top of the plains at some surface water. Next day we camped and had dinner at Tahoka Lake at a very small spring. That was the first time I had been to Tahoka Lake, though Holloway and I had been near there the winter before in our wild chases after buffalo. The next night we spent at George Singer's store, located at the head waters of Yellow House Canyon where Lubbock is now. The Singers had a small store and kept supplies for cowboys, a munition for hunters, and furnished lunches for travellers. I think Mr. and Mrs. Morrison slept in the house, but I slept out on the ground as I had been accustomed to do. They called it fifty miles to the Running Water Ranch.

We got there before night and I was a little tired, for riding horse back and keeping up with a buggy was a tiresome job. They go in a trot all the time and I had to keep up with them. Most of the time, I let my horse walk for about half a mile then I would spur him into a lope or gallop. Anyway, I was glad to get there after riding a hundred and fifty miles in little over two days. I was admiring the country for it was certainly fine all the way from Tahoka Lake clear on to Running Water. The surface lakes had water in them and the grass was just as fine as could be.

It did look good compared to that Big Springs country where I had just come from. Mr. Morrison, of course, wanted to show me all the good parts of the range. Next day we went north to the head of South Tule Draw, then turned west near where the town of Dimmit is now. We turned south to the head water on Running Water, then down the draw to the ranch, and I am sure I saw more grass on that day's drive than I had seen on the Colorado River in many a day. The next day we drove over most of their range. There were few cattle on the north part of the range, but, my, they were fat. We drove along the edge of the sand hills, for being in a buggy it was too rough in the hills.

At the southeast part of the sand hills, we had a little excitement. We thought we had found a fellow killing a beef. We could not see him good at first, but could see his horse. We could tell it was a man and we headed towards him. The closer we got, the more it looked like we had found somebody killing a beef. When we got close enough to see him well, we found it was a man named Jess Raulins, a buffalo hunter whom I knew well; he had killed a buffalo and was skinning it. We were relieved when we found out who it was. I knew Jess would not steal anybody's beef, for I had known him down in the Big Springs country.

He said there were three buffalo but when he shot one the other two ran into the sand hills and got away. I told him I was surprised to see him and supposed he was down on Sulphur Draw. He said it had gotten too dry down there and he had to hunt new range to find buffalo. We talked over old times while our team rested a little, for Mr. Morrison was a hard driver. Jess wanted us to go to his camp and stay all night, but we bid him time of day and headed for the ranch twenty miles away. It was then near sunset. We had a very good road and we got in about ten o'clock that night.

The Morrisons were there about a week and we drove out over the range every day for I enjoyed looking at the fine grass. I tried to get Mr. Morrison to ride horseback and let his team rest, but he did not like to ride horseback. After we had looked over everything, they went back to Big Springs where they took the train for Ft. Scott, Kansas. I missed them for Running Water was a lonesome place. At that time, there was not much passing.

Before I left the Slaughter ranch, we ordered some freight to be sent to Running Water.

A man named Ben Griffith and his partner, Aaron Clarkson, were the freighters. They had eight yoke of oxen apiece. They loaded at Colorado City and were three weeks coming. It had rained on them and the streams were up north of Snyder. They were loaded with lumber and post mostly, also some supplies for the ranch. We had to build corrals of post and lumber to brand all the cattle. The Morrisons had three thousand head that had to be branded and tallied, that is, counted; and ten thousand from the Slaughter Ranch.

In November, I took my outfit of horses and men down to the lower ranch to receive a herd. Gus O'Keefe was anxious to find out about things at Running Water. I got most of my orders through him, although C. C. Slaughter was general manager and Gus was supposed to be assistant manager. In fact, he was manager; you might say he was the whole cheese. He asked all about how I got along with the branding. I said it was what Sherman said war was. I said I had finished branding the Morrison cattle and the other Slaughter herd, something less than three thousand. We put circle on hips and shoulder of the cattle, and circle on both hips of the horses.

To brand that many cattle with cow chips, and some of them wet, is a job. He laughed and said he told them, meaning Slaughter, Morrison and Johnson, that would be a big job. He said he and Henry Mason would have another herd of two thousand head in a few days. He would let one of his men drive the herd if I wanted him to. I could have four mules, and a wagon and take a load of *mesquite* wood as I went. I said that would be fine for we had only one team at the ranch. John West and myself loaded that wagon to the guards with *mesquite* wood, the best firewood in the world, and headed for Running Water, just one hundred and fifty miles away. Now, that sure is a long ways to haul wood. We had a good team and made good time. We got in several days ahead of the herd and that gave me plenty of time to make all necessary arrangements to brand the cattle when they came.

Before I left the ranch to go after this herd, I asked "Uncle Jimmie," (we called him). O'Holoran, an Irishman, if he could make us a furnace with a grate in it to burn cow chips. He said he could and when we got in with this load of wood, Uncle Jimmie had the grate done and it worked fine. I gave Uncle Jimmie the job of keeping up the fires, and keeping the branding irons hot, and he did a good job of it. He would not let any of the other boys bother the irons or the fire. He did all that himself. He was a good old fellow. We made good time branding out this herd by having Uncle Jimmie to keep the irons hot. Bill Blake drove another herd up and when we got the cattle branded, we gathered a herd of beef cattle and Blake drove them to Big Springs for shipment and that wound up the trail work for that year.

It was then about the first of December. It had been a very busy year for me. I had made two trips up the trail to Indian territory and taken two herds to Running Water. We bought seventy-five head of young saddle horses. Having done lots of hard work, late that fall, they got very poor. Many of them ate loco (a weed causing some of them to go crazy) and, of course, they got very poor. We were forced to keep them in a small pasture and it looked as if they would all die if we kept them here in this open plain's pasture. I thought if I could get them in the breaks somewhere, I could save them. I went to Mr. Charlie Goodnight's ranch to see if he would let me winter them in Tule Canyon.

I went across the canyon to get to their ranch and I thought how fine that would be if he would let me Winter them there. He was away from the ranch when I got there and I had to wait two days for him to get home. I told him my troubles and told him the mustangs were so numerous that we could not turn them loose for they would take up the horses and stray off. He said he knew how mean the mustangs (wild horses) were, and said I could put them in. I told him I would put a man there to see after the horses. He was nice about it. We put sixty head over there.

A few of the worst locoed ones died, but I believe we would have lost half of them if we had kept them at Running Water. We got along very well with the balance of them at the ranch by feeding them corn. It was my first winter on the plains and, oh, it was cold.

Down at the lower ranch I had been out on the plains often, but could get back in the breaks when the blizzards came. It was different at Running Water. It was said the winter of 1883 and 1884 were unusually cold. Cattle just froze to death. On the seventh of January, 1884, I spent the night at our south camp with John May and Charlie Quilin, as they were staying at camp that winter. We had a good dugout, small of course, but warm in ordinary weather. It was so cold that night we could hardly stand it at all. Next morning, we got out and looked around.

The camp was near the southwest corner of the pasture and cattle had drifted to this corner by the thousands. Some were dead, some down and could not get up. That evening I rode the fence line out for a few miles. I saw dead cattle and dead antelope everywhere. The cattle had drifted south from the storm trying to protect themselves, but they struck the fence; they could not go any further. They would bunch up and some lay down, many of them to never get up again, for they would freeze. We lifted many of them, put them on their feet and rubbed their legs and some would walk, some would fall again.

The second morning, the storm was not quite so bad. We rounded up a big bunch and headed them north towards Running Water, twenty miles away. That was the nearest water. After we got them started and once facing the blizzard, the leaders would tuck their heads and travel very well. That gave those behind some protection from the wind. We left them in the evening still traveling towards the draw.

The morning of the third day was a very nice clear day; it was cold but no wind. We rounded up all the cattle we could find that could walk and turned them north towards the water.

It was a sight to look at. Along the south fence there was dead cattle everywhere. Nearly all the lakes or low places had dead cattle in them. It just made me sick to see it. There was just one thing we should have done if we could have withstood the cold, and that was to keep them on their feet. We could have driven them up the fence for a while, then turned and driven them back, or just anything to keep them from laying down. When they laid down, they would get numb so they could not use their limbs and, of course, freeze to death.

If I had to go through with that again, after learning about such things, I would cut the fence and let them travel, get my outfit and follow them. When the storm was over, I would drive them back. Of course, that would not save all of them, but it would save hundreds of them.

It was my first experience with fences up to that time. Everything had been run off the outside, what we called open range. Slaughter and Gus O'Keefe had instructed me to hold those cattle in the pasture for if they drifted back to Colorado River they would all starve, which I knew was so. So, I guess I did the best I could under the circumstances. After the storm was over I wrote to Slaughter at Dallas and Gus at Big Spring and told them all about it.

I told them I did everything I could do and if they would tell me anything else I would do that. I also wrote the Morrisons at Ft. Scott. I have often thought about those letters I wrote those fellows; they were blue and discouraging. Since I have had ranches of my own, how I would hate to get a letter from a man on my ranch like those were. My, I would be sick. I guess I should not have done it, but I was young then and did not know enough to keep any of it back. In a short time, I got an answer from Gus; he was the first to answer, and it was just about as discouraging as mine was. He started his letter by telling me to not be discouraged; it was mighty bad, of course, but he had had even worse luck.

Everything in the cowline that was not dead had drifted clear out of the country. They had no fences down there then, but they had cowboy scouts out all over the country south and west. Gus had just returned from a trip to Pecos City and there was "Lazy S" cattle as far as he had heard from. The cowmen in all the Colorado and Double Mountain country had a meeting in Colorado City to plan what to do. Gus had sent for Mr. Slaughter, but he had not arrived. He said they were to hold another meeting two days later and he would write me later. After reading his letter, I decided maybe I had not fared so bad after all.

About the time I got Gus's second letter, I got letters from Slaughter and Mr, Morrison writing me of the storm at other places. Mr. Slaughter sent me a newspaper telling of the awful storms and the hardships it would bring on cattle interests everywhere. It was said afterwards to be the worst storm in the history of cattle business. They said all the cattle were gone from the head of Colorado River, also from Double Mountains. There was some cattle that had drifted in there from the north a long distance. After the check up on things when their scouts got in and reported, they said cattle in most places were on water. They were getting water to drink, but no grass.

By the time the men held a few meetings at Colorado it was getting up in February. It dawned on them that something had to be done. So, they had another meeting in Colorado City an elected Gus manager to take charge of the entire outfit of cattle and men. People for hundreds of miles around were interested in the move, for everybody's cattle was in the drift. They were not to try to separate the cattle, just drive all cattle back to the Colorado River. There were twelve outfits, that is twelve wagons and about ten to fifteen men each, a boss to each wagon and fifty horses. I was not there to see it, but men have told me that it was the biggest thing they had ever seen.

I don't suppose anybody ever knew how many cattle there were, for they were dying all the time. I think they put two thousand as near as they could in a herd. I expect when they rounded up a bunch with anywhere near the right number the wagon boss would take them and go and make room for the next man. The idea was to get them out of that country as fast as possible, before they all died.

My brother Dave O'Keefe worked with the outfit. He told me when they first started to work, they put all hands together and drove everything, just drifted along. When night came all went to camp, but next morning the cattle were as far back south as they were the day before when they started. They changed that plan then and gathered a herd of two thousand and turned it over to one wagon boss, had him take his men and start out on the trail for the head of the Colorado River. They were starting from Pecos River somewhere below Pecos City, and when a wagon boss was far enough ahead to keep out of the way, they gave boss No. 2 a herd and so on until they reached No. 12. They then had to wait until No. 1 could get back from the Colorado. The big job was to get water for all these herds. Gus made arrangements with the T & P Railroad for water.

I think Stanton was the last place, then they turned north to Sulphur Springs on Sulphur Draw, then twenty miles to the head of Rattle Snake Creek, a tributary of the Colorado River. Getting the railroad to furnish water was not all of their troubles. They had to get lumber to make troughs to water these herds. They got good carpenters to make the troughs. They did not risk cowboys with that. Mr. Joe Service, now living at Canyon City, was one of them. He said they moved lots of cattle by his place. Brother Dave said it was the worst job he ever had. Cattle poor, and not much grass, horses pretty well ridden down, and all those things put together made it mighty bad.

After that bad drift they went to building fences and it was not but a few years until most of the country was under fence. Running Water Ranch was already fenced, and had been for about one year. Goodnight, Adair and the T. Anchor ranches had only been fenced a short time, one or two years.

## Chapter 7

As time went on the changes came, the country changed from open range to a pasture country and from a free range to a leased country. Cowmen were put to great expense to lease land and improve it. They formed companies and leased large tracts of land and built fine houses. Their extravagance broke many of them. Cattle were very high priced in the early eighties. But when the slump came a little later, it seemed that half the cattlemen were broke.

Some of the older and more conservative men did not run so reckless. I mean such men as Charlie Goodnight, Bugbe, Gunter, Munson, all the Slaughters, Merchant and Paremore, Day and Driskel, Reyalds Brothers, J. L. Vaughn, Jim Carter, and others of that type stood the strain and came out of the slump. I remember, though, that Mr. Slaughter got in some mighty tight places and he had to ship lots of cattle to pay up when his creditors began to press him for money. He would write to Gus, his manager, to know if he could gather any fat cattle and how many.

Gus would go over the range and give him an estimate of what he thought he could gather; generally, the order would come back from Slaughter to gather that number and more if possible. When I first commenced working for them, I wondered why a man like Lum Slaughter would ever get in a tight for money, but I learned that big folks get in tights same as little ones. Late in life, when I had to rustle money to finance my own little business, I concluded that everybody was in a tight all the time. It did not look so hard, though, when the other fellow is doing all the rustling and having to do all the managing and losing the sleep over it. I was sympathetic with them, for I never was much of a spendthrift.

I never could see why they bought a herd of cattle, pay some cash and make notes for the balance. They were buying cattle all the time; that is for several years. I knew those notes had to be paid with fat cattle. Steer money, as far as it would go, and then make a run on fat cows and heifers, which they did not want to do, especially on young heifers for they were trying to build up their herd. The young females were what they wanted to keep.

They were usually good cattlemen and good judges of business. When Slaughter used to come to the outfit, he and Gus would sit up half the night and talk and plan how they would manage. I learned quite a bit from them by laying awake at night and listening to their plans and schemes. Slaughter, of course, was at the head of everything, but he almost always wanted to get Gus's ideas too. Sometimes they would differ on certain things and would fuss around for a while. Both of their heads was full of plans and schemes.

They certainly did make a good strong combination, if they did differ sometimes. Slaughter would sit in his office in Dallas planning things; like buying someone out. That is, buy another herd of cattle and pay for them out of the steer money on the ranch. Gus would have a list on his books; of the number of calves branded for that year and the thing would not meet. Then they would get into a little noisy conflab. If Mr. Slaughter went ahead and bought them and if they got in a tight over it, which they often did, Gus would in a kind of half-hearted way say, "I told you you'd get in a tight."

Slaughter would always say, "Oh, well, we will work out of this." and they always did.

They bought a herd of fifteen hundred steer yearlings from Mark Linn. When those steers were four years old, they kept account of them as they were shipped and gathered all of them. That showed how well they ran their business. Slaughter engineered the thing; Gus worked out the details and ran the ranch. It seemed as if he could get more work done than anybody. He was a good judge of men. Slaughter had two thousand cattle at the head of Colorado River in 1879 and put Gus in charge of the ranch.

At that time Slaughter had half interest in a herd of five thousand cattle with John Hulum and had half interest in three thousand cattle with John Scarborough. He bought all his partners out. That gave him nine thousand head. In ten years, they built that herd up to near fifty thousand cattle. During that time Gus bought an interest in the herd and kept it a few years; then sold it back to Slaughter. He remained with Slaughter several years then he bought the C. A. Ranch near Colorado City. When I left the Slaughter ranch to take charge of the Running Water Ranch, I carried with me some much-needed experience that I had learned under these two cranks, as I sometimes called them.

One trouble I had in handling cowboys was that they would drink and gamble. I did neither except once in a while I would take a drink with them just to be sociable, but not often, and I never gambled at all. That made me unpopular with them to some extent. I soon found out the older men respected me for it.

Talking about gambling and drink makes me think of how easy it can get men into trouble. While I was on the Slaughter Ranch a bunch of boys went to Big Springs to a picnic and got to drinking and having a general good time. The north part of town was the Mexican part. These Mexicans had more dogs and more kinds of dogs than I ever saw. They had the first hairless dogs I ever saw. They had woolly dogs. You could hardly see their eyes. Of course, they had the common old dog, the kind you see over the country. In passing through town that whole bunch of dogs took after the boys. They could not stand for that and they went to shooting at the dogs and killed some of them and crippled some others.

Of course, the Mexicans did not like that. The Mexicans, some of them, came out with their guns but did not do any shooting. I guess they felt the boys were partly justified for killing their worthless dogs and let it go. The boys saw the Mexicans did not like it. They had all the fun they wanted, put spurs to their horses, and ran off. The Mexicans threatened to prosecute them but that was as far as they went. It passed off and I guess they soon forgot it.

After I left the Slaughter Ranch and went to Running Water some of the same boys moved their camp out near Stanton in Martin County. They got to drinking in town one day and shot up the town, as they called it—shot some chickens and dogs, shooting up in the air and having lots of fun. The citizens began to bunch up in the streets and looked as if they might interfere. The boys saw the people did not seem very well pleased with the way they were acting. They ran off as they did at Big Springs.

But there came a time when all of them did not run out of town, for the settlers got tired of such foolishness and shot back at them and killed one cowboy. They did not see why they should sit there and let a bunch of wild cowboys, as they wanted to call themselves, have so much fun at their expense. So, I imagine they did a little planning too. Next time the boys' plans failed to work for the citizens were ready. When the boys began to shoot chickens as well as other things (but not at the people), the Stanton folks began to shoot at them. They killed John Dogie and shot a hole through Henry Mason's hat. The bullets began to sing around the other boys' heads. They decided to get away and they did.

I thought it was just too bad that John had to get killed for he was as good a cow hand as there was on the Slaughter Ranch or any other ranch for that matter. He was kind-hearted and a good worker, always at his place when there was work to do. I think he was just about the best calf flanker I ever saw. He would just take a big calf almost a year old and, as we boys called, bust him on the ground. Well, we know he did not bust the calf, but I expect if the calf could tell it he would think he was almost busted. Well, when the news of John Dogie s death came to me at Running Water, I certainly did hate to hear it. After I thought over it, I said there was a good boy and a good friend gone wrong.

One time while I was on Running Water Ranch, we had a bad prairie fire. In all the prairie country, grass that was dry would just go like powder. The fire would sway and maybe jump fifty feet, lap down and the next little puff of wind leap way out yonder. Whoever has seen a prairie fire has seen it sway and jump. This time it burned off most of the Plains country through our section. I had ploughed what we called fire guards. Ploughing two furrows next to the fence and two more furrows about seventy yards away made land look as if a farmer was going to plough up his field. This made a ring all around the pasture eighty miles long and seventy yards wide.

Then I burned this seventy-yard strip out clean and that gave us good protection. We saved our grass, while the grass was burned all around on three sides clean up to the fire guards. The sand hills protected grass on the south side of our pasture. That left a scope of country with grass on it that extended to the south prong of Yellow House Draw where Lubbock is now, but there was no Lubbock then.

One fellow had about 3,000 head of cattle in this outside country. Many others had cattle there too, but this particular man decided it did not look good. In fact, he told someone he would winter his 3,000 cattle in the Running Water pasture. I had a cowboy attending the fall work, that is the roundups on Blanco and lower Yellow House canyon. He heard of what this person said. When the roundups were over my men hurried on to the ranch and told me about it. I said all right, we will watch out for him. So I sent this boy and another good boy, or men they were, to the South camp. I told them to do their riding early every morning and late in the evening. I said he would try to slip them in at night and as his herd was south, he most likely would undertake that side. We figured it would take him at least five days to drive cows and calves that far.

In about ten days the boys found where he had pulled up the fence post and drove the cattle over. There were sand hills nearby and they drove the cattle up in these hills, hoping we would not find them until they mixed among our cattle. But the boys found them early one morning. One of the boys rushed to headquarters to let me know about it. We soon rounded them up and cut out what Circle O cattle there were. *Circle* was our brand. We got through cutting or separating the cattle just before dark, put them through the fence and started driving them south. Lucky for us a strong norther came up. We followed them a mile or so and turned back to south camp, highly pleased with our day's work, for we were sure those cattle would drift to Yellow House canyon (40 miles to the south). This was in December.

The next spring when the roundup started at Circle Ranch, this fellow sent his wagon boss and outfit expecting to gather his cattle. He did not find a cow in the Running Water pasture. About a year after this a friend of mine asked this man who turned his cattle in on us what he thought when he sent his outfit to Circle Ranch expecting to get 3,000 cattle and did not get a cow. He said, "Them dog-gone O'Keefe's are always watching. If they can't be there themselves, they have got somebody else watching for them." I saw this man many times after that but neither of us mentioned this incident.

I figured I had spent lots of money ploughing and burning the guards and he had not done anything, and I aimed to protect it. I guess he figured he had tried to do something that he knew was not right and that he better just let it go at that. He had about 200 cattle in the Running Water pasture before that. I did not stop until we put every one of his cattle out. I would have let these 200 remain if he had not done what he did.

There was often some fellow trying to steal our calves and we had to be on the lookout for that all the time. Some people say that everybody was honest in those days, but I did not find it so. There is a strange fact about some people, especially a cow thief. He will do most anything for you, help you out of trouble or distress. If he owed you money, he would try to pay it, even if he had to steal your cattle to pay it with. So the saying that everybody was honest in the early days does not hold good in all cases. It was then as it has always been and always will be, some good and some bad.

Mr. Hasting said they commenced stealing cattle in Jacob's time. When Jacob put the ring-streaked Poplar, Chestnut and Hazel poles around at the water troughs so when the cows and sheep and the goats came to drink, the off spring was of similar spotted or off colour; some speckled and spotted, some brown, and some white. Mr. Hasting said Jacob first got Laban to agree to let him have all the off-coloured cattle, sheep, and goats. The way Mr. Hasting told it was just too funny. Mr. Hasting was not a Christian man. He said that it was as good a thing as old Jake wanted. He got Laban to agree to let him have all the off-coloured cattle, sheep and goats. He said the old scamp stole all of Laban's cattle; that was, he stole all the increase.

Then, he would say to me, "Now Rufe, suppose I did that with this NUN outfit. I could get rich that way."

Mr. Hasting would talk that way about things, and yet he was tender-hearted and a man of fine character; there was nothing little about him. In his dealings, he was always on the square. He was my neighbour six years while I owned the OBR Ranch. My pasture joined the NUN Ranch on the south. We would work each other's ranges together and were together a great deal. I often wondered whether he meant half he said, for he would say some hard things about the church.

One time I went up to their ranch to work their range. They had sent me word that they would start the rounding up on a certain day. I went up and got there the evening before they were to start. Mr. Hasting and Jack Rogers, their wagon or range boss, had just come in from Lubbock where they got their mail. I asked what was the news at Lubbock. It was then a very small town. Mr. Hasting said Lubbock never got any news except when the mail hack came in or when a freight wagon came in from Colorado City.

Then he said, "Well, yes, they are raising cane over there with a protracted meeting. Everybody seemed to be interested and going to the meeting."

I asked him if he went.

He replied, "Hell, no, there was nothing to it. The damn thing would have played out long ago if it had not been for the women."

They told him at the hotel they would continue services for another week He thought they had better be at work.

Mr. Hasting kept a buggy and team and he not only drove his own team but fed and attended to them himself. He was afraid the boys might not feed them properly. They were nice big brown horses. He called them Jimmie and Dan. I was with him lots and I never did see him drive faster than a walk. He would go out with the outfit, have his roll of bedding and stay out for weeks at a time. He used to have me to ride with him. We would move camps in the evenings after branding up the calves and he would want me to ride with him for company. I did not like to do it at first, but next day I told Jack Rogers about it and felt I ought to help drive the cattle for we had a stray herd all the time.

Jack said, no, he had plenty of help with the cattle and said he was glad for me to ride in the buggy to be company for Mr. Hasting as he was then near eighty years old. I felt better about it then though I did not want to throw off on my job. Mr. Hasting used to drive his team to Colorado City and go to Chicago. Then he would have his team to drive back from Colorado City to the ranch.

Dick and Tol Ware had a ranch near Gail, Borden County. Mr. Hasting nearly always had a jug with him. One evening he drove up to the Ware Ranch to stay overnight and there was the usual bunch of boys there. He brought his jug up to treat the crowd. There was a fellow there named Bill Birdwell, from Big Springs, a great big fellow with a big stomach. He was really out there to cure himself of the drinking habit. He told Mr. Hasting he did not drink. Mr. Hasting said, "Why in the hell don't you take your sign down then." Of course, meaning his big stomach. Of course, Birdwell and Mr. Hasting were good friends and understood each other's jokes. Poor Mr. Hasting. I often wondered if he ever changed in his belief about the Bible and Christianity. Bob Ingersol said that kind of religion would do to live by, but would not do to die by.

The following spring after the big drive, we moved a herd from Slaughter ranch. Cattle were poor and were badly scattered for the cold hard winter before had played havoc with the cattle business. It took lots of hard work for ranchmen to get their cattle back home. Our cattle at Running Water, that did not freeze during the blizzard, had done pretty well. Especially the steers. The first of June, they ordered me to gather all that would do for beef and drive them to Kiowa, Kansas, for shipment.

Kiowa was the end of the Southern Kansas Railroad at that time. I worked the range well and gathered six hundred. We headed north for T. Anchor ranch. The boys there directed me how to go over a dim road to Dixon Creek Ranch. It led out near where Amarillo is now and north near where Panhandle City is now located. The Dixon Creek pasture fence had recently been built. I was told the distance to this fence and I made a hard drive to get into that pasture to camp so if the cattle should run, I would have the fence south of me to prevent them from drifting south. We got inside and camped just before dark.

As I rode towards the wagon, I saw a man on horseback coming over the road we had just come over. I wondered who it could be, for we had not seen a man that day outside our own outfit. As he got to camp, I recognised Wess Slaughter, a distant relative to Lum Slaughter. I knew him well. He said we were the hardest outfit to catch up with that he had ever seen. He had left T Anchor Ranch that morning and said they had sent him to catch me and turn me back. I thought it strange they would turn me back after I was half way to market. Then he handed me a letter from Gus that read:

"Turn your outfit of cattle, horses and men over to Wess Slaughter and he will drive it on to market. Please tell him all you know about the route or of anything that may help him. You bring wagon and team and six gentle horses. We have bought you fifty more young unbroken horses. Bring a bronco buster with you if you can get one. Your Brother, C. A. O'Keefe."

After I read the letter, we had supper. Then I showed Wess my bed and told him to unroll it and lay down and rest awhile.

I went to help bed the cattle and arrange the guards for the night. I got back in about an hour. Wess had gone to bed, but was not asleep. We talked half the night,

I guess. I joked him some; I told him I'd like to trade jobs with him, that was, I would like to drive this herd on and him go back and break that herd of bronco horses. He said he did not want to trade for any bronco job. Of course, this was all in fun, and we made the best of it. Then I told him all I had found out about the route, which was not much. Next morning at daylight the cook called us.

After breakfast, I rode around the herd and saw that everything was all right then bade the boys goodbye and pulled out for Running Water Ranch a hundred and thirty miles south. The first night I spent at T. Anchor Ranch, and the second night I was back to headquarters. I did not see a man after I left the herd, only the men at the T. Anchor Ranch until I got to Running Water. Little did I think then that there would one day be towns like Amarillo, Panhandle, Canyon, Tulia. If anybody had told me then what we know now, I would not have believed him.

The only thing I saw on this two days' hard ride was a coyote den and I killed one pup. It was on a high ridge covered with tall grass about eight miles south of Terra Blanca Creek. From there on there was nothing to see but just plains country and antelope until I got in the neighbourhood of Running Water. Then I began to see cattle and I knew I was getting close to home. My, but I was glad when I got there, for I surely was tired. It always tires me worse to ride straight down the road than it does to round-up cattle. I get my mind on the work and it does not tire me so much.

It took me one day to get team and wagon ready. I took one boy with me. We changed often; that is, one of us would ride horseback and the other would drive the team. Riding in the wagon felt good to me after those two hard days riding. It took us about six days to get to the Slaughter Ranch. We got there in the evening. Gus came in next day from the outfit. As usual, he asked me all the questions he could think of. He asked how far I had gone when Wess caught up with us. I told him about half way. He said that was bad, but they decided it best for me to come back and take charge of these young horses. He asked if I brought a horse breaker with me.

I told him I did not bring a professional, but he was all right after a horse had been ridden one or two saddles. I said I had some good riders, but had to let them go with Wess. He said it would be several days before he would have a herd of cattle ready and I could stay at headquarters and handle the horses. If any should get loose with saddles on, they would be in the pasture. We could get them.

Next day I went to Big Springs and got several boys and left word with a friend to send me some more. I told him none but good riders need apply. Of course, in those days, boys hunting jobs would tell you they were good riders, but you had to try them and see. I got five boys first day. I wanted eight, but next day we rounded up that bunch of broncos. There were a few of them that had been ridden for they had saddle marks on them. I tried to pick out and divide them equally among the boys. I told them to remember them as they rode them and they would be their mounts. Each of them were to have six horses. I had them to put hobbles on them after they rode them.

We got along pretty well the first day for we picked gentle ones. But the second day we had fun when the rope would go over their heads. I don't suppose some of them had had one on since they were colts and were branded. My, the way they would snort, pitch and even fight. I told these new boys that when the rope went on a horse for them all to grab the rope and help hold him and the wild rascal would soon choke himself down. We would hold him down until we saddled, blindfolded him and put hackamore or halter on him.

The boy would then mount and two of us would get gentle horses and would do what we called herd him. That is, we would ride beside him and keep him from running over a bluff or into a dangerous place. Some of the boys got pitched off and some would let their horses get loose when trying to handle them. Sometimes we would have two or three horses loose with saddles on at one time.

We then rounded up the whole bunch of horses. We had a good corral to handle them in. I soon found out that I had a good lot of boys, two of them were dandy good riders and understood working with young horses. We had one horse in that bunch that was not a young horse. He must have been seven or eight years old. He would fight if he could get to you. We roped him around the neck and tied the rope to the snubbing post in the centre of the lot, then put another rope on his front feet and get him down. He did not pitch as bad as some of the others, but he was stubborn and mean. When the boy got on him and pulled the blind, he would try to bite the boy's legs. He gave us more trouble than any of them.

We stayed there in the pasture headquarters about a week then moved outside so we could ride these young horses and help roundup cattle. When we got to making long rides, they would get pretty tired; that soon took all the pitch out of them. It took about another week to get the herd ready to start for Running Water. That made about two weeks. The horses had been ridden and most of them were so each man could handle them by himself. Some of us were mounted on gentle horses so we could help the fellow on a bronc if needed. When we got to Running Water, they were what we called half-broken horses. We did have trouble when we first moved from Slaughter Ranch and away from the corral, for we had to substitute a rope corral by tying a rope to trees and enclosing them in this rope corral. For the first few times some of them ran over the rope and gave us a little trouble that way.

When we got on the plains where there were no trees or bushes, the boys would have to use one side of the wagon by tying rope to the wheels and one boy stand at the end and hold the rope. This had to be done every evening and morning. In the evening they had to be hobbled and, in the morning, had to take the hobbles off and catch a new mount; this also had to be done at noon. You might say it had to be done three times each day. The more they were handled the sooner they would get gentle. Handling them in these rope corrals had a good effect on them. Most horses after they find out that you are their friends, like to be petted and they soon respond to kind treatment.

Of course, at first, you have to be rough with them until you conquer them. They are somewhat like a child and they seem to know when you treat them right. Of course, all are not alike for once in a while there will be some that never have any sense. We had one in this bunch that was that way.

When Gus and Henry Mason finally delivered the cattle to me, which had been a big job to gather after the hard winter before had scattered them so badly, we only had about twelve hundred. I was very glad that I had a small herd to drive with those half-broken horses and new men, or rather, boys. When you had an outfit of that kind it made it pretty hard on the boss. These were a pretty good bunch of kids, anxious to learn. Before I started on the trail, I picked out two who seemed to be the best posted.

I put them at the front end of the herd, one on each side to keep the cattle pointed right and to keep them from scattering. I wanted to be at the back end to keep them from crowding the calves too much. We called that taking care of the drags. Sometimes calves would give out and we would haul them to the next stop, times the herd would be strung out half mile and when the calves would give out, I would send somebody up and have the pointers to stop the lead cattle.

We let the herd graze while the calves rested. Sometimes we would fix some way to haul them. One way was to stretch a beef hide under the wagon and tie the calf or calves, for sometimes there were two or three calves and if there were more than that it was just too bad. When we would get to the first water, we would lay up; that is, stay there until the calves rested so they could keep up with the herd. Sometimes it would take two or three days, this particular time we made a long drive from the head water on Tobacco Creek to head water on Yellow House. It's over fifty miles and we had to be out two nights without water. The first day at noon we were in reach of Tahoka Lake.

There was a small spring of fresh water there. I sent the horse rustler and cook with the wagon on to this spring to water the horses and get dinner.

The balance of us grazed the cattle slowly, for we had to take care of them for the long drive to Lubbock next day. We got within about five miles of the spring at twelve o'clock noon. I let half of the men go to the wagon and get dinner and change horses to come back and relieve us. We were still holding the herd near, where they had left us, only the distance they had grazed. Some of the boys thought we should drive up to the wagon. It was then about two o'clock. I sent these boys that had remained with me on to get their dinner. I took one of the boys that had had dinner and told him to stay at the back end and take care of the calves, not to let the cattle drive, but just let them graze as they wanted to and not let them string out as we had been. I would go see how we would go around the lake.

It was dangerous to let the herd get too near for when they could smell the alkali salt water they might get so we could not hold or control them, and to drink a lot of alkali water would kill cattle. I told him all this to give him a good scare. When I got my dinner and a fresh horse, I soon picked out my route. I told the cook to fill his kegs with water. He had one on either side of the wagon. I told him we would make a dry camp that night and to save all the water possible. He asked what I meant, for he was a new man of the plains.

I said, "I mean don't let anybody wash hands or faces except yourself, for we may run out."

When I got to the herd, I found the new boss, I called him, had done as I told him. I looked the calves over as they started out and they were all right. I told this new boss I did not know how they will look this time tomorrow. He asked how far it was.

I told him about thirty miles. I wanted to make a confidant of him, for I needed him.

I saw that he became more interested in it. His name was George May.

I said, "You stay at, or near, the front and don't let the cattle string out like we have been doing. We must keep them so we can control them. If you get in a tight place, you wave your hat to me and I will come to you. I will be back with the drags. In the morning you ride your best horse and tell the other boys to ride their best horses, for we may have some hard luck. We have got to make the best of it."

"I want you to take half the boys and hold the herd till midnight, and I will take the other three and hold them till daylight. That made four men for each guard, instead of two men as we had before."

I knew it was too risky for two men. Next morning, I had the cook up and the horses in the corral; everything was ready to move by daylight; in fact, we had the cattle traveling when daylight came. We got several miles of good traveling for a herd of cows and calves. We stopped and grazed as long as they would and let the drags rest. After that we threw them on the trail, we got good traveling out of them for ten miles, for the leaders had gotten dry for water.

The boys had to ride in front and hold them instead of driving. It was a case of holding back. At twelve o'clock we held up for dinner. We had to round them up in a close bunch in order to hold them. That done, I send George and his three boys to dinner while three boys and I herded the cattle. We were then two days and nights without water and those cows were restless. We had nearly ten miles to go to water.

Immediately after dinner we sent the cook and horse rustler on to water. We eight boys starved with that herd and just before sunset we drove the last ones into water. I let George take his three boys and get supper and change horses, but instead of going to supper it took all eight of us to hold and quiet them down. The balance of us did not get supper until late, then we had to go one at a time. Cows and calves just seem to almost go crazy after a long drive. One boy's horse fell with him that evening and broke his arm. I had had my own arm broken once. We got him to the wagon. I had the cook help pull his arm back till we heard it snap in place. We had nothing but salt and water to put on his arm to cool it.

We remained there two days to keep the cattle on the water, let them rest and hunt for any that might have gotten away during the siege. Cows and calves, if they can, will go back to where the calf last sucked his mother, for he will go back to get his dinner. I sent George May, for he had by this time gotten to be a good assistant, and one other boy back to where we stopped last time. They got one cow and calf.

I found out at Singer's store that it had not rained any towards Running Water.

I knew that meant another fifty miles drive to water and we prepared the best we could for it. We had water up the north draw of Yellow House. For three miles we grazed along up the draw and left the water in the evening and only went about three miles and camped the first night aiming to get near enough to Eagle Springs to get water for our horses. Next day at noon we went right up that draw ten or twelve miles. The grass was fine and we could not make much time. Some of the boys would get impatient and want to crowd them.

I told them, "No, don't do that; just let them have all the grass they could eat and then they would want water."

We would make good time for a dry cow will sure walk for water. So instead of our getting to Eagle Springs for noon, we got there that night. We had plenty of water for the horses and to camp with, but none for the cattle. The next day it rained and we had plenty of water. The grass from there on was good, but, my, how slow we did move. I guess five or six miles a day was as far as we would go. I let half of the boys at a time go to the wagon and sleep for we were all behind on sleep. We had been up most of the night for several nights. When we got in about twenty miles of the ranch, I left George May in charge of the herd. I wanted to get my mail and see how things were at the ranch, for I had been away a month.

When I got to the ranch, I found Mr W. D. Johnson there. Mr. Johnson was one of the owners of the ranch, the one that I had never seen. He was a coal mine operator in Iowa and Illinois. He also had interest in a cattle ranch near Vernon with his brother-in-law, Dick Worsham. He had come by there on his way out to Running Water. I spent that evening at the ranch and next morning Mr. Johnson and I went back to the herd in his buggy. I, of course, led my horse. We had lots to talk about. I found his main business was mining, but I asked him how he liked the cow business. He did not like it. The reason was we brand the calves in the spring and summer, turn them loose and never see them again.

He did not like that; if he had anything, he wanted it where he could see it and know that he still had it. He said he was going to sell out and quit the cow business. I soon found out he did not mean all he said, for just before that he said that this ranch ought to fence up a much larger country and form a big pastoral company and take in cattle to pasture. They could make more money off pasturing cattle than they could on what they owned. His two talks did not fit, but he was a good talker. I enjoyed listening to him. We got to the herd about dinner time, had our dinner; then we drove out and looked at the cattle as they were scattered and most of them laying down.

I told him you could see what we had here in this herd, for they were not trying to get away. He said, yes, that was what he liked and he enjoyed driving around among them. He asked me how many; I told him a little over twelve hundred. He said it looked like four thousand for they were scattered. He asked if we would get to the ranch that night. I was surprised and said, no, that we were eighteen or twenty miles from the ranch. I said we would camp tonight and tomorrow night; then the next evening we would be in sight of the camp. He thought we could drive them in this evening and asked why not start them in now (it was then about one o'clock and very hot).

I said, no, that those cows and calves were doing more good resting than anything they could do. The herd had to make two fifty-mile drives without water, it's been might hard on them and they need rest. I decided to let them lay there until three or four o'clock, then punch them up and keep grazing. That way we would get them two miles, maybe three, by camping time. I could tell he did not like what I said very well. He asked, if I was going with him to the ranch. I said, no, that I will stay with the cattle to keep the boys from driving the calves too hard. I would be over next day.

When I left the ranch a month before, I had left Jack O'Malior in charge. Next day when I got to the ranch Jack had just come in from somewhere. I asked him how everything was. He said it had been awful dry until the last few days, but everything was looking better. I asked him how he liked Mr. Johnson, our new boss.

He replied, "I don't like him a damn bit; he is an old fool."

Jack asked me how I liked him.

I said, "You remember Mr. Morrison told us Mr. Johnson was peculiar, but was all right after you knew him." I said that from what I had seen of him and heard him talk, I thought he would prove to be a regular blow hard and want to brag about what he has. I think the best way is just let him have his own way unless he gets to interfering with the work, then we might have trouble with him. He owned a fourth interest in the ranch and, of course, wanted to have something to say about things.

Jack said that was the trouble; he said too much. He asked me if Johnson wanted to boss me about the herd.

I said, "Yes, he told me I ought to drive the herd to the ranch in one evening, twenty miles. I told him it would take two or three days after that evening."

Jack said, "That's the way the old fool has been doing around here; he hasn't got any sense."

I said, "I think the best way to handle Mr. Johnson is to treat him nice and then go on and do the work like he was not there. That's the way I did the other day. He seemed to get along all right."

But Jack could not see it that way for they had trouble every once in a while. I found out Mr. Johnson was a very nervous man and full of energy, always wanting to be doing something and oft times he wanted to do the wrong thing. Jack O'Malior said he always wanted to do the wrong thing. As time went on, we learned more about Mr. Johnson. Instead of selling out as he had told me he was going to do, he kept his interest in the ranch and came out every summer. He was a trouble maker. Jack said that he had rather be bothered with the seven-year itch.

One time we were working, gathering steers, and were too busy to stop cutting cattle for dinner. It was three o'clock when we got through and turned the roundup loose down on the creek. I told Johnson that he, two other boys and I would stay and hold the cut until Jack could take the rest of the boys and get dinner, come back and relieve us. I could see he did not like it, but he did not make any kick about it then. Jack and his boys, four of them, ran a race down to the house about three miles. Jack sent one boy to round-up the horses while the rest of them ate dinner, so they could hurry back to relieve us.

It was surprising how quick they got back. Mr. Johnson said, by gad, he was going to dinner and started off in a trot. He never rode faster than a trot. Before he got there, he met Jack and his boys coming back as fast as they had gone. When I got to the house, the first place I went was to the well to get a drink, as all of us did. We had a milk house that opened out near the well. There was a nice milk trough for the cook to keep milk and butter in. She kept milk in crocks so the cream would rise on it. Then we would skim and churn it.

As I got my drink of water, I heard someone in the milk house and looked to see who it was. It was Mr. Johnson. He wore a long beard and moustache and the old dickens had cream all over his whiskers and moustache. The old rascal tried to laugh it off and be funny about it, but it was not funny to me. I went on and washed and was eating dinner when he came in. The cook was Mrs. Breeding and she waited on us at the table.

I said, "Mrs. Breeding, if you don't get much butter next time you churn, you just charge it up to Mr. Johnson for I caught him stealing your cream a while ago."

The other three boys laughed and enjoyed the joke, and to cap it off, Mrs. Breeding said that she thought something had been wrong with her milk lately. Well, the boys just roared. I was sorry that Jack was not there for he would have gotten more fun out of it than any of them. When we got out to where the other boys were, we told them about it. The whole bunch was mad about it. Jack said he was not surprised, "a damn hog would always be a hog."

Next day we rounded up on the opposite side of the ranch and, of course, Mr. Johnson was there. We would take it time about cutting, that is, two would cut for a while and then change and let two others cut; that way resting our horses. Mr. Johnson was no help because he would not let his horse run to head a cow. Johnson would ride in and cut out five or six head, heifers, cows, calves or just anything. I saw him do that a time or two. I had told him as well as all the boys, we did not want to cut anything but steers. This time I decided I would not let him do it. It just made a lot of hard work for we boys. I was mad at him for drinking the cream anyhow. I would not let the whole bunch go out. He asked what did I mean. I told him I meant to hold all those cattle back, but the steers.

I said, "Now make your horse jump at him and jump him out."

He said that his horse was no account.

I said, "I will change horses with you. I will ride your horse and you can ride mine."

He replied, "No, that son-of-a-gun would jump from under me."

The truth was, he could not ride a good cutting horse. I told him no one else was trying to cut the cattle in bunches and I did not want him to do it.

I said "You cut out six head to get one; there by making the work five times harder for the boys. If you will cut one at a time, it's all right, but you must not cut out a lot of cattle we do not want."

He said, by gad, he would go to the house; I told him that was the best place for him. That night he was all right and in a good humour. I expected him to be a little sore about it. I found out the old rascal did not care for us fussing at him. I think it was a part of his religion.

After Johnson left the roundup ground, some of the boys that heard me fussing about the cutting of the cattle told Jack about it and here he came around where I was, just dying laughing.

He said, "I thought you said you could get along with him."

He asked why Johnson went off. I told him Johnson said if he could not cut like he wanted to, he would go home. I said that was the best place for him.

Jack said, "The damn old fool would fight."

I asked him how he knew it. He said because he told him one day down at the corral, if it was not for his age, he would give him a "damn good whipping."

Old Johnson said, "Young man, don't you let my age have anything to do with your business."

Jack was so tickled he could hardly tell the story. I told Jack that I knew I was riding a better horse than Johnson, and if he wanted to fight, he would have to catch me first. I knew he could not do that. It was funny to see how the other boys collected around to find out what all the fun was about. Some of them came in from the back side of the roundup. They all bunched up and enjoyed the fun. Our horses were tired, anyway, and a little rest did them good.

I told the boys, "Jack said he had rather have the itch than have Johnson around, and now we were rid of the itch, let's get to work."

They were a dandy lot of boys, not a lazy bone in their hides. Every one of them knew his place. One of them said that he guessed the old devil would go to camp and drink up all the cream again. I don't know if he did or not, but we were glad to get him away from the herd for we had all we could do without being bothered with him. We had to night herd these steers as we gathered them. It's hard work to round up a bunch and night herd with eight men and that was the reason we were careful not to let anything in the herd that did not belong. We were gathering one- and two-year-old steers to be delivered at Buffalo Springs, Texas, to the Capital Syndicate Company.

## Chapter 8

Before we were through gathering the steers, the two Morrisons and their wives came to the ranch and brought orders for me to start the cattle north, that Mr. Slaughter and his wife were on their way and would follow me up. I left at noon one day and the next day I found water in the middle of Tule Draw and camped there that night. In the evening all of the men, not any women came, camped with us. We killed a nice fat calf for supper, and after dark Mr. Slaughter sent a boy to the herd to tell me to come to the wagon he wanted to talk with me. He asked me if I could deliver that herd. I told him I could drive them up there, but I had rather that he would deliver them, to see to the business end of it.

He said he thought I could do it all right. I said that I will try, at least, to do my best. He could not go and said Johnson wanted to go, but would do more harm than good. He then said he would stay at the ranch a while. He would get Johnson and the Morrisons to help him drive a lot of cattle to Tule Draw as the grass was fine there. That would keep Johnson busy and keep him from going with me and the boys. He did not want to hurt Johnson's feeling and asked what I thought about the plan.

I said, "If you will do that, I will take care of this herd and deliver them in as good shape as possible."

None of the boys liked Johnson anyway. Of course. Slaughter and I were off talking to ourselves. After we understood each other about Johnson, we went back where Johnson and the Morrisons were and talked in a general way. He was an old trail man himself.

Slaughter was a great man to ask questions. He asked me if I knew the way to go. I told him I knew how to start and to get to Tierra Blanca Creek where we would water first. I would stay there to scout and see what was ahead. He said that was right, always know where is your next water. He also said to watch the boys with the drag end of the herd, not to let them crowd them and not to try to make fast time. I was glad he said that so Johnson could hear it. He asked when I thought I would be back. I said I thought inside of three weeks. He said he, Morrison and Johnson could round up and drive a herd from Running Water to Tule Draw and put them on good grass.

I said, "Well, that would be fine; but you fellows are getting a little old to turn cowboy."

I joked them about getting young again.

Slaughter said, "Well, we will drive them slow and take plenty of time so as not to hurt them."

Then he asked where would be the easiest place to gather good sized herd. I said just west of the ranch at the mouth of the north draw. They would be easy to start from that point and let them drift up the north draw to the first bend, then point them out on the east side of north draw. I said that you can get three thousand there with little riding. Someone said it was getting bedtime. We looked and it was eleven o'clock. I told them I would divide my bedding with them. Slaughter laughed and said, "I'll bet you have not got enough for yourself."

"He thanked me and said they had brought their own bedding with them. I bade them goodnight and started to bed. Slaughter said "Wait a minute; I just thought of something. Gus O'Keefe and Campbell had some trouble at Spring Lake over the ages of steers, and if Campbell receives your herd, he may try to give you some trouble. Yours is a good class of cattle and you ought not to have any trouble, but just make the best deal with them you can."

That was just like Slaughter to think of business up until the last moment. I had told the cook to have breakfast in time to eat before daylight so we could get an early start.

Next morning as soon as it was light, I rode to see about the herd. I told Jack to graze them north and I would go back to see Slaughter, for he would think of something else to tell me.

Jack said, "I hope they don't let old Johnson go."

As I got back to camp. Slaughter and the others were finishing breakfast. Slaughter asked if the cattle gave much trouble in the night. I said no, that we had penned some of the mean ones a night or two before we left the ranch. He said that always helped. Then he cautioned me again about Campbell and the Syndicate outfit.

Johnson said, "Yes, by gad, you want to watch that outfit. I am afraid they will try to work you."

I thought, my, I wonder if he will go anyway. I was so scared I did not stay long for fear he would take a notion to go. One thing I did know, if Johnson took a notion to go the jig would be up. I bid them goodbye and they all wished me luck. I felt good riding away without Johnson. When I caught up with the herd, Jack asked if I got rid of old Johnson.

I told him yes, "and it's up to us now. Let's get them up there and deliver them in as good shape as possible. They have trusted this herd of nineteen hundred cattle to us, now let's do our best."

I looked on Jack as my main man and helper. I told him what Slaughter said about Gus and the Syndicate outfit having trouble and to be on the lookout.

He said, "I will be right with you."

I have thought often about how funny it was soon as we would get rid of one trouble, we began to look for some other trouble. We were both glad we had gotten rid of Mr. Johnson. Now, we were looking for or rather wondering, if trouble was in store in delivering this herd. We grazed the cattle for two hours, but kept them going north. We were beyond where our range cattle would graze. It was too far from water, so we had plenty of time to talk before we put the cattle to traveling. We mentioned what a nice country it was to handle a herd of cattle.

I said there was just one thing lacking and that was water, for after we left middle Tule, we did not find any more water until we got to Tierra Blanca Creek. There had been rain enough to make grass, but not enough to put out surface water. We had a good time, nothing to do but watch the steers fill themselves. About nine o'clock they began to travel. I told Jack and Lee Shipman to work at the head of the herd and I would be at the back. If they got in trouble to wave their hats and I would come to them. We soon had them strung out and traveling good. We travelled ten or twelve miles. I told Jack to take the wagon and camp about two miles ahead of the herd; he and his three boys to change horses and come to relieve us. I knew we were several miles from water, but I knew we would get good traveling out of the cattle when they wanted water.

At one o'clock we were all through with dinner. I told the cook and horse rustler to follow the herd. We had not gone but a few miles when we could see the breaks of Tierra Blanca Creek. Then we had trouble holding the cattle back to keep them from running. I sent all the boys up to the front end but one, and he and I did not have anything to do but follow up. About four o'clock we got in on the creek, about ten miles east of where Hereford is now located. It was a fine place to water a herd. Deep blue holes of water, deep enough to cover the backs of the cattle. Some of them would jump off the banks and some were crowded off. They would swim around and drink as they went. It is a pretty sight to see a dry herd have such a feast. We camped that night and remained on the creek next day until watering time.

Luck was with us, for the Syndicate outfit sent a man to pilot us up the trail. He told us we would find a good lake of water about ten miles ahead. We left Tierra Blanca about three o clock in the afternoon. We made a dry camp that night and made it to the lake by ten o'clock the next day. From there on we found lake water until we got to the Canadian River. I asked Jack if he had had much experience in crossing cattle over streams and especially quick sand. He replied, yes, and that he had had plenty of trouble. I had found it the same way. I told him to hold up the leaders about a half mile this side of the river and we would round them up in a close bunch. That way the drags would push the leaders in and we would keep crowding the drags.

"You pointers stay at your places at the point and I think we will make it all right."

We worked it that way, had every man, eight of us, to his place. We did not have any trouble like Dick Malone and I had down in the Indian Territory on the same river. We were about twenty miles above Tascosa when we had a surprise. We saw the chuck wagon go across without bogging at all. We had expected trouble with it. We had the sixty horses driven right behind the cattle and the chuck wagon to follow them. The cattle and loose horses seemed to pack the sand, for it was almost as solid as the road out on the prairie. Our pilot, the Syndicate man, piloted us to a spring branch where we camped for dinner.

We were then inside of the Capital Syndicate lands. We found plenty of water, but very little grass. The best and all the grass we had at this place was in the river valley or on some of the creeks, tributaries to the Canadian River. They had not had rain and the range had been heavy stocked the winter before. The cattle had just been thrown out and they were finishing up the fencing preparatory to stocking it.

I wondered if the country was like this all the balance of the way up, for we were about one hundred miles from Buffalo Springs. I looked up our pilot to find out. He said most of the trip would be hard on account of it being dry. He said for thirty or forty miles it would be like this. I told him we would drift along and not drive much, for as I saw it, we had to depend on the creek valleys for grass. He said there was another creek about eight miles from where we were. I decided we would graze over there for dinner next day. I asked him what was the name of that creek. He laughed and said it was Ponthadeiwa and said it means in Spanish, "plenty of water." We had nothing else to do that evening but kill time and let the cattle eat up what grass there was.

I asked him all about the country, for he seemed to be well posted. He said this creek led in our direction for several miles and if I wanted to stay on the best grass that it might be the best route, but it would be a little further. I said I did not want to lose too much time, but I did want grass for these cattle and so a few miles wouldn't hurt. He changed his route just a little. He said then the Syndicate Company had a camp about twenty miles ahead and he was to go on ahead of me and report when I would get there. We found the grass some better. Our pilot led us to a good camping place and ate dinner with us, then said he would go on to their camp, report, get a fresh horse and come back and meet the herd next day. Before he left, he gave directions how to go to the next creek. He called it Alamocetus.

Next day we grazed over and found plenty of water, but not much grass. Our pilot brought two other Syndicate men with him. A Mr. Owens, the boss of that division of the Capital Syndicate outfit, had with him Mr. Ruck Tanner. Mr. Tanner was a typical cowboy; he showed it in his looks and ways. He was a very sociable fellow, had plenty to say and cracked jokes. As we followed the cattle along, he asked me if the boy they sent down to meet me had been much help to me. I told him he certainly had. By his being along, it allowed me to keep all my men with the herd as well as myself and did not have any trouble at all to find water and camp sites, of course, we had to make pretty long drives to water, but he could not help that and he told me the grass would be short after we got to the Canadian River.

I said, "You need not be afraid to send this fellow to meet any herds you have coming, for you can't beat him. He pays close attention to things, he knows directions well for he did not miss any point he aimed to make."

Tanner said he had known this boy a long time and he knew the country well. He was glad they had sent the right man. I asked Mr. Tanner if he was manager here for the Syndicate. He said no, that Mr. Owens, yonder, was manager. He was just a straw boss, that is, he was their wagon boss and distributor for the herds. I asked him what he meant by distributing the herds. He said that as the herds were received and branded at Buffalo Springs they had to be placed on water and grass. He said it was a job to find the grass, that right now water was mighty scarce at Buffalo Springs. He said I had good cattle and asked how many. I said that I counted them off the bed ground yesterday morning and had all I started with. He laughed and said, "Good cowboy," then said he had to go and left me.

I then went up to Mr. Owens. He was a different looking man from Mr. Tanner. He wore a white starched shirt and looked as clean as if he had just jumped out of a band box. I was surprised when I saw he did not have on knee pants. I tried to like him; I asked if he was the manager. He said, "Yes sir."

I saw he was observing the drags pretty close. He asked, "Where did you get those calves?"

I told him we raised calves down on the Running Water Ranch, that was the way we made our living.

About that time the cattle were getting well in on the creek to water. I said, "Mr. Owens, we will stop here and check up my horse."

I told him I was glad they had come to meet us and that I hoped we would have better grass from there on than we had the last few days. He said that I would be disappointed, for it was very dry. I asked him how far it was to Buffalo Springs and he said about seventy miles. He did not have much to say and seemed to be a little bit hard boiled. I told him the breaks looked as if it should be a good cattle country, but seemed that it had been badly over stocked. I still could not get much out of him. I began to think the best way to do a fellow like that was to let him soak a while. I let him alone for a while. Not long after that, the cook hollared chuck. I asked him to come and eat dinner with us. He thanked me and said his wagon was just above our camp on the creek, which I could see, and he would go up there for dinner.

Before we separated, he asked what time I would move camp. I saw it was about twelve o'clock and I said about three or four o'clock. I said, if I have seventy miles ahead of me, I can make that in three days for my cattle are pretty well rested. He asked me not to move until he got back, that he wanted to talk to me after dinner. I replied, all right and we both started off in a lope. I wondered as I rode to the wagon, what he wanted to talk about. I had tried to get him to talk for the last two hours. I imagined he must want to kick about the yearlings (calves he called them). I reasoned that his partner Mr. Tanner had complimented me on having good cattle, then I wished it was Tanner I had to deal with. I told the boys to let the herd graze where we were until three or four o'clock. After dinner I crawled under the wagon for a rest and waited to see what the white boss wanted.

About two o'clock, Mr. Owens and Mr. Tanner came. I noticed at a distance they seemed to be talking very interestedly. First thing I thought of, he is telling Tanner about those calves he saw. I guessed they are hatching up some trouble for me. About that time another man galloped up and introduced this third man to me as Mr. Campbell, a cousin to the Mr. Campbell that was the general manager of the Syndicate at Yellow House Ranch. I had met the other Mr. Campbell, but this was the first time I had met Mr. M. C.

M. C. was quite a talker and a very pleasant fellow. I found out from him that he had just delivered some cattle to this company at Spring Lake. He said he met Gus O'Keefe while he was delivering a herd at the lake and we had quite a visit. After a while, Mr. Owens asked me how would it suit me to deliver my herd there and brand them. I said I did not know about the branding, but I was willing to count them out to him. He said, no, we could count them as we branded them. I said that will take a lot of time. He asked how many men I had. I said eight mighty good hands.

"How many have you," he asked Ruck Tanner. Ruck said eight and said we would have plenty of men. I said, no, we would have to hold two herds. That way it would take four of my men to hold those branded; then they might mix up again.

I said, "I don't like the plan."

He said, "You make me a proposition then."

I had Jack posted to stay and hear the talk as well as his men. I told him I would help him brand the cattle after he had received them.

I said, "I will cut out the one-year-olds from the two's and then you can look them over until you are satisfied. We will move them far enough apart so there will be no danger of them mixing and count them. Count the other bunch and you give me a receipt for them, then I will take my outfit and help brand."

He said, "Suppose we lose some of them."

I said, "We have both outfits and we can round up the country until we get them, but if we should miss a few head, they will be here in your own pasture and you can get them later."

He said his company did not like to receive them until the brand went on them. I replied, "That way it will take two men all the time to check them as they are branded and if we make any mistakes, which we will, then that stops the whole outfit of sixteen men. Now, why not do the counting before we start branding, then get in the pen and put the hot stuff to them. You have no shute and I tell you it's no child's play to rope nearly two thousand steers and brand them. If you will do as I suggested, I will undertake it. First thing, the cattle will be at your risk, that is, if any are killed or crippled by roping them. They are your cattle."

Mr. Owens asked Ruck what he thought about it. Ruck said it looked like a fair proposition. He said, "As Mr. O'Keefe says, it's a good big job to rope and brand over nineteen hundred cattle. By doing that we will have lots of men, then the classing of the cattle on the prairie might cause some trouble."

"Well," I said, "You would have the same trouble in the pen, then you would have to stop the whole works."

He said that was so. Then Owens asked Campbell what he thought about it. Campbell said at Spring Lake the other day, Gus O'Keefe wanted to class and count the cattle before they penned them. Campbell did not want to do it that way and said that it took up lots of their time. He said they not only took up lots of time, but it was so hard of the cattle, throwing them to examine their teeth. M. C. said if he was doing it, he had rather receive them before beginning the branding because he thought it saved time and was a better way. M. C. Campbell helped me out. At first, I thought they had brought him along to work against me, for Mr. Slaughter had told me about Gus and Barbeg Campbell having their trouble.

After M. C. made that statement, I said, "Mr. Owens, it is up to you now."

He said he had been studying it over and concluded that it was the best way.

I said, "Now you understand you are to give me the receipt for them when they are counted and not when they are branded?"

He said, "Yes."

I then asked the others if they understood it, and they all did. I told Mr. Owens I would have the boys scatter the cattle out to eat what little grass there was. We would graze just as long as they could see tonight, and by two o'clock the next day we would have them separated and ready to look at. I told Jack to lope up to the herd and tell the boys our plan and for him to stay with them to see that they got the best grazing they could find. I felt better, for Mr. Owens had warmed up to me and was more talkative. But still, I knew there could come some trouble in classing the cattle. I felt glad that M. C. was not against me; that was worth something.

When the boys found out what we had done, it was the talk around the camp that we would soon turn back towards the ranch. They were getting tired of the trail and too much night guard. Some of them said they never wanted to see another trail herd. You could hear all kinds of remarks and they did not mean a little of them. I told them they had lots of hard work to do before they were done with the herd. They said they did not mind to work in the daytime, just so they could sleep at night. I said that two more nights, I believed, will wind it up. They were tickled at that.

Next morning, a little after sunrise, we were cutting the herd. I told Jack we would put two boys in the herd at a time, then change off and let their horses rest, for him to save his horse and we would finish them up. Well, I never saw boys work better than they did. Every man seemed to know we were about through and did his best. For two hours we held the herd up close together and that forced all the little cattle, one-year olds, on the outside and it was easy to cut two and three, sometimes a half a dozen, at a time. Jack said that if old Johnson had been there, he could have cut these yearling in bunches, but he rather cut them one at a time than have to put up with Johnson.

Well, we had lots of fun as well as hard work. Tanner and his men came pretty early and helped out. About nine-thirty I told Jack we would finish up. I soon saw the boys had made a pretty good job of it, so we did not cut very many. Then I told Jack we must look close in turning, that is, cutting the yearling herd, for that was what we were interested in. We found a few two-year-olds in the yearling herd, but they had run in no doubt. The boys hadn't cut them in. By twelve o'clock we had them ready and they looked through the two-year-olds and said they were satisfied. Then they rode in the yearling herd, but they had found mighty small

I said, "Mr. Owens, there might be a few that are not quite a year old, but look over there, there is one, two or a half a dozen that are almost two-year-olds."

He said, yes, that was so, and asked Tanner what he thought about it. Tanner said the two-year-old bunch was all right, but a few yearlings were just a little short, ages, but as Mr. O'Keefe said, there were some long ages and taking the average, he thought they were all right. Owens said, all right, they were ready to count them. It did not take but a little while to count them. He gave me a receipt for so many one-year-olds. I don't remember the exact number, but it was the number we started with, over nineteen hundred. I asked how we should handle them. He said he would leave that up to me.

I suggested we leave the big steers where they were with two men to hold them and put the one-year-olds on the water with three men to hold them until the balance of us had our dinner. Then we could put about half of the yearlings in the pen and go to branding. Then put all the balance in one herd and let them graze until we branded the bunch out. Owens said his men could hold one bunch.

I said, "We will hold them this evening and you can hold them tomorrow."

That was understood and we all hurried and ran a race to the wagon for dinner. We all had fresh mounts after dinner. We put about six hundred yearlings in the pen and the fun began. We had four men on horses that roped the yearlings by the hind feet and dragged them down. The boys would jump on their shoulders and we would brand them in a hurry. We got Mr. Owens, the white shirt gentleman, to tally. We branded one hundred and twenty the first hour, or two steers per minute. We could not keep that up. We stopped and rested a few minutes, then tackled them again.

We were just two days branding them. We commenced at noon and got done at noon. For convenience, we had camped both wagons at the pen and had gotten better acquainted. We got along fine. Mr. Owens was a very agreeable gentleman after I learned how to take him. Mr. Tanner was agreeable from the first. In the evening we bade them goodbye and they went one way and we went the opposite. I never saw either of them again.

We camped that night about twenty miles from Tascosa. Next morning, we got to Tascosa and camped and bought some clean clothes. Most of our shirts had gotten torn off branding those steers. There was a mercantile firm there named Cone and Duran. Mr. Cone was an American, Duran was a Mexican, and it was said they made a good combination. It was a surprise to me to see so large a stock of goods as they had in a country store like that. I had heard a lot of the stories about the bad men of the west congregating at Tascosa and the killings there and Boot Hill Cemetery. Billy The Kid and others used to make their raids on the Canadian River above Tascosa and drive off whole herds of cattle. That was all in the past when we were there. Billy The Kid had been killed seven or eight years. Some of our boys said we needed not be afraid if he had been dead that long.

A man named Jess Jenkins, who operated a saloon, took great interest in telling us some of the past history of the town. He told us the number of men that had been killed there with their boots on, but I don't remember the number. He told many other interesting stories about the Indians and Mexicans of the early days. I am sorry that I did not make some notes on some of the things he told about. He told about the cowboys strike that happened a few years before we got there. He seemed to have known them. He said, some of the would-be bad men, started the strike so they could get more money, but it was short lived and most of the leaders lost out and left the country.

After taking in the sights at Tascosa and spending one night there, we started for Running Water. Nothing unusual happened, only we had several good rains and it delayed our traveling on account of the muddy roads. Grass was coming up at the ranch and things looked much better than when we left with the herd three weeks before. I was glad to get back; although it was just a dugout, it seemed like home to me.

Mr. Slaughter and Mrs. Slaughter had gone back to Dallas. Mr. Johnson, the trouble maker, had gone to his home in Iowa. Mr. Newt Morrison and his family were still there, and, of course, Mr. Morrison wanted to know how we got along with the herd. I told him and he wanted to know if we got there with the full number we started with. I told him we did. He then wanted to know if we had any trouble making the delivery. I told him we made it all right and showed him the receipt. It showed about one hundred and fifty two-year olds more than one-year olds and he seemed well pleased with it.

He and I fixed up letters to Slaughter and Johnson and rushed them with the receipts to Slaughter and a copy to Johnson. In due time, we got a nice letter from Mr. Slaughter acknowledging the receipt of the letter and check, also saying he was pleased with the count. We did not hear from Mr. Johnson. Mr. Morrison said it did not make any difference for he would be kicking about something anyway. We did our part and wrote him, now it is up to him to do his part.

Jack said "it was a damn good thing we did not hear from Johnson for he would want us to go back and count the cattle again/"

I told Mr. Morrison I had told him everything I knew. Now, I wanted him to tell me how they got along moving the cattle over on the Tule Creek. He laughed and said, "You will have to get Lucian to tell you."

Lucian was his son, a young man about twenty years old. He was a very talkative boy and he did enjoy telling about the way they got along for weeks afterwards. He was always thinking of something they said to each other, mostly between Johnson and Slaughter. His father and uncle did not take much stock in the fussing, for they had been dealing with Johnson several years. They said to let Johnson have his own way. But Slaughter did not think that way. He said if Johnson would do right and not talk and do things against the interest of the ranch, whether it was like he wanted to do it or not, it would be all right.

But he was not going to sit still and let him do detrimental things to the ranch. He said Johnson could not cut a cow out of a roundup. He was always in the way and made more work for the boys to do. He was not going to let him do that. Lucian said Slaughter told all of them, Johnson among the rest, for all to work together and round the cattle up in a close bunch so they could get them under control. They did not have much help, just the three Morrisons, Slaughter and Johnson. Slaughter started out up the creek to pushing the cattle together and the other men followed. All but Johnson. He went the other way, poking along and hardly turning any cattle at all. Slaughter and Morrison soon got a good-sized bunch together.

After a while, Slaughter looked down the creek where Johnson was, and instead of Johnson riding fast and trying to hold the cattle up so they could round them up, he was just poking along letting the cattle pass him and scatter out down the creek. Lucian said that when Slaughter saw that, he took a slicker or rain coat in his hand and ran around and got ahead of Johnson's cattle and ran into them with that slicker hollering and yelling at the top of his voice. Lucian said he liked to run the cattle over Johnson. I expected that was what he wanted to do. That soon put the cattle together and then they did not have much trouble, but that did not fix it with Slaughter for he was still mad at Johnson.

He told him to get back home and stay there and told him he should not have anything to do with the management of that ranch. Being mad, he said too much, just as we all do when we get mad. Lucian said Johnson went on poking around the cattle. He got so mad after a while he got in another fuss with Slaughter about him saying he should not have anything to do about the management of the ranch. By that time Slaughter had gotten over his mad spell, for Mr. Morrison had been talking to Slaughter. Slaughter apologised to Johnson and they fixed it up, that is for the time being.

Within the next few days, they had a big rain and there was no need of moving the cattle. Slaughter went back to Dallas and in a few days later, Johnson and Tom Morrison left. I was real glad I was not there while all the fussing was going on. I think it was about the first of July when I got back from delivering the steers to the Capital Syndicate Company. We went in to camp for a while and scattered the saddle horses out to get them on good grass and to fatten them up a little. The boys all rejoiced over Johnson being gone more than they did over getting to rest.

The rest did not last long, for about the twentieth of August I went to Big Springs after a herd of cows and calves. Cow and calves always meant trouble and took lots of patience for they were so slow. They were not so bad this trip, for we had plenty of rain and, of course, plenty of grass and water. Cowboys were generally happy when there was plenty of grass and water because the work was easier. The August sun got mighty hot and the calves suffered. We did not have a cook going down with the outfit but was to get one at town. Big Springs.

We had a pretty hard time finding a man to do the cooking. He had cooked for a trail outfit before; he said he was not feeling very well, but he would be all right in a day or two. We found out from others that he had been drunk. I thought when he got out of town where he could not get whiskey he would soon sober up and be all right. He was a good wagon cook when he was able to cook. Most of the time some of us would have to cook and hitch up the team. We were but a few days receiving the cattle, for the most of them were already under herd.

We went up the same old trail I had been over many times. By Battle Snake Creek, Wet Tobacco Creek and Dry Tobacco; then we went on the plains and had plenty of lake water from there on. This was one trip we did not have to be so careful about passing Tahoka Lake for we had plenty of rain everywhere. After we passed Tahoka, the next place was Singer's store on the Yellow House Creek, where the town of Lubbock is now. We did not have the trouble at Yellow House Creek as we had had with other herds before, for we had plenty of water. We got the cattle all there in good shape and from there on up the north prong of the Yellow House Draw the grass was fine. We did not drive, just had to graze. I thought of the other trips when I had been along there. We would have to hold the cattle back for they would be so dry for water.

We had a good trip except for the cook. We could have sent him back in a wagon, but he kept saying he would be better in a day or two. We were sorry for him. I felt that when we got to the ranch, and he could take better care of himself and have a woman to cook him something he could eat, he would improve. When we got within about twenty miles of the ranch, we sent a boy with him to the ranch. We were two or three days getting the herd to the ranch, but the cook had gotten worse. I sent a man to Estacado after Dr. Hunt, that was fifty miles. Dr. Hunt was the Rev. J. W. Hunt's father who is now president of McMurry College at Abilene, Texas.

Dr. Hunt got to the ranch next evening, looked the sick man over and asked how long he had been sick. I gave all the information I could. I told him he was not feeling well when we left town with him. I told him he had had a little whiskey until a day or two before. Dr. Hunt said that was what he needed, a stimulant, but he did not believe he would live long. He died late that evening. We got Dr. Hunt to stay and help us bury him. The next day we took some lumber from a small grain room and made a box coffin. We buried him about a quarter of a mile west of the ranch. That wound up the last drive for the Slaughter ranch, for that completed the full ten thousand head Slaughter was to put in on the ranch deal.

## Chapter 9

When I first came to Running Water, we got our mail at Epworth. Mr. Horatio Graves lived there with his family and kept the post office. His wife was post mistress and he was mail carrier; he did not carry it very often. It was thirty miles from Graves to Estacado to get the mail. When I found out how inconvenient it was, I told Mr. Graves if he could fix it someway so I could carry the mail I would help him out. When he could not go, I would go or send someone. He said he would appreciate that very much and appointed me mail carrier. After that we would go one trip and he one trip and that was better. Mr. Graves was the only settler at that time in the country.

In a few years settlers began to come in and settle on Tule Draw twenty-five miles north of Running Water. The first were Trus Gray, William Conner and his brother, L. G. (that afterwards moved to Randall County and started the town of Canyon City), Mr. Parrish, Mr. Settles and Jake Brown. These men received their mail at the Running Water Ranch just like we had gotten ours at Epworth a few years before. All of these people on Tule Draw had cattle.

About that time Mr. Maxwell settled on the Running Water Draw twenty miles east of the ranch at some Hackberry trees. He was a sheep man. It was not long after Maxwell came until Mr. E. L. Lowe settled there. After that they came in pretty fast and the Fort Worth and Denver Railroad was building west as far as Clarendon. I went to Clarendon and bought a load of ranch supplies from Wood and Dixon, general merchants, and they had it delivered to the ranch. Not long after that, the railroad pushed west and Wood and Dixon went ahead of the road and put in a branch house at Amarillo.

They carried everything usually found in a general store and operated it in a very large tent. If you happened to not have a camp bed, they would loan you some blankets and let you sleep in their tent store. Mr. Conrad was in charge of the store. A man named Kenny had a restaurant and soon after that Tuck Cornelus came up from Snyder, Texas and operated a general wagon yard. Then Burns and Walker came up from Colorado City and opened a general supply store. Cone and Duran came down from Tascosa with a general supplies store.

From then on, the people came in fast and they soon had a good western town. For several years Amarillo was the largest cattle shipping point in the country. When the country began to settle around Amarillo and the railroad pushed on west, the cattle shipping went to Canyon and Hereford and on out to Bovina, which was the main shipping point for many years. At one time, Bovina was said to be the biggest shipping point in the world. While these towns were building, Plainview was being settled although it was eighty miles from Amarillo and sixty miles from the railroad.

At Canyon City, Maxwell and E. L. Lowe had Col. R. P. Smyth to survey and lay out the town of Plainview. A cowboy that was working for me at the east camp of Circle Ranch, reported to me that they were going to build a town down at the hackberry thicket. I told him I would eat all the town they would ever build down there. I thought the settlers would stay a year or two and go back to their kinfolks, but they had come to stay and they proved to us that we had a pretty good country out here.

Of course, it was not to the best interest of the cattlemen for the country to settle and it was natural for them to oppose it. It went like all other new countries, when the proper time came the settler took the country away from the cowman. The old saying proved true in this case. First the Indian, then followed the buffalo hunter, the Texas Ranger, next the cattlemen and then the actual settler. The country had to go through all these stages before the chain was completed. All of them at times had pretty hard going.

The hunter, as Dave Crockett said, had a hard time blazing the way for future generations to follow, but he liked it. They had the Indian to contend with, also the wild beast, sickness, sometimes death among their friends, (friends that meant something) and many times starvation staring them in the face. I guess they all learned to like jerk meat (dried meat) for I can't see how they could carry enough of any other kind of provision on their long trips. I don't think we appreciate those old pioneers as much as we ought to, for theirs was the hardest of all.

Then came the early day cowman, but very different from the present-day cowman. I have heard those old fellows tell how they used to sleep out in the brush to guard their horses at night to keep the Indians from stealing them. They did not sleep much for it was too dangerous to risk going to sleep. My old friend, Jim Carter, that died at Dimmit many years ago, used to tell me some of his early experiences with Indians. He told of one particular time when he took a boy who was in his teens to help guard their horses. They were supposed to take time about, one guard at first then wake the other one; but he said as soon as they got settled down and everything was still, the boy went to sleep and snored so loud he as afraid the Indians might hear him. He was sure it would never do if the boy went to sleep and him too.

He said an hour or two before daylight he heard an Indian make a loud noise, or grunt, and in just a few minutes he heard another answer from the opposite direction. He said he thought it was time to act. He pulled the boy's hair and pinched him and finally got him awake. He thought he had made so much fuss the Indians heard him and did not try to get the horses for when daylight came the horses were in a lot and he found Indian tracks. But the Indians were not there.

During the Civil War, in Shackelford County, the Indians drove off a bunch of the neighbourhood cattle. The men all got together and followed them. The Indians got a good start and left a dim trail. They got across the Red River. The white men kept spies out and located them late one evening. That night they surprised the Indians, killed some of them and got their cattle. They immediately started back to Texas and drove hard to get out of the Indian country for fear they would make up a band. They did not sleep much until they got across Red River, then they would relieve each other and get some sleep.

Mr. Carter said one thing impressed him on that trip—they had a small calf that would give out every day. He could not keep up with the herd and they had no way to carry him. They just left him behind one day. That night the little fellow came dragging in to the herd and found his mother. After that when the calf would get tired, they just let him have his own way and every night he would come in to the herd and bawl for his mother. That was the way they got him to the ranch.

The story that interested me most was about his looking after stock one day and got out on a big prairie. He rode up on a high point to look as they always had to. He saw five men. His first thought was Indians. He looked around and located the nearest timber and started to it. As soon as he turned toward the timber, they turned that way too trying to cut him off. He knew that was one of their tricks, but said they were generally afraid when you got in timber. He beat them to the timber and ran right on down into a dry bed of a creek. The Indians were right after him hollering and yelling as loud as they could.

He had figured they would stop at the edge of the timber, but no, here they came and two of them were getting near enough to shoot at him. He knew he would have to fight them. He saw an abrupt bend in the creek ahead of him. He threw the bridle reins over his horse's head and jumped off with his pistol in his hand and jumped behind this bank.

The Indians were running so fast that they could not stop their horses until they ran so near to him, he shot the two leaders off their horses. He said the other three were not so bold, but they did not want to give it up and kept shooting with their bows and arrows. Each side stayed behind trees and he thought he shot another Indian, at least they gave up the fight.

That was late in the evening. When dark came, he followed the creek a few miles and made his way to the ranch. He said that was the closest call he ever had. I think sometimes about we younger cowboys. If we had had to go through such times as Jim Carter and many others, whether we would have wanted to have been cowboys or not. I can see that men get used to things and I imagined they would say afterwards that things were not as bad as they looked. He said he took deliberate aim at those Indians as he would have at a wolf. He was glad when they quit shooting at him. I am telling this story to show how different it was in Jim Carter's time.

My first trip to the west was to Eastland in the year 1878. The next year, '79, I went to Mitchell County near where Colorado City is now on Champion Creek. I had two brothers, Gus and Dave, working on a ranch for Waddell and Biler. Waddell was manager; they had seven thousand cattle and to me that sounded mighty big. I spent about three months there. They talked some about Indians. It had been about two years since they had some fights further north with the Indians. I was too busy with my ranch plans to let that bother me. I guess I planned to kill all the Indians if they bothered my ranch. One thing I forgot to figure; that it would be many years before I got this ranch and as many hardships to go through with as most of the others.

The early day settler and farmer had his hard time, also the pioneer merchant.

I remember what a hard time George Singer had to keep his stock, also Dockum, Charlie Holmes, and Dr. Hunt at Estacado. I remember if George Singer bought just a little merchandise, some outfit would come along and buy it all at once. If he laid in a good supply, it would be his luck that nobody came. I am sure it was a hard job. After Crosby County was organised, Stringfellow and Hume opened up a good store at Estacado and carried a good line of everything and a little later they opened a branch house at Plainview. Mr. Thornton Jones was manager.

Later Mr. McClelland and son had the second store at Plainview. Mr. Rawlings was the next merchant, later Vince and Welter. Then came R. C. Ware. Another year or so J. N. Donohue bought in with Mr. Ware and formed the company of Donohue and Ware. While all of this was going on in Plainview, people were coming in and taking up land in the country. I bought two sections southwest of Plainview and improved it. J. N. Morrison was in charge of the Running Water Ranch, or Circle Ranch then.

Later I bought one and a half sections more land, making me three and a half sections. Most of the country was taken up by people filing on school land and leaving it unfenced. That left the country open from the old T. Anchor pasture to Yellow House at Lubbock.

## Chapter 10

In January, 1890, I married Miss Lizzie Kiser and we settled on a little ranch six miles southwest of Plainview. I had at that time four hundred cattle, mostly two- and three-year-old steers. Although it was small, we used it to the best advantage. Of course, we built many air castles, or dreams, as my wife called them. She laughed at me many times and said I built my air castles too high and too many of them. I argued; if I did not build any air castles, I did not get any ranches. We had lots of fun over what we were going to do.

As time passed, we soon saw that being married carried a great deal of responsibility with it, but I continued in the steer business. I bought steer yearlings and calves at weaning time and held them for market at three-year-old. By hard work and close management, I built my little herd up some; but it looked mighty slow to me. My wife told me I must have more patience.

I had some good friends among the cattlemen that helped me a great deal. Among them were the Bryan boys. Bud Oldham, Knight and Slaton, Leach Brothers, Trus and Ted Gray, Will Connor, Bob Lemmons, Dick McQuirter, Carl Roberts, Jim Cox, and others over the plains country. Of course, we were all helpful to each other. I doubt if there was ever a set of men that would go as far as the cowmen did to help each other, also to help anyone that was in distress or in immediate need. If it was at all in their power, they always extended a helping hand. Few of them ever turned anybody hungry away. I am sure that their liberality is the cause of many of them being in a hard shape today. Many were broke by helping someone else.

After we were married, my wife's mother gave us some chickens. We got along all right with the chickens until garden time came in the spring. We had net wire around the garden, but the hens would fly over into the garden. We both knew that people clipped chickens' wings. We did not know they just clipped one wing. We clipped both wings. I guess we thought like the fellow did about the medicine; if a little would do a little good, a lot of it would do a lot of good.

We told her mother about it and had a hearty laugh about it when we found out we were just supposed to clip one wing. She scolded us for not knowing. It was just about the same as if we had not clipped either wing. We doubled the wire on the fence. We learned then to clip one wing the next time.

I had a boy named Sherrod Durham working for me. My wife said we would have had a good garden if Sherrod and myself had not trampled things to death going over to see if the plants were coming up. I made a good crop of feed that year. We had lots of rain and things were prosperous, but the next year was dry and the grasshoppers came and made it still worse. I went in with Mr. Morrison and we shipped some of our oldest steers to Flint Hills in Kansas. We were gone about two weeks and when we got back, we had gotten good rains all over this part of the plains. The grass as green and soon very fine.

I saw I had made a mistake. The country was settling up all the time and like the song, "*Times Are Not Like They Used To Be*." I began to build more air castles. I could see I would have to either sell my cattle or find better range for them. I figured with my friend J. N. Donohue on several propositions on a good-sized ranch, but we never did quite get together.

A little later, Gus O'Keefe bought the Fish Ranch in Dawson County. He had moved his family to Colorado City and offered me the job of running his ranch and run my own cattle on the ranch with his cattle. He had seven thousand cattle and I had six hundred cattle. I had lost money on the cattle I had shipped to Kansas and I did not want to get caught in another trap like that. After I had investigated my brother's proposition of running his ranch, I decided it was all right. I came home after looking it over and told my wife I had built more bubbles in the air. She asked what I had gone into now. I explained to her the proposition. She agreed with me that it looked good. She asked if I thought I could manage the ranch.

I told her I knew I could. I then told her I had figured out two plans. One was, I would build her and May (our baby) a house in Plainview and they would be near her people, or she could go with me and we all stay on the ranch. I told her we would have a good comfortable house, but the one bad thing was it would be lonesome for her. The nearest neighbour was twelve miles to the Bishop and Godair Ranch. I was mighty glad when she said, of course, she would go to the ranch so we would all be together. It was a good move for us; it was a lonely place for a woman and baby, of course. That part of it was bad, but I tried to console my wife by building more castles in the air; telling her we would make enough in a few years to move to a school, which we did.

I managed the Fish Ranch two years, then bought a ranch just north of the Fish Ranch. I had eighty sections of land and one thousand cattle. I made another trade. I bought five hundred cows in October and got all unbranded calves. The spring calves had been branded, but the summer and fall calves were not branded. About two hundred head were thrown in; I bought the five hundred cows for thirteen dollars per head. Just a year after that I sold all the dry cows out of that brand for twenty-six dollars per head.

I began to believe that my dreams were about to prove true about my ranch. It was not all sunshine though, the lobo wolves got bad in that country and they killed many calves. The spring that I bought this ranch, I drove two thousand steers, one- and two-year-olds, for myself and Gus to Evans, Snyder, Buel, and Company Ranch on the Canadian River twenty miles north of Miami, Texas. I went over the same trail a part of the way from Running Water to Panhandle, that I travelled eight years before and the country had changed very much. One would hardly think it the same country, it had settled up so much.

I got back to the Fish Ranch in June. My wife was at Plainview all that spring and summer. Her mother died during that time, then we got her youngest brother, Ed Kiser, to go live with us. That made it very much better for all of us. This ranch was known as the OBR Ranch as that was the brand I kept up. Ed was a new cowboy, that is, had not done much of that kind of work. At first, he said he did not believe he would ever learn to be a cowpuncher and for that very reason he tried that much harder and made about the best hand I ever had. He always tried to do his best. He was honest and whenever he told me anything I knew it was so. He never tried to deceive anybody.

We had some pretty hard times, but after getting the dogs we had lots of fun. We seldom went out but what we killed something, a bobcat, coyote, or something. The big lobo wolves were the ones we were after. They were the fellows that were killing the cattle. Along about that time they were settling the country north of us. That was Oklahoma, southwest Kansas, Colorado, Nebraska and it was claimed this ran the lobos out of that country. I saw thirteen lobos in a bunch one morning early. I suppose too early for them to scatter out. Well, that was too many big wolves to look good. I began then to make inquiry how to get dogs. Mr. Galbreth, a ranchman of Double Mountain, had been running dogs after these lobos and he let us have some greyhounds. We made it hot for Mr. Wolf for a while.

Ed or I was always out at daylight with the dogs. Greyhounds run by sight, that is, they don't trail anything and can only follow their game as long as they can see it. One morning we rode up on a sand hill and saw three big lobos not more than two hundred yards from us, then the race started. The dogs soon ran up to one of them, but he was so big the dogs could not throw him. They would grab him by the hind legs and check him but the wolf would bite and snap them off. While the dogs were bothering the wolf so much, we would almost keep up on horseback, but we could not get close enough to rope him until we had just about run him to death. He ran some distance and came to a favourable place and on hard ground, then we crowded him and caught him.

After we killed this wolf, we found we had run him nine miles. We knew the distance to the fence was ten miles and we were just a mile from the fence with the dogs. As this was the first lobo, or big wolf, we had caught, we took the hide for a keepsake. He had not been dead but a few minutes until he was stiff. We had run him to death. Our horses were so tired they could hardly stand still. Just as soon as we killed the wolf, we hastened to take our saddles off our horses and let them cool. By the time we had the wolf skinned, our horses and dogs were rested some and ready to go.

We found out that it required eight to ten miles to run a lobo own. It was said, if you run one eight miles and did not catch him, he would die. It was claimed that had been proven by finding their carcass near where the boys would lose sight of them. The wolf sometimes would turn around a sand hill and give you the dodge, in other words, play hide and seek with you. We had some good horses and we certainly did ride them. We ran every lobo as long as we could see him. They can run faster than a horse for the first few miles, but by not running too fast at first a horse can last longer.

The idea was to just stay in sight of them until the wolf began to show signs of weakening, then crowd your horse and rope the wolf. There were always some chances against you in running wolves. Sand hills, tall grass and bushes almost the same colour of a wolf's back made it hard to see him very far. The sand hills were so numerous he would dart from one side to the other and leave you in doubt which way he had gone.

The wire fence was another hindrance and it used to look like everyone I would get after would head for the nearest fence, But I guess it just seemed so. It made lots of work and exposure, but that was set off by the pleasure we got out of it. We looked on work with pleasure then. These dogs furnished the fun. Eight greyhounds made a pretty sight. We would run our horses mighty hard trying to keep up with the dogs. We killed quite a number of them before we got the dogs. We would see wolf tracks and see where they had killed calves, but we seldom ever saw the lobos. Nearly every morning we would see fresh tracks in the sand and dust at the water trough.

Ed said if I would help him fix the wagon down near the water trough, he would sleep in the wagon and could kill some of them at night. I said they were too sly for that. I think they would smell you and be shy of you. He said well, we are only two hundred yards away at the house, they could smell us that far.

The more I thought about it the more reasonable it looked and we got the wagon with sheet on down near the water. Ed went down after dark and spent the night in the wagon. Next morning, he came up to the house grinning all over his face. I knew he had had some luck from the way he was grinning. He said he killed one lobo and two coyotes. I told him he would have to show me. I was tickled just about as much as he was. He slept there several nights but did not kill another lobo at the trough. He killed many at other places and several coyotes (the small wolves). He had lots of fun that first morning talking about it. One thing he said, he would only kill lobos from then on, but he failed. One reason he did not kill anymore, I got the dogs soon after that and of course the dogs kept them scared away.

When we first got the dogs, we both went hunting with them. We ran every wolf we saw and ran him just as long as we could see him. We would think of that saying, maybe he would run off somewhere and die. They were dealing us misery and we tried to deal it back to them. After about one year's use with the greyhounds, we got some bloodhounds. They could not run as fast as the greyhounds, but they could run much longer and too, if Mr. Wolf got out of sight or turned any corners around the sand hills, that did not bother the bloodhounds. They would just pick up the trail and keep right on after him. If he camped or laid down to rest, they soon over took him and had him going again.

We caught many of their young and some of the old ones. These hounds were on their trail so close that we made it so hot for them that they must have left the country, or at least, a lot of them for they kept getting more scarce. One thing, nearly all the ranches had dogs and of course, that just made too many dogs. I guess it looked to a wolf that everywhere he went he met the dogs and lots of them drifted to some other country. Still, we must have killed about all of the young ones. Every ranch in the country was reporting many killed. While we had these dogs to kill lobo wolves, we killed many coyotes and wild cats.

We must have rid the country of all the wild cats for they were easy caught. One very dry year we had a bad prairie fire which burned off most of the country from my ranch, ten miles south of Brownfield, clear into Yellow House Draw near where Lubbock town is now. It made it hard on Cattlemen and their business, but we could see how to run the wolves better for most of the grass had burned up clean. In just a few days after the fire we had good rains and the country was soon in good shape again.

We had a cowboy named Brit Clair who worked for us one summer. He was a good boy and a good worker. After he left me, he worked for Mr. Bone a near neighbour to us. Brit and another boy were hauling wood one day. Brit went ahead of the boy with the wagon and went into a thicket of Oak Bushes and there was a panther laying asleep in the brush. It was so thick the panther could not get out any other way only to come by Brit and he had an axe in his hand and killed the panther, I never have seen Brit since he killed the panther. I understand he married and now lives in Terry County and doing well. I am sure he deserved to do well for he was a good boy while he worked for me. Terry County was not organised when I moved away in '89. I had ranched in Dawson and Terry Counties about nine years.

Ed Kiser was with us seven years and many things happened during those years. Ed and I fought the wolves a good part of the time. He helped me move my first herd of cattle from Hale County of the Fish Ranch in Terry County. His mother was living then and he came back and lived with her two years. When she died, he came and made his home with us. I remember about the funniest joke Ed got on me was one time he and I were building some fence and we were going back and forth on horseback. We would come back to the ranch at noon and at night. We carried such things as we would need on our horses.

One day Ed had some stakes and I was to carry the post hole digger. My horse objected to my carrying the diggers on him because the diggers rattled and scared him and he threw me off. Ed was sitting on his horse with a load ready to go and was enjoying the fun. After he got through laughing, he told me to give him the diggers. I said, "No, I am going to make this rascal carry those diggers." I was pitched off three times trying to carry those diggers. Ed said he bet on the horse and the horse won. The way he threw me was, just as I put my weight in the stirrup, he would whirl to one side and I could not hold to him and hold the digger at the same time. He still tried to whirl from under me, but after I let Ed have the digger, I could mount him all right.

I have been thrown off several times that way, for the horse whirls from under you before you get on him. To avoid that, we hold him by the cheek of the bridle, then as he whirls, the rider goes with the horse. I raised horses a number of years and we had lots of fun breaking the young horses. Young horses are not so hard to handle as old unbroken horses. Horses that pass four years old unbroken and never have been handled are usually hard to break. After our daughter, May, now Mrs. Joe Ryan, was old enough to go to school, we moved to Canyon City and left Ed in charge of the ranch.

He had one boy with him all the time and he tells of many experiences they had. They still found some lobo wolves, although it had been some time since they were at their worst. Ed caught several in steel traps, also shot and killed some. People began to come into that country and I thought it would go like Hale County, settle up and high taxes would follow as it always had followed every country. I sold out to R. M. Clayton and R. B. Pyron. I had done very well for the time I was in Terry and Dawson Counties. I went there with six hundred cattle and built up my herd at one time to twenty-six hundred. We had a dry year and I was forced to sell off nine hundred stock cattle which I did not want to do. Drouths force us to do things sometimes that we had rather not do.

I kept my steers sold off as yearlings after that. That left more range for the cattle. I expect the wolves killed four or five hundred cattle for me during the time I was there. They did not only kill calves, but would kill grown cattle at times. I suppose there would be times when they could not find calves. The only way I knew, would be to see cows with hams cut. In that way the cow can't travel, then they get them down and a bunch of wolves soon kill them. I never saw them kill a cow, but have seen them eating on them after they were killed. I have seen cows with hind legs badly bitten. I was sure the wolves had done it and other cattle would fight them off.

The old-time buffalo hunter said some of the wolves would fight in front or at their nose. Some other wolves bite their hams until the buffalo could not travel. Those big wolves knew how to get well fed. They always got it unless man was in their way. They often did their killing at night and man would ride out next day and see the dead cow and the only thing man could do was to pull his hair and cuss. That did not hurt the wolves. They had their bellies full and they might be ten miles from there by that time.

Wolves were our worst trouble while I was there, but I must not overlook snakes for they were numerous and we were scared all the time.

None of us were bitten by them but the dogs were bitten often and several horses were bitten by them. We found that common soda was good for a snake bite. Take a sharp knife and puncture the wound until it would bleed well, then bind it up with soda in a rag. While snakes were bad on this ranch, they were not so numerous as they were on Rattle Snake Creek that I used to be on many years before with Lum Slaughter. It seemed they were at the root of almost every tree down there. It seemed funny that I had gotten back so near the same place where I had my first real ranch experience.

While I was on this Terry County ranch, I often passed the old headquarter ranch at German Springs. I don't think I ever passed there but what I thought of rattle snakes. I understand that country is settled up now and I wonder if the children haven't all gotten bit by those pesky snakes. While I am telling rattle snake stories, I have one more. They used to tell me that prairie dogs would fill their dens up if a rattle snake went in them. I always doubted it until I tried it one day. I saw a rattle snake crawl in a dog den. I got a stick about four feet long and slipped to the hole and began pushing dirt in the hole about like I thought a dog would do. In a few minutes here the snake came but seemed to be very watchful and careful. He looked like he was trying to discover what was causing that dirt to fall in the hole.

I lay flat on the ground to keep him from discovering me, but I guess he must have made out that there was an enemy around for he went back in his den. I tried it at other times and shot them by having my gun ready before I began the show. I have tried it at other times and they did not come out. I think they got wise and could tell the difference between a man pushing dirt in and a dog scratching it in on them. After my experience with them I have always believed that story. I have seen prairie dogs filling up their dens and he packs the dirt with his nose and it will be packed as hard as *adobe*.

Lum Medlin, a buffalo hunter told me that he was slipping up on a bunch of deer to get him some meat and of course kept hid in the bushes. He thought one of them acted very peculiar and seemed to be watching something. He could tell it was not watching him for it was looking in the opposite direction. He decided to not kill the deer until he found out what it was all about. He got close enough that he could see the deer's movements good. He had heard they would kill snakes and he sat there quite a bit.

After a while the deer made a jump or two and lit right on top of a rattle snake, then right back again. He repeated the same thing several times but said he got so interested in the fight that he let the deer get away without killing one but he got to see the deer kill the snake. The deer, a big buck, seemed to hold all four of his feet close together. He just seemed to bounce instead of jump. That snake was mashed to jelly. He could not tell if it had bitten the deer, but he could not see how it could with all that pounding going on.

It seems that nature provides everything some means of protection. The poor old rattler might have crawled up while the deer was sleeping and bit him and caused death, but he missed his opportunity and when the deer began bounding on him with all four feet it was too late. The rabbit depends on his speed for protection, but if he sleeps too late, he gets caught.

About three years after I sold out in Terry County, the county organised and of course settlers came fast and soon spoiled the country for ranch business. I did not stay out of the ranch business long, until I bought four leagues of Deaf Smith County school land. It lay in Lamb County and Bailey County near where Sudan is now. Ed Kiser was in with me in the deal. He owning one fourth and me owning three fourths.

We bought it from Massie and McManns of Floydada at one dollar and twenty-five cents per acre, on twenty years' time, five *per cent* interest. It was quite a job to improve that ranch being so far from the railroad. Bovina was our nearest railroad point. Forty miles to haul freight and there was lots of sand to haul over. Water was pretty deep and uncertain. The loco was just awfully bad. Loco was a weed resembling alfalfa and if the horses and cattle took to eating it, it would make them go crazy and many of them dwindle away and die from the effect of it.

Ed was with me about two years and I bought his interest in the ranch. He went back to Hale County in the east part of Lamb County and bought land and married Miss Alice Beasley. They lived there many years and raised four children, two boys and two girls. Later they bought more land at Running Water and still live there and are doing well.

After Ed left me, it was rather hard and lonesome, but I had to try to get along without him. That ranch was hard to get to from all directions but it was a good small ranch, had some sand on it but it did not get into the main sand hills. I owned four leagues of land and had three thousand acres, leased and usually carried one thousand to fourteen hundred cattle, owing to the amount of rain we got.

After Ed left me, I leased it out to Benson and Fritz Hudgins for three years. After my daughter married Joe Ryan, I got the ranch back. Joe was with me for a while. We stocked the ranch with eleven hundred two-year-old steers. We bought these steers in November and Joe Ryan and Buddy Thompson branded them about the last of November. About January the first, we began feeding them one pound of cotton seed cake every other morning.

When weather was bad, we fed them every day. We soon got them trained to come to the wagon when we called. At first one man would drive the team and another man would drive the steers into the feed ground. It was not long until all we had to do was call and if they were within hearing distance here, they would come. I bought six hundred of them from Mr. Bronson of Midland and he fed them cake the winter before and they soon taught the others to eat cake.

I gave twenty-eight dollars a head for them in November and sold them in June the first, next year, for fifty dollars. A funny thing happened, a man came down from Denver, Colorado, in February and offered me fifty dollars for them. I would not take fifty, I wanted fifty-five. He stayed overnight with me and slept with me as we were short of beds at the ranch. I thought sure he would take them in the morning, but he did not. He said he would receive them April the first and ship them to Denver, and feed them on the best pulp. I did not sleep good that night studying whether to take his offer or not. I reasoned that I might get sixty dollars at the cattle convention at El Paso. I let my man go and took my chance on El Paso, but not a bid did I get at El Paso.

The market had gone down and there was nothing to do but hold them, which I did. In May, I sold them to the American Beef Company of Denver for fifty dollars per head and delivered June the first. I lost four or five dollars per head on them. It shows we can't always tell about the market, but my fifty-five was not much out of line. At the time I made it according to other sales that had been made early, but I had made a very nice profit, about twenty-two dollars per head in about eight months. That was war times and high prices. We did not often make such profits.

After that, I bought eight hundred steers from John McElroy of Odessa. He had a drouth in his country and had to move his cattle to new country and moved them to New Mexico, sixty miles above Roswell on Pecos River. He had one-, two- and three-year-old steers. He thought he had nine hundred, but fell short about one hundred. That did not make so much difference. I figured I could soon pick up three hundred more. I told McElroy I would take the cattle, but he must deliver them. He said he could not do that for he had to move back to Odessa for he had had some good rains and had some cattle to move back home. I said I did not like to go back on the trail again and tried to talk him into delivering them.

But he stood pat and said he would not drive them back to Odessa unless he could deliver them there. I decided it was about the best I could do, so we traded and I caught the first train out and went to the ranch and got my outfit and moved the cattle myself. It took us nearly two weeks to make the trip. They were very good cattle but had been in the drouth and were starved a little. I put them on good grass and they came out wonderfully. I moved them in July.

The next Spring, I sold all the threes and that left me the coming yearlings and twos. I had bought up enough other yearlings to make up my number about twelve hundred. I liked to handle steers much better than stock cattle, only sometimes they were scarce and hard to buy. No one could make a profit and of course that was discouraging. I had tried stock cattle and raised my own steers, but hard cold winters, drouth, long distance to haul feed made it difficult to handle cows and calves.

During the eighteen years I owned the Door Key Ranch, I changed several times from steer business to cows and calves. I had Walter Ridgeway with me about seven years. I used to talk quite a bit with him about which was best. We both liked steers the best, but had much trouble at times to get bargains. Ridgeway said when we raised steers nobody wanted to buy them and when we wanted to buy steers nobody would want to sell them. It did seem pretty much that way. The reason I changed about often, I adopted a plan of buying the cheapest and the most suited to times.

It was difficult to tell what steers would be worth in two years from the time I bought them at yearlings. Sometimes the woods would be full of buyers. I found that new buyers were the hardest competition, for they were out to buy whether they got bargains or not, and some of them would give as much for a sorry bunch of steers as they would for a good bunch. Sometimes I had to buy them high to get them.

One time when loco had been bad, I decided to get rid of my stock cattle. I traded all my grown and mature cows and bulls to Walter Sullivan for all his calves and yearlings, both steers and heifers. I don't remember the price, but cattle were cheap then. We had a price on each class and adjusted the difference in money, but the difference was not much. When we got through making the exchange I had about nine hundred, a regular duke's mixture. Some steer yearlings, some two-year-old steers, and some heifers. I planned to spray all the heifers the next spring. Ridgeway said he had heard of men swapping horses, but it was the first time he ever saw them swap cattle.

After we made the exchange, I stayed with Ridgeway a few days to help him get them located. I left him in charge of that outfit with a boy to help him and went to Olton and Dimmit and bought up five hundred more in small bunches. I bought from the Kiser boys, Fred Shrier, Jim Hooper, Luther Williams, Mr. Cowart McGill, Herb Dickson and others in Lamb and Castro Counties. I made a trade with Walter Sullivan to help me bunch up these five hundred and we branded them at his ranch ten miles west of Olton. A Mr. Dodson had the first store at Olton and Mr. McClung had the blacksmith shop.

When cowboys got hungry, they would go to Mr. Dodson's store and get canned goods and crackers for lunch; spend the night with some friends for that was the custom then. When I drove in with my last herd, I went ahead of the cattle and found Ridgeway at the ranch. He said everything was all right, only the calves walked a great deal for about a week, but had settled down now and were looking better. I told him that they always did that when they were weaned in the fall. It was December. I told him to get his horse that I had another bunch to count to him.

When we met the herd I saw they were strung out good for counting. I told him to go down one side and I would go down the other; we would see if we had them all. We found they counted out all right. We mixed them up with the other cattle. We figured I had a few more than I set out to buy. I did that in buying in bunches. Ridgeway said I had too many cattle for the pasture, which was about twenty thousand acres. I said these are small cattle and they won't eat as much as grown cattle and in January we will cut out the poorest and feed them cake. He said we might save them that way. This was the first time we fed cotton seed cake; we managed it very well, but we did lose a few cattle.

We had some work next spring spraying those heifers. Ridgeway was a pretty good rough carpenter and we got a carpenter to help him build a good chute and a squeezer to handle the cattle with. Ridgeway had never seen any spraying done before, but I had for I sprayed one thousand on Running Water Ranch, also about that many on the Fish Ranch, so it was not a new thing to me. I used to say when I was working under Gus and Lum Slaughter,

I was getting some valuable experience that would help me in the years to come and it had come now. I would tell Ridgeway about that and tried to teach him, in my feeble way, how to manage and he seemed to take to it pretty well, for he made me a good hand all the time he was with me. He left me one time and went to Oklahoma and bought a farm, but he did not stay there a year. He came back to his old job with me again. I was glad to get him back, for I could always rely on him.

One time I had a remnant of cattle, about four hundred. They were a part of the sprayed heifers. I sold them to Dick Walch. I tried to get him to receive them at the ranch, but he said he had no outfit to go that far after them, but he would have some boys to receive them at Dimmit, Castro County. He had leased the old T. Anchor pasture and said he could handle them from Dimmit, I went to the ranch and told Ridgeway what I had done and we had about a week to get to Dimmit with them. I asked if he could find two or three extra boys to help us. He thought he could, but when he tried, he could not find anyone.

He said we could handle them. He had one boy at the ranch, I knew we three could get them over there for it was only fifty miles. I wanted to see how he would plan it. I said, all right, I will leave it up to you. He said well, somebody might come along, but if they did not we could let the boy drive the team and lead three extra horses and he and I drive the cattle. I said what will you do with your extra milk cows. He said turn the cows and calves together for we will be back in two or three days. I said that was fine, we would do as he said. I had already decided that was just about what we would do, but I was glad he planned it.

The first night we penned the cattle at Bill Hassel's ranch, Spring Lake. We got along fine only the boy did not understand about how to go on ahead and keep stray cattle out of the way. I told Ridgeway to just change his plan a little and he take the team and wagon and when he found cattle that would bother us to stop and help us by. After that we had no trouble. The second night we had to night herd. We divided the night into three guards, we put the boy on last guard so if he lost them, they would not be far away at daylight. The boy said the cattle were no trouble.

Next morning, we got to Dimmit. Dick Walch was there with three cowboys to receive the cattle and it did not take long to count them out. It just took five days from the time we left until we got back to the ranch. Dick Walch wintered those heifers in the canyon east of Canyon City. He told me after that they wintered fine. Dick was the easiest man to trade with I had met in a long time. I had told him the cattle were three years old and I wanted thirty-two and a half dollars if he would take them all. The cattle were all around the water when we looked at them. Not over thirty minutes later he said he would take them. I thought that was a quick trade.

Getting back to Ridgeway, some cowboys would not have wanted to drive the wagon, but it was just like him to do whatever was for the best interest. One time after that I had George Foster to survey out my four leagues of land into labours of one hundred and seventy-seven acres. We could not find a man to cook for the outfit. Ridgeway said he could do the cooking and carry the chain too. I said, if you will, I will give you a dollar a day extra. He said he did not want the dollar extra but he would cook. I gave him credit on the books for his extra work. He was that way about everything on the ranch. He was certainly a good trusty man and I hope he has done well.

I think that survey I had made on my four leagues, 17,712 acres, turned out to be an unwise thing. I had the entire tract cut up into labours and iron pipe at each corner thinking I would sell it to settlers, but kept it eight years after than then sold it in a body at last. Well, that was like many other mistakes I had made. We just have to pay for them, but I find that the fellow that doesn't make mistakes, doesn't make anything else because every man that does any business makes some mistakes. I made a mistake when I sold my land, but I thought I was doing a big thing when I sold it for fourteen dollars per acre. I paid one and a quarter for it eighteen years before.

I had used it all that time for cattle grazing, but to offset that, I had paid interest and taxes and the taxes were climbing the last few years I owned it. Lum Slaughter used to say, whenever they go to building courthouses in a county you had better move your cow ranches for, they would eat you up with taxes. Mr. Slaughter lived to see the change come that made it so you could not move because there was no place to move to. The west settled up until there was no more west.

You had to stay where you were, or quit. He used to say keep all your young heifers and raise all the cattle you can, there might be times when prices would be low, but they always come back. I guess if he was alive today in 1933, he would say sell off your steers and old cows and get out of debt and wait for the rise for it will sure come. I doubt that at this time.

That is something that everybody had to guess at and have to risk their own judgment and the best of them will make a mistake once in a while. Slaughter said, if you make a mistake work the harder and try to overcome it. It was good advice and one that I have always tried to follow, but made many failures. Gus used to tell me to not be so scary. He would laugh at me and say you have good judgment, go on and use it. I said, well, Dave Crockett said "Be sure you are right then go ahead." How could I always know when I was right. He said I would have to risk something. He said that to me one time when we were on a trade.

Gus had four hundred cows branded and he wanted to sell them to get them out of his Fish Ranch. He called them an off brand and was anxious to sell them. I had lots of grass and knew I could handle them all right. I asked what he wanted for them. He said he would take thirteen dollars per head and throw in all the unbranded calves. I said, "Here I am, as usual, broke. I haven't got that much money." He said he would sell them to me without a dollar and take my note at eight *per cent.*

I said, "I will pay one thousand dollars cash and take them." This was in October and there had been no calves branded since May or June and I knew there was a good many unbranded calves. I asked him when he wanted to brand them. He said when we roundup to gather beef. There had been beef cows sold just before that and had brought thirteen dollars. That was a basis for price at the time. In one year, I shipped all the dry cows out of the herd with the other cattle and they brought twenty-six dollars per head. I sold nearly enough to pay them out when I made the payment. Gus said, "Now suppose you had not bought them."

I said, "Dave Crockett said it was all right to buy them." And we had a lot of fun over it. He was glad I had made money on them, but nobody knows which way a cat will jump. I told Gus that was one time I was right.

I bought those cattle the year William Jennings Bryan was running for President on the silver platform and things were running at a low ebb. That was one reason I bought the four hundred cows so cheap and one other thing, Gus had two thousand steers that he bought in old Mexico from the Terrasus Ranch two years before. He wanted to sell them and up to the time I bought the cows in October, he had not had an offer on them. I told him "No wonder no one would bid on them for they were no account." I said, "The idea of you and W. T. Scott buying such cattle." Scott had gone in with him and had bought two thousand for each of them. They kept them two years and we worked together in rounding-up and branding. I would take my outfit and help him and he would help me.

I told Gus that Dave Crockett did not tell him to buy those Mexican steers. I joked him about those steers. I told him he ought to be ashamed to bring them and put them in a nice herd like the Fish cattle. I said "You accused me of being too scary, which was so but," I said, "it was a pity you did not get scared just before you bought that outfit." This was all in fun and he would join in and laugh just as hearty as I would. Of course, I never said anything against the cattle to outsiders, but I sure did rub it in on him. I would ride in the herd with him behind one of those steers and tell him I could cover that steer's whole body with one thumb. I said, "There is nothing to him but horns, hoofs and his tail." I said if you took them away from him, there would be no steer.

Henry Mason was Gus's foreman and he heard us having so much fun and said, "That is right Rufe, shoot it into him for he had no business buying those damn things." That was all in fun too. Henry said we would have to put up with the damn things two years. Henry and I guyed him so much about them, he said if we would let him alone, he would set us up the first time we went to town and promised to never buy another Mexican steer, and he never did that I know of. The reason he bought those steers over in old Mexico, he could not buy them at home worth the money and was forced to buy these. He said it was against his best judgment. I noticed he was never forced to buy any more of them. In the fall that Bryan was defeated, Gus said he was glad Bryan was beat. He said Bryan was the cause of the slump in the cattle market. I told him Bryan was the smartest man in the United States.

We would have friendly arguments about it and neither of us knew anything about politics. Henry said Bryan did not make the Mexican steers. Gus and Henry drove the steers to Amarillo two weeks after McKinley was elected. Cattle prices shot up to several dollars per head. He sold his steers to Charlie Jones a buyer for Commission House in

Kansas City and came out all right. I was just as proud of it as he was because I was afraid, he would lose money. Gus came back to the ranch laughing and said I told you when they got Bryan out that everything would be all right. I said that was just them gold bugs in New York and Washington withholding their money, but gold or no gold, he did not risk anymore Mexican steers. He traded in cattle most all the time; but after that Mexican deal, he traded in Texas raised cattle.

One time we bought one thousand steer yearlings near Colorado City. Gus found them and wanted to know if I wanted some of them. I told him I could handle four hundred. Cattle were cheap then; eleven dollars per head. He said he would buy them if I would go drive them to the ranch. I told him to have them delivered at Colorado and I would go after them; the cattle came from south of Colorado City. I received them the first day of April and started to the ranch the next day. It was a very dry time; dry all the fall and winter before. About the only thing the cattle had to eat was shin oak bushes. Along the river bank was a little new grass, but mighty little. It was that way until we got to the plains.

There we found good old grass at the head of Mesquite Draw. We made good time for there was no grass to eat and no use to stop. Some of the cattle were very thin, but we did not lose any. My but the way they did eat grass when we got on the plains. We came up through Bush and Tiller's Ranch, the Triangle H. Ranch on the Colorado River and we saw hundreds of dead cattle on account of the drouth the winter before. It's funny how things happen. We came down over this same trail with a herd of beef cattle in November of that same year. We had had lots of rain from the time I passed in the spring and the grass was just as fine as could be.

It reminds me of what J. L. Vaughn said one time, Texas can promise less and do more than any country and at other times promise more and do less. It certainly did not promise much that April when I drove that herd of yearlings through the Triangle Ranch. I had seen the country look mighty dry before, and, of course, like Mr. Slaughter said about the cattle business, when they were low and things looked discouraging, to stick that much closer to the business for they would come back and be better than ever perhaps. But as I looked on that bare ground the first part of April, it looked to me like the grass roots had all blown away. I tried to figure out what would become of that country.

## Chapter 11

When I moved to Canyon City, I bought some bank stock; Mr. S. F. Sullenberger and L. T. Lester organised the First National Bank and wanted to scatter the stock among the citizens. John Hutson bought some stock, Judge Thacker from Tulia was a stock holder and assistant cashier. Mr. Lester was president and Mr. Sulenberger was cashier. It was the first bank in that part of the country outside of Amarillo. They did fine business. Mr. Lester liked the banking business so well, he had branch banks at Lubbock, Floydada, Tulia and Bovina.

It did look like a good time for banks. Mr. J. N. Donohue moved to Canyon soon after that and wanted some bank stock and I sold him my stock. He was also in the hardware business with Stringfellow and Hume. Jack Campbell, J. D. Gamble and I bought out Wright and Gamble, general mercantile store. It was originally the Smith and Walker store. We organised the Canyon Supply Company. We sold stock to Irvin Hunt, J M. Black, W. T. Moreland, William Baird, C. T. Word and L. C. Lair. We elected Irvin Hunt as manager and we did a good business. Irvin said he sold goods by the wagon load.

I told him that was the easiest money I had ever made. He and Frank Wheelock had been in the mercantile business at Lubbock for several years. I had known him there and I worked to get him as manager of the Supply Company for I had confidence that he would make good and he did. We had competition in Pipkin Donaldson and Olham, they ran the other general mercantile business, but were nice men, and like us, seemed to realise that there was room enough for all. So far as I know the two outfits got along well.

We remained at the old stand of Smith and Walker on the southeast corner of the square for a short time. We decided in our board meetings that the northeast corner would in the future be a better location than where we were. Myself, Dr. Black and W. T. Moreland figured and planned quite a while and decided to buy three lots at the northeast corner of the square. The first thing we had to do was to locate the persons that owned them. We found that Dr. Stewart owned the corner and soon located the owners of the others. Then we got their prices and figured with them.

It was then like it has always been, if a fellow wanted to buy anything it seemed high. We hesitated for a while for it was a new venture to each of us; we had made our money, what little we had, in the cattle business. This thing, buying town lots was new to me and I told Black and Moreland so; they said the same thing. We had lots of fun over it in our little meetings we held in the back of the store. Mr. Moreland worked in the store, hence he was busy in the daytime. He used to laugh and say he would sic me and Dr. Black on them for a trade to buy their lots. Dr. Black and myself would scout around in the daytime and if we found out anything, we would make a date with Mr. Moreland and have our special meetings in the store.

I remember we got two propositions from the owners. One was for cash and the other on terms. We would get together and figure which was the best. Lots were cheap then compared to what they were later. We finally decided to pay cash as we would be saving some money. We were all a little scary for it might be a failure. I don't remember now the exact amount that we paid, but it was near one thousand dollars for the three lots.

We had a plan on foot then to put the bank on the corner lot and the Canyon Supply Store on the second lot. Later came the T. C. Thompson Hardware Company and we were all interested in that Company. We organised the Canyon National Bank and elected R. W. O'Keefe, president, J. M. Black, vice president, and I. L. Hunt, cashier. We opened up in a small frame building for the time being. This building was located east of and just across the street from the Hudson Hotel. We occupied that building until the building was completed at the northeast corner of the square. That is where the First State Bank is now, (1936.).

It was sometime after the bank moved into the new building before the Supply Company could move on account of getting material to finish the building. After I. L. Hunt left the store and went to the bank, they elected C. P. Hutchins, manager of the Supply Store. He was manager about two years then Oscar Gamble was elected manager, which he held for several years. He was a good man, also a good manager; but as time went on and conditions changed, we did not make the profits either in the store or in the Canyon National Bank. It seemed for a while the Thompson Hardware Company was doing better than the others, then it would change back.

I had a ranch in Lamb and Bailey Counties at that time and I would go down there sometimes for two or three weeks at a time. When I would get back, I would visit with the boys at the bank and each of the stores and it was a great pleasure when I would find things looking good. They were a good bunch of men, all of them anxious to succeed and make good and they were very conservative.

Mr. Roy Wright came in later as assistant cashier. He was very conservative and an experienced banker from Greenville, Texas. He and Irvin Hunt made a good team. Dr. Black had lived at Canyon many years and he knew almost everybody in the country, which was a great help to the bank. He had been in the ranch business and he said to me one time he had been in the sheep business, but he was not very proud of it. His friends joked him some about being a sheep man; he did not care for their joking, but rather enjoyed it. Said he would go into it again if there was any money in it.

At the Supply Store they had Oscar Gamble as manager after Irvin Hunt went to the bank. Mr. Alley Hunt was bookkeeper, Mr. W. T. Moreland and Henry Gamble as regular clerks and of course had others. Mr. Jim Gamble was clerk part of the time; but he was, as I told him, a retired merchant. He said no, but a broke merchant. He had been in the mercantile business several years with Mr. Wright. He used to tell me a great deal about their early experiences back in Tennessee.

I remember one funny story he told. He said they bought out a little store in the country and put one of their clerks there to run it. They called it Bird's Store. There was not much to it and the young fellow got mighty tired of staying over there. One day they sent another boy over to relieve him for a day or two, and the fellow came to town. While there, some man had a dog that had killed some sheep in the edge of town and they were going to kill the dog. This boy heard of it and he asked them to not kill the dog, said for them to just send him to Bird's Store. That would be just as bad as killing him.

Jim Gamble told me about Bob and Alf Taylor, brothers, who were both running for governor of Tennessee. Bob was a Democrat and Alf a Republican. Jim said whenever the Taylors went to town to speak, while they were campaigning, everybody was there to hear them for they knew they would have some fun. Jim Gamble was a good entertainer, easy to get acquainted with and he certainly was missed from the store. He still kept his stock in the store and was still lots of help to the store. I called him the scout for the store and Dr. Black scout for the bank. Anyway, we had a good bunch of men. Next to being a cowboy, I enjoyed it better than anything I was ever interested in.

One other experience I had while at Canyon; Mr. J. N. Donohue, J. A. Wallace and myself organised a telephone company. We bought out L. M. Falkner and repaired the line then running to Tulia and Plainview. We did not keep it very long, I think about a year. We figured it would take lots of money and we did not have that much confidence in the undertaking. We sold out to J. E. Nunn of Amarillo and we gave up the best thing in the country. Mr. Wallace did not want to sell, but Mr. Donohue or myself did not know much about that kind of business and we feared it would take too much money for an experiment. I have talked that deal over with Mr. Donohue many times since. It turned out to be one of the best investments either of us could have made. That was another mistake I made.

I had one other very interesting thing to happen while I was with the Canyon National Bank. The bank made a loan on a bunch of cattle that proved to be rather slow pay and the board of directors decided to see if we could buy the cattle even if we lost a little money for, we did not want to bring suit or collect it by law. The directors sent Dr. Black and myself to make the best deal we could with the man. I told the directors I could handle the cattle at what they were worth or at market price.

I had a ranch then. I told them I would get horses and wagon from there to handle the cattle in case we bought any. Dr. Black said he would go and take his son, Will. The distance was about one hundred and fifty miles. We decided that we three could drive a small bunch of cattle, but if there were too many, we would rustle more men. When we got there the party had found a buyer for all the steer cattle but could not sell the cows and calves, about a hundred head of them. We bought them after he sold and delivered the steers. We got our check for the steers. We started with our little outfit and had to drive slow on account of some young calves. We would take time about driving the wagon. We had quite a lot of fun about who would cook for the outfit, but I told the doctor that since we did not have much to cook it would not be much of a job.

I think we were gone about three weeks for we had to wait for the fellow to roundup and work his range. I enjoyed every bit of the trip; Dr. Black and Will said they wished it had lasted longer. One thing, I noticed we were good and hungry when we got back to my ranch. Walter Ridgeway was a good ranch cook and they had milk and butter, chickens and eggs and we were behind on all of those things. Dr. Black remarked after we left, that he bet Ridgeway and the boys were glad when we got filled up and left. I told him the boys were glad when we came, but sorry when time come for us to leave for at that time Door Key Ranch was a lonesome place. The nearest neighbours were five miles away and the nearest railroad point was forty miles, at

Bovina. These boys were always glad when I came and if somebody came with me, that suited them all the better.

I don't think I ever enjoyed at trip more than that trip I took with Dr. Black and his son, Will. Dr. Black was there just like he was everywhere else, willing at all times to do his part and Will was just as good. The doctor and I would go on ahead just before camping time and select a place to camp and tell Will to let the cattle graze up to the wagon. We had three horses saddled all the time. If the range cattle got in our way, we could all mount and turn the range cattle off the trail. Windmills or watering places would give us some trouble, but we handled it fine. We called Will the boss, he was a boy then about fourteen years old and he was a good one.

I told Dr. Black we three could drive a herd of one thousand cattle. He laughed and said "Owing to how far we had to drive them." When we got back to the bank and reported what we had done and turned the check in for the steer money, the directors seemed pleased that we had at least collected most of the debt, although, the bank had to take some loss. Then we told them about me wanting the stock cattle I had agreed to take. I told the directors I would leave it with Dr. Black to say what they were worth and Dr. Black set the price a little below what we had to give the party for them in order to keep out of a law suit with him. After everything was agreed on, I settled with the bank for the cows.

One other experience we had while I was connected with the Canyon National Bank, was during the depression in 1907. We had fifty thousand dollars on deposit in a bank in a certain city. This bank got into trouble by having loaned heavily to some South American coffee producing company. It seemed that country had been hit hard by the depression and they could not make satisfactory settlement with the bank. We were doing our business with this bank, A bank examiner came along and found them out of order and closed their bank and, of course, it closed with our fifty thousand dollars.

We called a meeting of the directors and decided to send Irvin Hunt to see what he could do. He came back in a few days and reported that he had found where we could arrange for the necessary funds to carry on our business for the time and also found out that it was thought our correspondent bank would soon be open again. They did open in a few months and allowed us to draw out five thousand dollars a week, but no more than that amount. We soon got back on our feet again, but it gave us a scare that we did not forget. After that we kept our money scattered in different banks.

During the time I lived in Canyon, I made very nice profits dealing in town property in a small way. When the Santa Fe Railroad built south out of Canyon, I thought; I could see that it would have a bad effect on the town and I made an effort to sell out all my unimproved property, but I failed to clean it all up. Soon after that they got the West Texas College located there. I contributed two thousand dollars to it and soon after that I sold my residence and moved back to Plainview. I then owned a ranch of four leagues of land in Lamb and Bailey Counties, near where the town of Sudan is now located.

It was much nearer to the ranch from Plainview that from Canyon and it had been our home before. We had made many friends while we lived in Canyon and I surely did hate to leave them but I thought it best from a business stand point, I had some trouble in getting located in Plainview as the town was on a boom and property was high. I made a trip to Lubbock to see about locating there but found prices still higher there. So, I went back and bought lots in Plainview and built the home we are now living in. We had been away from Plainview ten years and things had changed wonderfully. Many had moved away and some had died and it looked like all the children had grown up. I told Mr. J. L. Vaughn that one day and he said I ought not to have moved away at first. He said I might have known I could not make a living anywhere else, for he said I belonged at Plainview. Mr. Vaughn was a great hand to crack jokes, but a fine man and a good friend of mine.

When I went back to Plainview to look for property to buy, I met Mr. Vaughn. He asked me if I was there to try to beat somebody out of something. I told him yes, and I wanted him to help me. He said he would not help me beat anybody, but he would help me get a place and he did. One day after that he said bargains were harder to find than he had thought. He said it looked to him like everybody had gone crazy. I found a small house and rented until I could buy or build. My wife and I went around to look at the different property. Mr. Henry Skaggs told me about some property near his home and that he would like to see us locate there close to them so we could be neighbours.

I went home and told my wife about it and it turned out to be a place that we had already looked at and we both liked the location; but had been told that the place was not for sale. Next day I saw Mr. Skaggs and told him we looked at the place and had understood it was not for sale. The man that owned it had very recently bought it with intention of building a nice home there. Mr. Skaggs asked if we liked the place, I told him we did if the price was right. He said if I would let him have a few days he would find out and let me know.

I told him to go ahead and in just a few days he called me down to his office and told me the place could be bought as the party had changed his mind about building. He got the party to price the place. Mr. Skaggs said it was too high. Skaggs found out what the party gave for it a few months before and I told Mr. Skaggs to offer him what he gave for it with ten *per cent* interest added to it. In a few days we closed the deal.

The next thing then was to get the house built. My wife had a plan sketched off for the house that she had put in lots of time on and by making some little changes she had it ready. The place had an old house on it and the man had moved it out on one side of the property. After I bought it we moved in this old house and lived in it until we could get the new building completed, which took much longer than we had bargained for. When we moved into that old house, we thought we would just be there a few months, but it looked like they would never get the house built. We said we did not have much to move therefore we would not have much trouble; but we all decided before we got through with it that we did not want to move anymore.

As for myself, I had moved around on ranches a good many times, but about all we had to do then was to shut the door and call the dog. It is very different when one has to move a lot of household goods that have been accumulating for years. We made the old house as comfortable as possible under the circumstances and we had to stay there six months.

I made my first trip from Plainview to the ranch which was over about the worst road one can imagine out through the sand hills. It was fair until we passed Hale Centre and to Hart's camp, and there we struck Yellow House Draw.

There we entered the old cattle trail leading to Mexico by way of Sod House, to Salt Lake, and New Mexico and it looked to be the most crooked road in the world. I had been over it many times back in my earlier cowboy days, but I was riding horseback and went my own way then and, of course, did not notice all the crooks and turns, but riding in an automobile was very different. I guess John Chisholm never thought when he was driving his first herd of cattle over that trail, that he was laying out a road for automobiles to follow fifty years later. It had high middles, *mesquite* roots, stumps, sand and wash outs; to say nothing of the crooks.

Sometimes we would have to leave the road and go up or down the little draw that ran into the main draw. We would go sometimes a quarter or a half mile to find a place to cross, then wind back through the *mesquite* brush until we would find that crooked road again. The next time I went to the ranch and for a long time after that, I took an axe and a spade with me so we could dig out and we often needed them.

A little later, the people at Brownfield laid out a road from Brownfield to Hereford. It ran about due north and passed a few miles west of where the town of Olton is now. I went that way some, but it did not help much for the bad sand was west of where this road crossed Yellow House Draw. I found out that Mr. Phelps White had made him an automobile road leading from Yellow House to Portales, New Mexico. I tried that route to Yellow House Ranch then out on the Phelps road as far west as the Louis Lester Ranch, later Bassitt Ranch, then I had no road for fifteen miles to my ranch. We had hard land but very little sand. This route by Yellow House proved to be the best route, but much further.

It was a bad job for several years to get to the ranch in an automobile. Later when they got a mail line from Plainview to Olton, I kept a saddle horse at Olton with some friends. I would ride a horse from my ranch to Olton and put the horse in a pasture for the next trip and ride with the mail carrier into Plainview. Mr. Ogg was the mail carrier for some time and I have ridden many times with him. He and I used to make that trip some mighty cold days. Mr. Ogg was a fine man.

One thing I noticed about Mr. Ogg; he was always in a good humour. It made no difference how cold or muddy it was, he was just the same. He would tell some joke and laugh about it and say, "Oh, well, it could be worse." He would tell about how cold or how muddy it was at some other time in the past and in that way we would pass the time fine. The distance did not seem near so long. We would leave Plainview about five or six o'clock in the morning and get to Olton about twelve. I think he changed teams three times on the road.

As I go to Olton now and note the changes, it does not seem possible. Then it was settled with stock farmers from one section up to ten sections to the family. Each ranch had a small farm and in native grass pasture. I was at Olton recently and the whole country has been ploughed up into farms with the exception of the sand hills south of

Olton. A very small grass pasture for each farm, usually forty or fifty acres, seldom ever more than a hundred acres. Olton and all that part of the country west of Olton as far as eight or ten miles was in the original Running Water Ranch and as far south as the north prong of the Yellow House Draw.

We had what we called the south camp located at Hart's camp on that draw. We called it eighteen or twenty miles from headquarters to the south camp, but since the country has settled and has been surveyed out, they claim it is not that far. Anyway, it used to seem like a long ways when the blizzards were blowing and we would have to drift the cattle from the south fence and get them back to water on Running Water Draw. Many cold nights I have spent there during the storms for I soon learned after I went to that Running Water Ranch that when a blizzard came it would drive all the cattle to the south fence. Then wherever they would strike the fence, they would drift along the fence to the Yellow House Draw to Hart's camp.

We kept two men at the south camp to keep the cattle worked back from the south fence, for they would get in the corners of the fence and bulk together and trample the weaker ones to death. When fifteen thousand cattle got together it was too many cattle for two men to drive and so I tried to always be there to help get the cattle back to water. Sometimes we would drift them along until dark would overtake us. We would leave them strung out and traveling and hoping they would go on to water and many of them would go to water but lots of the weaker ones would stop as soon as we left them. We used to guess at how many would be back to the south fence next morning and the next morning we would find some at the south fence and find them all along to where we had left them the night before.

We would generally find the drags of that bunch and the poor things, some of them could hardly walk. Some of their feet would be frozen and some of them would be left to die. It would almost make a man sick to have to look at them, but all we could do was to try to take care of those that could walk. Try and get them to water, usually when they had been out the second day without water, when we would get them within a few miles of water they would go to it.

Even if the norther was still blowing, they would tuck their heads and face it to get to the creek to get a drink. We would have to break the ice often. My, it was a cold job. I think I suffered more from cold the first two winters I was on the Running Water Ranch than all my experience in the ranch business. That was in 1884 and 1885. I have worked with the cattle trying to get them back to water and keep them from bulking in the south side and I would not notice how cold it was until we would leave the cattle and start to camp. Then find that my ears and toes were almost frozen. By rubbing our ears and pounding them we would get up circulation.

I remember we would sometimes get off our horses and walk and stamp along to get our feet warm. We most always had heavy Arctic overshoes and certainly did need them, though I have known boys that would get caught without overshoes and get corn sacks and open them out good and straight then wrap them around their feet. It made a very good substitute for overshoes, that was, if it was a dry snow, but if the snow was melting it did not do so good, for the water would soon get in next to their feet.

The blizzard would cover up our tracks and at night it was very easy to miss our way. We used to joke each other about what we would do if we could not get to camp that night. We would all agree that it would not do to lay down or undertake to sleep. There were many things we did not always agree on, I used to think of all the good warm places I had ever been in, in my whole life, and it may seem strange to say, but I would often think of my mother. Henry Grady was not the only one that thought of his mother when he got in a tight place, for I would think of mother's good warm feather bed and especially the feather pillow.

Down at the camp I knew no feather bed or pillow was waiting us. I would spread a blanket on the ground and put my pants under my head for a pillow. Speaking of putting my pants under my head makes me think of John May. When we were on the trail or the boys were doing night herding, John always put his boots and pants under his head and I believe he could get up and dress quicker than anybody I ever saw. He was the only man I ever stood guard with that could beat me to the herd. I have seen many boys that I could get to the herd and send the first guard in before my partner would get there.

But John was one partner I knew I had to get a move on myself to get there even with him much less beat him. At times in summer time, John would light his pipe before he would get on his horse, then I could beat him. We used to run races to see which could get to the herd first. John always put his boots on first thing when he woke up to go on herd, then put his feet through his pants legs while he was sitting on the edge of the bed. Then as he arose from the bed, he would pull his pants up as he was walking to his horse. I used to tell him I believed he slept with his clothes on.

He was a fellow that took great interest in his work and made no difference what he was doing he did his part. He did not want to let anybody beat him and that was so different from some others. His brother George was very much like him and was just as good a hand, only was not quite as quick as John. I have had some boys in the outfit that were so slow we would wake them up fifteen minutes before time so they could get up, then sometimes they would be late.

I used to feel sorry for some boys that had never stood guard much. They would be so sleepy we would have to pull the suggins down and shake them. Many of them would be good boys and want to do his part, but they could hardly wake up. We would joke them about it the next day and most of them would tell us to just pull him out next time. That would usually be young fellows in their teens. They required more sleep than the older men do. Nobody ever had to pull either of the May boys out of bed.

One time after the XIT, or Capital Syndicate outfit, started up their ranch at Yellow House, I sent John May over there to represent us and get what cattle we had there. That was after they built their fence and naturally fenced up all the cattle that was on their land. A man named Campbell, called Bar B Q Campbell, used to have a ranch in the Indian Territory. His brand was BQ, hence he got that name. He was manager and sent me word when they would round-up and cut the strays out. John was gone about two weeks. When he got back, I asked him how he got along, he said fine, he got something over one hundred cattle. Then he told me about the amount of material they had at Yellow House, Wire and post were piled up until it looked like you were at a railroad station. He said he bet they had five acres of wind mills. Then he said "Unless they have lots of money they will soon be broke."

I said, "No, they won't go broke for they are the richest outfit in the country."

John said no outfit could spend money like that and get by. I asked him how he liked Mr. Campbell. He said, I will tell you what happened then you can form your own opinion. Some cowboys went in to Campbell's office to get their pay checks and they never thought about taking their hats off in the presence of Mr. Campbell. Campbell told some of them that all cowboys must have been born with their hats on, and, of course, he got the ill will of some of them. Others said they had just as soon put in their time tipping their hats as doing other work, and so it went.

John May had been clerk in a store for his uncle in Limestone County, in fact, manager of the store. Did much of the buying and he based his ideas on that about running the ranch. John was an extra good rider and while he was working in that country store, boys in the neighbourhood would gather there often on Saturdays and ride unbroken horses. John could not get to ride on Saturdays because he would be too busy, but would get some of his friends to bring horses on Sundays so he could ride them. There would always be a crowd of boys there to see the show. There would sometimes be ten or twelve boys on unbroken horses. Sometimes they would get pitched off, then they would have to get some gentle horses to catch them.

Before I leave off about Mr. Campbell, there are several funny things that happened while he was connected with the ranch. Gus O'Keefe was delivering a herd of steers to him one time at Spring Lake. They had a mixed herd, that is, all ages from one to four years old and they sometimes had trouble agreeing on the ages. One day Gus claimed one for a two-year-old and Campbell claimed it for a one-year-old. Finally, Campbell told Gus he would leave it to one of Gus's own men to pass judgment and say how old the steer was. O'Keefe told him all right; O'Keefe had a fellow named Mode Cooch working for him and Cooch was just a bunch of wit.

Campbell asked him to tell them the age of the steer. Cooch looked on a minute or two and there was a big four-year-old steer standing nearby. Cooch said, "Mr. Campbell, do you see that big red steer?"

Campbell said, "Yes."

Cooch said, "Yes, well he is not as old as that steer."

It took Campbell on such surprise he hollered to the man at the gate to open the gate and let them go. He said he ought to have known better than to leave it to a crazy man. Campbell liked Cooch so well that he hired him to work for him. He first asked Gus if he would object to him giving Cooch a job. Gus was glad for him to get a job. He was a dandy good cowhand, but no much of a business man. He always wanted to have too much fun, but Campbell wanted him for what he knew about the cattle business for Cooch was then nearly fifty years old. Campbell was buying and receiving cattle all the time and needed just such a man with experience to help him.

One time while Cooch was working for him, Campbell sent him south ten or fifteen miles to meet a herd and help them to water. Campbell had dug a well that developed a very weak flowing well and did not furnish much water. Campbell told Cooch to take the herd to the little artesian well, as he called it, to water. Cooch was suspicious of the well, he had never seen the well but the boys said there was not much water there. He decided the best thing for him to do was to go see and as soon as he saw it he knew he could not water there. He rushed off at top speed to meet the herd and turn them west to some surface lakes that he had seen that had plenty of water.

He had not more than got the herd pointed towards the lakes and in the opposite direction from the little well, when he saw Mr. Campbell coming in his buggy under whip. He drove up to Cooch and asked why he did not take the cattle to the little well. Old Cooch told Mr. Campbell he could drink that water as fast as it came out of that well. That buffaloed Campbell a bit and he said, "Now, Windy." He called Cooch, Windy. "How long can you drink that water as fast as it comes out of that well?" Cooch said, until he starved to death for water. As much as Campbell fussed at Cooch, he always liked Cooch and they were just as different as could be.

Campbell was an educated man, at that time holding a high position and had charge of one of the biggest ranches in this country or any other country. Three million acres of land and plenty of money to stock it with was no small thing. Of course, he made his mistakes just the same as everyone else. One among them was, when he wanted the cowboys to tip their hats to him when they came in his office. Just imagine a big rough cowboy before Campbell tipping his hat to him. Mode Cooch himself was just about the roughest and toughest looking cowboy I ever saw and could act a fool to perfection, and yet he had more sense than half the cowboys.

When he wanted to be tough, he could play it to a fine point, and yet if you put him in town and dressed him up, he was a fine-looking man. I told him one time I did not hardly know him, he looked like a dude. I told him he looked like Mr. Campbell. He enjoyed the joke as he always did. He grabbed me by the hand as I had not seen him in several years, and said. "Rufe, I saw Bar B Q not long ago and what do you reckon he said to me?" I, of course, had to tell him I could not imagine what he said, unless, he was fussing at you about some of your jokes. No, he was in the best of humour I ever saw him, he replied.

Campbell said, "Cooch it has been a long time since I saw I saw you and I want to tell you something. Someone has been telling that I stole a million dollars from that XIT outfit. They told a lie about it for I did not steal over half a million dollars and people ought not to lie about things that they don t know about."

Cooch told me that and just enjoyed the laugh. As a general thing, he did not laugh much himself, for he would tell or make the jokes and the other fellow would do the laughing, He said he and Campbell had a fine time visiting and it had been several years since they had seen each other. When they separated Mr. Campbell told him if he ever came to Wichita, Kansas, to be sure to come to see him. It was funny to me for two men as different as Campbell and Cooch to ever care about seeing each other again. Mr. Campbell, strictly business, and old Cooch just the opposite and did not care a thing for a dime.

All he cared for was fun and yet he did good work and knew all about ranch work and so far, as I know he was truthful. One bad fault he had was nearly always telling some joke and taking up other boys' time, when often they were needed to help hold the roundup. I used to get worried at him for that, but I was like Mr. Campbell, I liked the old boy. When he was not telling his stories he was as good a cowhand as there was in the country. If Mode Cooch is living today, he would have been a good helper for Will Rogers, for he could keep the outfit laughing all the time. If the old boy had training in that line, I mean in the show business, he would make a good clown. He was a man that never did forget anything. It has been thirty-three years since I have seen him (1936.) I never heard of his death if he died.

So much for Mode Cooch and other old-time cowboys.

But the future cowboy will be different. Instead of riding the range to hold his cattle when the blizzards come, he will have his cattle in the barn or under a shed eating hay and grain and cottonseed meal. Instead of cattle drifting over the range trying to find protection, there will be fewer but better cattle. Instead of waiting until a steer is three or four years old for market, he will be ready in one or two years.

It's wonderful how the country has changed: first the buffalo and the Indian, then the Hunter and the Texas Ranger and Soldier, then the Cattleman or Cowboy, the Farmer and the actual Settler, then the Railroads.

We will have to wait and see what comes next.

www.ingramcontent.com/pod-product-compliance
Lightning Source LLC
Chambersburg PA
CBHW031620160426
43196CB00006B/210